THE
21 IRREFUTABLE
LAWS OF
LEADERSHIP
TESTED
BY TIME

THOSE WHO FOLLOWED THEM . . .
AND THOSE WHO DIDN'T

JAMES L. GARLOW

ASSISTED BY GERARD REED

OLIVER NELSON™

THOMAS NELSON PUBLISHERS®
Nashville

A Division of Thomas Nelson, Inc.
www.ThomasNelson.com

Published in Nashville, Tennessee, by Thomas Nelson Publishers.

Published in association with Yates & Yates, LLP, Attorneys and Counselors, Orange, California.

ISBN 0-7852-6493-0 (hc)
ISBN 0-7852-0675-2 (sc)

Printed in the United States of America

04 05 06 07 08 PHX 5 4 3 2 1

THE
21 IRREFUTABLE
LAWS OF
LEADERSHIP
TESTED
BY TIME

Dedicated
to
Carol

my wife, my mate, my lover, my counselor,
my confidante, and my friend

CONTENTS

FOREWORD

I f you enjoyed my book *The 21 Irrefutable Laws of Leadership* you will love this book. This book takes the 21 Laws to the next level and shows you practically how these laws have worked in the lives of those who have followed them and how leaders have failed because they have ignored them.

The 21 Irrefutable Laws of Leadership Tested by Time is a must read for anyone who is or wants to be a leader. Jim Garlow is a leader. In 1995 Jim followed me as Senior Pastor of Skyline Wesleyan Church in San Diego. The twenty-first Law of Leadership is the *Law of Legacy*. I did not want just anyone following me at Skyline. I wanted a leader, someone who himself would leave a legacy. I wanted someone who could take Skyline to the next level, and Jim Garlow has gone above and beyond what I could have expected. He has taken Skyline to the "mountain" (its new location), attendance has grown, and finances have increased since Jim has been in charge.

With his degrees in historical studies and his understanding of leadership, he is very qualified to write this book. You will do well to read and study this book time and time again.

In each chapter, Jim gets straight to the point in showing you how the laws apply to you, and he highlights practical leadership principles that can be referenced quickly. If you are willing, you can learn and apply these lessons and principles, and it will help make you into the leader God intended you to be.

If your heart is like mine you want to grow into the best leader you can possibly be and impact as many lives as possible. This book is the tool to help get you there. The information is helpful, profound, clear-cut, and loaded with hope. It doesn't matter if you've been a leader for 10, 20 or 30 years or more, or if you have just begun to get your feet wet in leadership. This book will help make you into a better leader. It's that good!

John Maxwell
INJOY
Atlanta, GA

ACKNOWLEDGMENTS

The "21 Laws" are borrowed entirely from John C. Maxwell's book, *The 21 Irrefutable Laws of Leadership*. I am extremely grateful to John for permission to use the 21 Laws as the foundation (chapter titles) for this book. And I am immensely grateful for the continual encouragement and counsel he provided during the time I was writing.

More importantly, I thank John for his gift of leadership training that he has made available to millions. I am one of the many who have benefited so much from his teachings during the last two decades. And most importantly, I will forever be indebted to him for entrusting to me one of his most precious treasures—the pastorate and the wonderful people of Skyline Wesleyan Church in San Diego. For all of the above, I say a deeply felt "thank you, John" for being an example, an encourager, a "cheerleader," and a friend.

I am deeply indebted to Dr. Gerard Reed of Point Loma Nazarene University of San Diego, California. Without him, many portions of this book would have never existed. My training has been in *church* history. Gerard's training has been in *both* church history *and* secular history. In addition, he is trained in political science, philosophy, and theology. Gerard was the first one I called when this book project became a reality. We dreamed together. We outlined it together. And then we divided up the individual articles to be researched and written. Gerard's "thumbprint" is all over this book. His thinking and phrasing are evident in the sections on American presidents, explorers, Native Americans (of which Gerard is one,) philosophers, and emperors. I am so grateful for the privilege of partnering with him in this project. "Thank you, Gerard," for the journey we experienced!

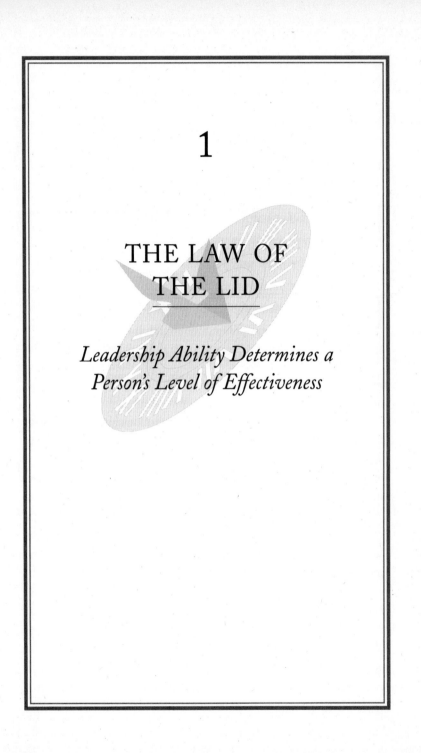

1

THE LAW OF
THE LID

*Leadership Ability Determines a
Person's Level of Effectiveness*

PRINCIPLES OF
EFFECTIVE LEADERSHIP

History is exciting. It is also a teacher. In fact, history is a *great* teacher. By looking at the successes and failures of those who have gone before us, we can hopefully avoid their errors and gain from their strengths.

History is revealing. We can tell much more about a person's effectiveness after he is gone than while he is still alive. History reveals a person's impact.

History can be ruthless, illustrating that an individual gave his life away to things that do not retain value. Or history can be complimentary, showing that an individual's life "investments" are bringing a great "return."

History irrefutably shows who understood the principles of leadership. Negatively stated, history points out those who did *not* grasp the principles of leadership.

History has a way of revealing the Law of the Lid, which states that "leadership ability determines a person's level of effectiveness." Who were effective persons because they knew how to lead? Who were the ones with an opportunity for effectiveness, but were not effective because their leadership skills did not equal the challenges they faced? Who were those able to switch occupations, yet rise to the top in each new setting? Who were great leaders in one arena, yet experienced disappointing failure in another due to the lid?

Leadership skill is the difference between success and failure; it is the difference between creative vitality and mediocre maintenance.

TEST YOUR EQ (EFFECTIVENESS QUOTIENT)

Think for a moment of the persons you know who are most effective. Who are they? What have they accomplished? How do they do it?

Now think of the persons you know who have been least effective, persons who failed to accomplish their mission, who alienated many of their followers in the process.

What one thing was always present among the persons who are effective? And what one thing seemed to always be absent among the persons who are least effective in carrying out their assigned task? The answer will probably not surprise you. It is leadership.

Now let's make it more personal. What is your EQ? What is your effectiveness quotient? Look back over the last year or two or three. Look back over the last decade. Have you been effective? Have you accomplished what you set out to accomplish?

If you have been effective, it is for one reason. You are a skilled leader. I know it is not pleasant to hear this next sentence, but the reality of it remains true. If you have not been effective over the last five or ten years, the reason is that you lack leadership skills. But the good news is, you are reading a book that will help you in that area, and as your leadership ability increases, so will your effectiveness.

How would you rank your level of effectiveness over the past years on a scale of 1 to 10, with 1 being very ineffective and 10 being extremely effective? Is it a 2? Is it a 6? Is it a 9? Whatever you rank your level of effectiveness is also your level of leadership. If your level of effectiveness is a 4, your level of leadership is a 4. If your level of effectiveness has been a 9, then your leadership level is likely a 9. The bottom line is this: the level of effectiveness you experience in your life is directly proportionate to your level of leadership.

> **PRINCIPLE OF EFFECTIVE LEADERSHIP # 1:**
> *Leadership Always Shows*

⅛

RONALD REAGAN

Leaders cannot hide. Leadership always shows—regardless of the occupation or the setting in which one finds oneself. An example is Ronald Reagan. Simply stated, Reagan was unable *not* to lead. Succinctly stated, he was a skilled leader. And as such, he was unusually effective. One writer, Dinesh D'Souza, author of *Ronald Reagan: How an Ordinary Man Became an Extraordinary Leader,* rates America's fortieth president as one of its greatest, right below Washington and Lincoln. How did this happen? Why is he listed among the greatest of the presidents?

THE LEADER-STUDENT

When Reagan was a high school student in Dixon, Illinois, and a college student at Eureka College, his athletic and acting skills quickly emerged. His popularity as a student and the accompanying leadership skills were early signs of what was to come.

THE LEADER-ACTOR

Reagan was an actor. But he was much more than an actor. He was a leader, being elected the president of the Screen Actors Guild. How many actors are taken seriously enough to be elected to public office? Very few. But Reagan was not only skilled in his profession; he was a skilled *leader*. And leadership skill determines the level to which one may rise.

THE LEADER-POLITICIAN

In 1966, he won the governorship of California by more than one million votes, and he was reelected in 1970. One decade later, he was elected president of the United States. Even his staunchest critics acknowledged his ability to inspire people to follow him. Those who opposed him desperately attempted to portray him as an intellectual lightweight—simply an actor-turned-president. But they could not dismiss him. Why? Because he was a highly skilled leader, and as a result, he was effective.

Leadership shows—always—whether one is a sports announcer, an actor, or a governor. Certainly not every great leader will become a governor

4

or president. But leadership shows. Like cream, it always rises to the top. And the level of leadership ability determines the depth and breadth of one's effectiveness.

POPE JOHN XXIII: THE DARING LEADER

Leading an organization—even if it's small—requires skill. But a large, established organization is especially difficult to change. How would you feel if you were leading one of the world's oldest and largest organizations?

And what if that organization was not one in which you could readily hire and fire, as you can in corporations? What if that organization was a charitable organization, where the rules are much more challenging? That's what a man named John faced in the late 1950s. And his story is one you ought to know. It will help you in developing your leadership skills.

A MOST DIFFICULT LEADERSHIP CHALLENGE

Few things are as difficult to change as a religious denomination, especially when it is the largest and oldest. They are as cumbersome as turning a large ocean liner without the benefit of a rudder or propellers. In 1958, no organization was as large (900 million adherents) and as old (sixteen hundred to two thousand years, depending on how you date the beginning) as the Roman Catholic Church. But skilled leaders have impact. And Pope John XXIII was a skilled leader.

Pope Pius XII had led the Catholic Church for nineteen years, from 1939 to 1958. To some, the Catholic Church seemed irrelevant and entrenched—out of contact with the masses, incompatible with modern life—and its worship services were conducted in a language that few understood. But leaders change things. Prior to 1958, John XXIII had had successful ministries in Rome, Bulgaria, Greece, and France. But his greatest challenge came on October 28, 1958, when he was elected pope of the largest religious body in the world. To this seemingly atrophied and antiquated system of leadership came a leader who was visionary and energetic—an effective agent of change.

PRINCIPLE OF EFFECTIVE LEADERSHIP # 2:
Effective Leaders Are Change Agents;
They Change Their Environment

Within ninety days of his election, on January 25, 1959, John XXIII called for the convening of the Second Vatican Council in 1962, for the purpose of renewing and reinvigorating the Catholic Church, no small task. This massive conference was held in Rome, in four different sessions during the fall months of each year from 1962 to 1965. It was a rare event, occurring only twenty-one times during the last two thousand years.

Some people regard the Second Vatican Council as the most important religious event of the entire twentieth century, and perhaps the most significant event since the Protestant Reformation of the early 1500s. It opened the window and let a fresh breeze blow into the Catholic Church, invigorating Catholics and drawing the respect of many Protestants.

The Catholic Church suddenly became more open, more responsive, more pastoral and caring, and considerably more relevant to it adherents. Worship services became more understandable and had more meaning. The church began to speak to issues of modern life. The pope miraculously opened a warm and embracing dialogue between Catholics and Protestants, previously unheard of.

Virtually no one could have anticipated the renewing and change that those years brought. But they underestimated Pope John XXIII, the warm, compelling, energetic leader. His impact was global. Why? Because one's level of leadership determines one's level of effectiveness, and John XXIII had the highest leadership skills. When he died on June 3, 1963 (long before Vatican II was over), the remorse was felt globally, even by Protestants who would typically have been emotionally detached. One of the world's most effective leaders had died.

※

JOHN ADAMS AND JOHN QUINCY ADAMS

Let me test your memory. How many father-son teams have served as presidents of the United States? Answer: two. George H. W. Bush and

George W. Bush; and John Adams and John Quincy Adams. Let's examine the presidencies of the Adamses and assess their leadership skills based on their effectiveness.

GIFTED

The second and sixth presidents of the United States both came to that position thoroughly gifted and prepared—or so it seemed. John Adams (1735–1826) and John Quincy Adams (1767–1848) were an exceptionally gifted father-son team.

AMAZING ACCOMPLISHMENTS

John Adams, the nation's first vice president, was elected to succeed George Washington as president in 1796. John Adams seemed groomed for the presidency. His accomplishments are impressive:

- an excellent student at Harvard
- a superb thinker with a skilled grasp of political thought
- a scholar well-read in constitutional history
- a leader in the Continental Congress of 1775
- a strategic player in drafting the Declaration of Independence
- vice-president, elected in 1789
- assistant to Washington in uniting people behind the Constitution in the 1790s
- a man of integrity

But like all of us, Adams had weaknesses too. He was:

- sometimes egotistical
- pompous
- occasionally bullheaded
- ridiculed as "His Rotundity"
- a bit stuffy

7

Benjamin Franklin included both strengths and weaknesses when he said Adams was "always honest, often great, but sometimes mad."

ADAMS AS PRESIDENT

In 1796, John Adams was elected president of the United States. It was a close election. He barely defeated Thomas Jefferson, who became his vice president (and opponent). With all his great strengths and brilliance, Adams tackled the presidency. But it proved a daunting task.

INABILITY TO DELEGATE

John Adams was unable to delegate. If he couldn't handle an issue, he allowed no one in his administration to tackle it. He tried to do most everything himself.

UNWILLINGNESS TO REMAIN AVAILABLE

But that was only a part of the problem. He not only failed to delegate authority, but he was difficult to find when he himself needed to exercise it! He loved his home in Quincy, Massachusetts, and was unusually unhappy in Philadelphia, the nation's capital at that time. Consider the contrast between Adams and the previous president, George Washington: George Washington spent 181 days at his home during his presidency; John Adams spent 385 days at his home during his presidency. John Adams spent a shocking one-fourth of his presidency *away* from the nation's capital, in Boston, in an era without phones, faxes, computers, or any other means of communication faster than horse travel! He was an absentee president.

COMMUNICATION WEAKNESSES

In addition to being unwilling to delegate and being absent, he suffered from inadequate communication skills in regard to foreign policy issues with France. Failing to communicate quickly and openly about what later became known as the XYZ Affair, he had to deal with an unhappy public. He later communicated more openly. But his delay cost him political pocket change.

INDECISIVENESS

President Adams was also indecisive. France had seized three hundred American ships and expelled the U.S. ambassador, Charles Pinckney. Congress appropriated millions for war. But strangely enough, President Adams refused to ask for a declaration of war. He hesitated, equivocated, and delayed. To his credit, he negotiated a treaty in 1800, and the nation was spared a war with France. But his delay came at a high political price: the division of his own party.

LACK OF DISCERNMENT

John Adams failed to restrain overly exuberant supporters. He didn't seem to understand that the actions of his friends were costing him credibility with the people he governed.

His supporters in Congress, during the anti-French clamor for war, passed laws designed to suppress criticism of governmental officials. The Alien and Sedition Acts, passed in 1798, sought to make it more difficult for foreigners to become American citizens and granted the president extensive powers to simply expel or imprison dangerous aliens or seditious critics of the administration.

Free speech and free press were suddenly at risk. Critics called it the "Federalist Reign of Terror." Newspaper editors were rounded up and sentenced to jail terms. Even a Vermont congressman, Matthew Lyon, was imprisoned for "libeling" the president! Lyon was reelected to Congress while in jail.

> PRINCIPLE OF EFFECTIVE LEADERSHIP # 3:
> *Ineffectiveness Always Results in Loss of Leadership*

As the war hysteria subsided, the Alien and Sedition Acts were rarely enforced, and in time they would be repealed. But they seriously tarnished the image of President Adams. When he could and should have restrained his partisans, he stood by and allowed the very foundations of a free people to be threatened.

What was the reaction of the public? They turned him out of office. When he ran for a second term, he was defeated. He lost by a significant margin to Thomas Jefferson.

Inability to delegate, absenteeism, communication deficiencies, indecisiveness, and lack of discernment have one thing in common: they all indicate a lack of leadership skills. Was he honest? Yes. Was he bright? Yes. Was he good? Yes. In fact, he was a great man. But he lacked the leadership abilities to match the challenges. For John Adams, or for anyone, effectiveness is determined by leadership ability. Tragically, his effectiveness was far less than it might have been. The reason? Lack of leadership, for leadership determines one's effectiveness.

LIKE FATHER, LIKE SON

Two decades later, John Adams's son, John Quincy Adams, became the nation's sixth president. He had a loving father who guided him. His mother, Abigail Adams, was one of the most outstanding women of colonial times. John Quincy inherited much of his parents' intellectual brilliance and Puritan ethic.

John Quincy Adams's accomplishments even exceeded those of his father. He:

- served as private secretary/interpreter to Francis Dana, American envoy to Russia, at age fourteen.

- attended Harvard.

- was admitted to Boston's legal bar.

- held diplomatic posts in Europe.

- studied in Paris, becoming fluent in French.

- was sent by President Washington to the Netherlands and Portugal.

- was regarded by Washington as the best officer in the foreign service.

- helped negotiate the Treaty of Ghent in 1814 under President Madison, ending the War of 1812.

- was appointed secretary of state by President James Monroe.

- helped secure a treaty (the Adams-Onis Treaty in 1819 which was finally ratified in 1821) with Spain, which added Spanish Florida to the U.S.

- helped formulate the Monroe Doctrine in 1823, a bold and imaginative proclamation concerning the entire Western Hemisphere, serving notice on Europe.

NOW FOR THE EFFECTIVENESS TEST

What kind of a president would such a talented person make? When he was elected in 1824, one would have expected him to become an outstanding president. To that point, he had enjoyed uninterrupted success in various ventures. Unfortunately, he did not meet expectations for continued success.

Four persons ran for the presidential office in 1824. One was the hugely popular Andrew Jackson, "Old Hickory," the hero of New Orleans. Jackson won the popular vote, but not a majority in the electoral college. As the Constitution prescribes, the election was tossed to the House of Representatives, where Speaker of the House Henry Clay finessed Adams's triumph.

LACK OF DISCERNMENT

Using poor judgment, the new President Adams appointed Clay as secretary of state. This action angered many who detected a corrupt bargain in the whole drama, a sort of tit for tat. So angry was John Randolph of Virginia that he challenged Clay to a gun duel, which was fortunately nonlethal. But Adams did not fare so well. The new President Adams had sacrificed trust, a leader's most valuable asset.

LACK OF RELATIONSHIP SKILLS

President Adams also demonstrated weak relationship skills. Much like his father, he proved exceptionally able to offend and alienate people. At an official reception, he met General Jackson, who graciously greeted him and offered his hand. Petulantly, Adams stood immobile, disdaining Jackson's gesture, and replied in a manner designed to offend.

EMPHASIS ON THE NEGATIVES

In Adams's first public speech as president, he exacerbated his leadership challenge by highlighting the negatives of a hard-fought election rather than uniting the country behind him. In his inaugural address, he seemed almost apologetic, acknowledging that he was "less possessed of your confidence . . . than any of my predecessors." He validated that lack of confidence during much of the next four years!

ADAMS HAD MANY WONDERFUL QUALITIES:

- He was a hard worker, rising between four and six o'clock each morning.

- He took long walks in order to maintain physical health.

- He faithfully read the Bible with a desire to following its teachings.

- He had many noble aspirations including Clay's "American System," calling for a national university and an astronomical observatory.

- He desired to develop western lands and to federally fund a national transportation system.

PRINCIPLE OF EFFECTIVE LEADERSHIP # 4:
Noble Goals and Hard Work Are Important,
But They Do Not, in and of Themselves, Make a Good Leader

John Quincy Adams wanted to do good. He was a good man. In fact, he worked hard. But he failed as a leader. He failed to understand what his constituency wanted and needed.

FAILURE TO "READ" HIS CONSTITUENCY

John Quincy Adams did not understand what Andrew Jackson represented—the rise of the common man. Ordinary people, in growing numbers in the West, had little interest in the president's refined ideals. They wanted a government more attuned to them and their needs. They saw in Andrew Jackson an emblem for the nation they desired.

COMMUNICATION WEAKNESSES

Samuel Eliot Morison makes this insightful observation regarding Adams: he "was a lonely, inarticulate person unable to express his burning love of country in any manner to kindle the popular imagination."[1] As leadership expert John Maxwell so often says, "He who thinks he is a leader, but has no followers, is only taking a walk." Adams' leadership failures cost him his "followership."

PRINCIPLE OF EFFECTIVE LEADERSHIP # 5:
Being a Nice Person, Although Important,
Cannot Make One a Leader

Respected rather than loved, John Quincy Adams had little chance against Andy Jackson, Old Hickory, the man of the people. So they denied, by a landslide, Adams's bid for reelection, and Jackson won the election of 1828. Jackson "out-leadershipped" Adams!

Much like his father, John Quincy Adams illustrates the ceiling principle. Utterly competent on one level, he failed to grow with his opportunities and failed to effectively serve as president. And that effectiveness hung on one thing: leadership.

PRINCIPLE OF EFFECTIVE LEADERSHIP # 6:
Effective Leaders Adapt

CHARLES FINNEY

Leaders adapt. One of the great tests of leadership effectiveness is how quickly they adapt to changing situations. One person has said that there are only two constants in life: God and change. God, the Bible teaches, does not change. But everything else does. In fact, change is a constant, always occurring. Leadership, in part, is the capacity to adapt quickly to a changing environment.

How well do you, as a leader, adapt? How well are you able to change with your circumstances? Charles Finney's incredible adaptable leadership is a lesson in effectiveness for us all.

TRANSITION # 1:
FROM LAWYER TO EVANGELIST

Charles Finney (1792–1875) is a prime example of unusual effectiveness because of his unique leadership ability. He practiced law in upstate New York in the early 1800s. After an encounter with God in 1821, he made a significant career change, leaving the practice of law and becoming a preacher. Using legal language, he exclaimed that he was on "retainer for . . . Jesus Christ to plead His cause." Within a few years he became the Billy Graham of his era, holding enormous citywide crusades in New York City, Philadelphia, Boston, and many other cities. Huge crowds flocked to hear him from 1824 until 1832.

TRANSITION # 2:
FROM EVANGELIST TO PASTOR

Health problems surfaced, which forced him to stop traveling. But that did not diminish his influence. He demonstrated his leadership skills in three churches he pastored: Second Street Presbyterian Church, and Broadway Tabernacle, both in New York City, and First Congregational Church in Oberlin, Ohio. If pastoring great churches was his third career, it certainly would not be his last.

TRANSITION # 3:
FROM PASTOR TO COLLEGE PRESIDENT

By 1851, he was the president of Oberlin College. But this fourth career only catapulted him to his next career move, the one of which he was most proud.

TRANSITION # 4:

FROM COLLEGE PRESIDENT TO SOCIAL REFORMER

Oberlin was not an ordinary college. It was way ahead of its time. And that was due to the unusual foresight of Charles Finney. Oberlin was the first college to admit women—a move previously unheard of. And it was also the first college to admit blacks—equally foreign to the academic world. The admission of blacks to an otherwise all-white institution preceded the civil rights movement by more than one hundred years!

The conditions of America helped propel the convictional Finney to his fifth career: social reformer. Under Charles Finney's creative leadership, women and blacks gained unprecedented opportunity. Finney's fervor was contagious. Students and townspeople were infected with the dream of equality for women and blacks. And some of that came with a bit of excitement and opposition.

FINNEY'S SOCIAL REFORM DISCIPLES

One of the most celebrated events occurred in 1858 when a fugitive slave named John Price was being shipped back to his master in the South. One quick-minded person frantically rang the chapel bell at Oberlin College, alerting the whole town of a crisis. As a result, a crowd of several hundred abolitionists gathered and decided to storm the hotel in nearby Wellington where Price was being held before being taken to a train. The rescue attempt proved successful. The grateful freed slave was taken back to the city of Oberlin where he was helped by J. H. Fairchild, the man who succeeded Charles Finney as president of Oberlin.

How could a man go from being a lawyer to a preacher holding large citywide crusades to a pastor of prestigious churches to a college president to a nationally known social reformer (and I didn't even mention his successful career as a writer), all the while succeeding? The answer, as you may have guessed, is quite simple: exceptional leadership ability. If Charles Finney had had ten careers rather than the five mentioned, he would have still been effective, because leadership ability determines one's effectiveness.

ULYSSES S. GRANT

Ulysses S. Grant (1822–85) was a superb soldier. Though a less than exemplary student at West Point, he graduated from there and later served admirably as a young lieutenant in the Mexican War.

Grant understood failures as well. He:

- was forced to resign from the army to avoid a court-martial for drunkenness.

- failed as a farmer.

- failed as a real estate salesman.

- failed as a merchant.

His wife, alone it seemed, trusted and believed in him during those dark days. They loved each other intensely, and their four children added warmth and blessing to the Grant family.

When the Civil War erupted, however, he resumed his military career and quickly proved himself a capable officer, moving steadily upward through the officer corps. Close associates, once they learned to look beyond his often sloppy attire and casual manners, something of a western characteristic, found that he exuded an inner strength, a quiet way of working with men, something akin to his skill at handling horses. Victories at Vicksburg, where he fought a brilliant tactical battle, and Chattanooga—decisive for the North's triumph in the West—led President Lincoln in 1864 to make him general-in-chief of the Union armies. He developed the strategy and fought the battles necessary to defeat Robert E. Lee and the Army of Northern Virginia.

Describing Grant, Lincoln once said, "He is the quietest little man you ever saw. He makes the least fuss of any man I ever knew. I believe on several occasions he has been in [the Oval Office] a minute or so before I knew he was there. The only evidence you have that he's in any particular place is that he makes things move."[2] And that's what Lincoln wanted in a general—the ability to make things move!

NOBLE AND GENEROUS IN VICTORY

Lee and Grant were a study in contrasts at Lee's surrender at Appomattox Court House. Grant, dressed in muddy, "rough garb," looked much the same as he did on a battlefield, dressed in a private's shirt, "his feelings sad and depressed," noted one observer, "at the downfall of a foe who had fought so long and valiantly." Lee was dressed in his finest uniform, replete with a red sash and jewel-studded sword, as befitted a Virginia cavalier. Grant waited courteously in the conversation—hesitant even to discuss the surrender until Lee brought up the topic.

The surrender terms required the Confederate troops to go home disarmed, but free so long as they obeyed the laws of the United States. But Grant wanted to maintain the honor of those who were surrendering. He:

• allowed them to keep their swords.

• provided food for the famished Southern soldiers.

• insisted they keep their horses and mules for spring plowing.

When news spread of the victory, Grant, out of respect for the South, insisted that bands stop playing and flags stop waving. "The war is over," he said, "the rebels are our countrymen again." Writing many years later, Englishman Winston Churchill stated, "This was the greatest day in the career of Grant, and stands high in the story of the United States."[3]

> PRINCIPLE OF EFFECTIVE LEADERSHIP # 7:
> *Popularity Is Not a Substitute for Leadership*

With the war over, Grant naturally enjoyed the nation's acclaim and adoration. Republican Party delegates gathered in Chicago and unanimously nominated him, at the age of forty-six, on the first ballot, as their candidate for president in 1868. The Republicans, of course, stood for Lincoln and the Union. The Democrats were identified as the party of secession and slavery. So the election, like the Republican Convention, went to Grant.

LACK OF EXPERIENCE

Entering the White House, Grant confessed that he had little experience or expertise with which to handle the nation's grave problems. "It was my fortune, or misfortune, to be called to the office of Chief Executive without any previous political training," he noted in his final message to Congress.[4] He'd only once voted for a presidential candidate, and he'd taken little interest in the nation's political affairs. The experienced soldier was a political novice. The valiant warrior was a confused statesman.

LACK OF VISION

Given his inexperience, Grant needed to master the constitutional system. Instead, he remained largely immobilized, thinking Congress should take the initiative in most aspects of government. He thought of himself as something of an aide to the legislative houses, more of a ceremonial figure (akin to a monarch in a parliamentary democracy like England). "I shall have no policy of my own to enforce," he said in accepting his party's nomination.[5] Having no policy of his own, unsure of how he should act, he understandably did little of consequence.

A WEAK TEAM

And tragically, T. Harry Williams says, "he surrounded himself with mediocrities, incompetents and scoundrels."[6] A few appointees, such as Ely S. Parker—a Seneca who served him during the war as a staff officer, then headed the Commission of Indian Affairs—proved worthy choices. But many betrayed his trust.

This list of betrayals is painful:

- His private secretary (chief of staff), Orville Babcock, misinformed him, kept him in the dark, and planted evil rumors in his mind.

- Other federal officials enriched themselves at government expense, making Grant's administration one of the most scandalous in American history.

- James ("Jubilee Jim") Fisk Jr. and Jay Gould, scheming to get a corner on the gold market by buying up all the bullion available, used the president's brother-in-law to gain access to Grant and persuaded him that the nation's well-being would be harmed if he released any of the federal Treasury's gold reserves.

- Grant trusted Fisk and Gould, thus driving the price of gold to absurdly high levels and precipitating Black Friday and a national panic in 1869.

There were other scandals and failures involving railroads, tax swindles, Southern Reconstruction disasters, and corrupt politicians in the civil service.

PRINCIPLE OF EFFECTIVE LEADERSHIP # 8:
*Honesty, Although Necessary,
Is Not a Substitute for Leadership*

When the election of 1872 approached, Republican critics of Grant mounted a serious challenge to him, but he managed to gain reelection and serve another term. But he primarily occupied the office, doing little to alter the complexion of his administration. To the end, though personally not corrupt, he either failed to understand or refused to believe the degree to which his associates and appointees betrayed him. Throughout his life, few doubted his honesty or courage.

Following his presidency, deeply in debt and struggling with cancer, he toiled heroically to write his memoirs of the war in order to pay his debts. He could have declared bankruptcy, and few would have blamed him. But he was an honorable man, and he did his duty.

LEADERSHIP *DOES* INDICATE ONE'S EFFECTIVENESS

The highly competent general, the admirable individual, entered a venue for which he was unsuited. And he failed miserably. In his own words, in his final message to Congress, he said, "Failures have been errors of judgment, not of intent." Sadly enough, however, good intentions never suffice on the battlefields, the athletic arenas, or strenuous testing sites where actual goodness is secured. Consequently, historians often rank Grant near the bottom of American presidents.

Ulysses S. Grant was honest, honorable, and decent, clearly some of the marks of leadership that will be listed in another chapter. And undeniably, he was a profoundly successful general, demonstrating superb leadership qualities. Unfortunately, in the office of the presidency, his leadership ability did not match the task at hand, and that void determined his ineffectiveness. Grant, in his last place of service, experienced the devastating impact of the Law of the Lid.

WHAT ABOUT YOU AND ME?

But our concern is not with President Grant. He died more than one hundred years ago. Our concern is with you and me. None of us can escape the Law of the Lid.

Our leadership ability *does* determine our personal impact. Here are some questions: In what areas have you been effective? What leadership principles caused your effectiveness? In what areas have you been ineffective? What leadership laws did you violate?

If you are not sure how to answer the last question, keep reading.

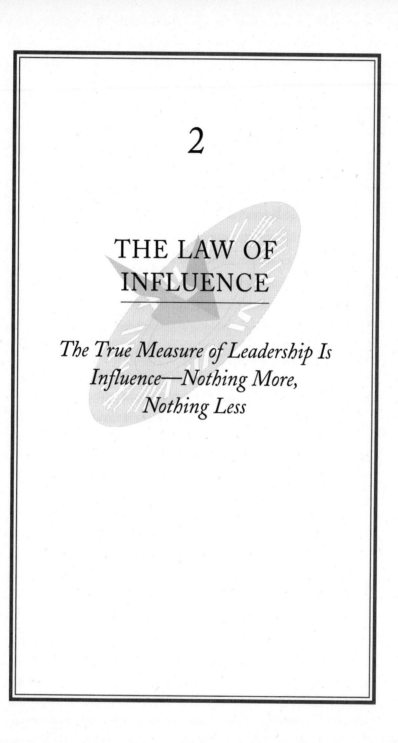

2

THE LAW OF INFLUENCE

The True Measure of Leadership Is Influence—Nothing More, Nothing Less

Principles of
Influential Leadership

H ave you ever wondered why some names are remembered throughout history? Why do others just disappear from the pages of history? The answer is influence. And how do you spell influence? It is spelled l-e-a-d-e-r-s-h-i-p. Leadership ultimately is influence.

Here is a question for you. Answer either yes or no. In order to be a leader, must you have a "position" of some kind? As you may know from reading John Maxwell's *The 21 Irrefutable Laws of Leadership*, leadership is not about holding a position or having a title. It is ultimately about influence. The person who has the influence *is* the leader.

You may have a position. You may not. But if you have influence, you are a leader.

✐

THEODORE ROOSEVELT

While writing this chapter I flew to Rapid City, South Dakota, for a speaking engagement. Although most Americans have probably never visited North and South Dakota, I think they are beautiful states. Near Rapid City is the famous Mount Rushmore. One of the four presidents honored in that carving is Theodore Roosevelt. The location is appropriate for the man, for TR (as he is often called) had spent some of his most enjoyable years on his North Dakota ranch, working with cowboys and hunting with experienced woodsmen in the mountains to the west.

ONE OF THE MOST QUOTED SPEECHES

In 1910, at the Sorbonne in Paris, Roosevelt gave a speech that has been quoted by leaders ever since. It depicts his vigorous view of life and contains a profound challenge to everyone who reads the words today:

> It is not the critic who counts: not the man who points out how the strong man stumbles or where the doer of deeds could have done better. The credit belongs to *the man who is actually in the arena*, whose face is marred by dust and sweat and blood, who strives valiantly, who errs and comes up short again and again, because there is no effort without error or shortcoming, but who knows the great enthusiasms, the great devotions, who spends himself for a worthy cause; who, at the best, now, in the end, the triumph of high achievement, and who, at the worst, if he fails, *at least he fails while daring greatly* [italics added], so that his place will never be with those cold and timid souls who knew neither victory nor defeat.[1]

Listen to those words: "the man who is actually in the arena," "at least he fails while daring greatly." Those words ignite human hearts. That is the language of a leader. Those are the concepts of an influencer.

THE ARMY THAT INFLUENCE BUILT

War with Spain erupted in 1898. Roosevelt, then assistant secretary of the navy, volunteered to help recruit a special corps for the war. He believed that we should drive Spain from the Western world. He and his good friend Dr. Leonard Wood had often talked of the need to help Cuban revolutionaries free the island from Spain's control. Since both men had considerable experience on the frontier, they envisioned leading a group of rough-and-ready frontiersmen to battle.

Three cavalry regiments were to be raised from among the wild riders and riflemen of the Rockies and the Great Plains. Roosevelt proposed that Wood head up the endeavor, serving as colonel, with him assisting as lieutenant colonel. The group was officially designated the First United States Volunteer Cavalry, but the public soon labeled them the "Rough Riders."

PRINCIPLE OF INFLUENTIAL LEADERSHIP # 1:
Influencers Attract

Congress intended the recruits to come from four territories: (1) New Mexico, (2) Arizona, (3) Oklahoma, and (4) the Indian Territory. But men started volunteering from everywhere. Applications poured in! TR was a leader. And leadership is measured by influence. Succinctly stated, influencers attract.

Wood originally planned to admit only 780 to the regiment. The number was later raised to 1,000. In addition to the "rough" westerners, men began joining from the East:

- athletes from Ivy League colleges such as Harvard and Yale (although he could take only one in ten Harvard applicants!)
- members of men's clubs in New York and Boston
- policemen who had served with him when Roosevelt was police commissioner in New York
- many members of wealthy, prestigious families

Those signing up weren't lightweights either. They knew what they faced. It was said that they turned out to be exceptionally good soldiers because they had thoroughly counted the cost before enlisting.

PRINCIPLE OF INFLUENTIAL LEADERSHIP # 2:
Influencers Attract Persons Like Themselves

When Roosevelt himself arrived in San Antonio, he found that Wood had gathered the would-be soldiers, and he liked what he saw. They were described as: a splendid set of men; western men; tall and sinewy; with resolute; weather-beaten faces; with eyes that looked a man straight in the face without flinching.

No better soldiers could be found anywhere, TR declared. They were physically and mentally tough, used to foraging for themselves in the wild, unafraid of anything. And what type of people did TR attract? People just like himself. That is one of the laws of leadership. It worked for TR. It will work for you. You will attract people like you.

In a remarkably brief amount of time, the Rough Riders were ready to fight. From Texas they boarded trains to Tampa, Florida, where the cavalry were informed they would leave their horses behind and serve as foot soldiers in Cuba. Although they were called Rough *Riders*, they wouldn't be riding to battle! From Tampa they took a troop ship to Cuba. There they joined the American assault force.

THE REAL TEST

Finally, it was time for war. The Rough Riders took part in the battle at Las Guasimas. But the moment that is etched in history is the Rough Riders' charge up San Juan Hill in their march to Santiago. The rigorous discipline of Roosevelt's army paid huge dividends. Although the fighting was at times intense, the Americans prevailed and freed Cuba from Spanish rule. The impromptu "army that had been built by influence" was victorious!

PRINCIPLE OF INFLUENTIAL LEADERSHIP # 3:
Influencers Affirm

In Roosevelt's description of the fighting, he constantly praised his men by name, pointing out their heroic acts, their unflinching perseverance, and their commitment to the cause. We have to remember that Teddy Roosevelt freely trumpeted his own accomplishments throughout his life. He was hardly reticent or shy to talk about himself. But when he talked about the Rough Riders, he rarely praised himself. He praised his men. He described their stoic acceptance of death, their daring in battle, and their willingness to follow orders.

ANOTHER TEST

Once the combat ended, a graver struggle began as his men suffered from malaria and yellow fever. But they never complained. Fortunately, they were soon ordered back to Florida, and the grand Rough Rider adventure concluded.

Roosevelt wrote that as his men headed for home, they were much thinner than when they had enlisted. Many of them had wounds. Others had fevers. The medical doctors who tended to them made a surprising discovery. When they cared for other soldiers, they saw that the soldiers would sometimes fake injuries they did not have. But the Rough Riders were the opposite. They downplayed their injuries, sometimes stating that they needed no medical attention. The medical team had to exercise extra care, since some who claimed that they were fine were, in fact, quite injured. The Rough Riders were truly a most unusual lot. TR had produced one of America's finest fighting units up until that time.

THE LEADER'S GOOD-BYE

Roosevelt's farewell time with his men was emotional. The men loved their leader. They had looked forward to the challenge. Now it was over. In their final moments together, TR let them know how proud he was of them. But in typical TR fashion, he warned them not to rest on the laurels of the past. They would be viewed as heroes for ten days. Then they would have to work as hard as ever.

TR's Rough Riders had a gift for him. They presented him a bronze statue—*The Bronco-buster*—cast by the famous frontier artist Frederic Remington. He considered it the most "appropriate" imaginable gift. TR was "deeply touched" by his men's affection. He wrote tenderly in his book simply titled *The Rough Riders*: "Is it any wonder that I loved my regiment."[2]

PRINCIPLE OF INFLUENTIAL LEADERSHIP # 4:
Influencers Model the Sacrifice They Expect from Their Followers

---

TR cared for the men he led. And they knew it. He was a leader. Leaders touch. They inspire. They invigorate. In summary, they influence.

Leaders draw others to themselves and their causes, even when the cause is difficult. Roosevelt's cause was one that demanded a tough love, which calls men to risk their very lives in serving a higher good. Only leaders can inspire others to that level. There's a name for it: influence.

Roosevelt's zest for life, his commitment to justice, and his willingness to share the hardships and dangers with his men enabled him to effectively recruit and lead the adventurous band. And his courage proved infectious. Writing later in his *Autobiography*, he confessed, "There were all kinds of things I was afraid of at first, ranging from grizzly bears to 'mean' horses and gun-fighters; but by acting as if I was not afraid I gradually ceased to be afraid." He learned that a man can rise above his fears. And in leading the Rough Riders, he personified the leadership and the courage needed for a military operation.

⚜

POPE INNOCENT III AND ST. FRANCIS

A most profound and intriguing example of this leadership principle comes from the Middle Ages. There were two men:

- One of them held one of the most powerful positions—if not *the* most powerful position—in the world.

- The other one had nothing, no position at all. In fact, what little position he *did* have, he insisted on giving up!

These two men present quite a study in contrasts. Here is what is amazing:

- The first man—the one who held the position of great power— is virtually unknown today. He had a mighty position. And he did have influence of sorts for a time. But he had little long-term influence.

- The second man—the one with no position of authority—has had enormous influence. This man who had nothing went on to influence the entire world. His reputation is held in highest esteem to this day. Amazingly, his name is known globally today, some eight hundred years after he lived.

Now, I ask you: Which one was a leader? Of course, the man who was without a position yet had enormous influence. Now, let me tell you the story of these two men: Pope Innocent III (1161–1216) and St. Francis of Assisi (1182–1226). Here is the account of these two individuals who lived at the same time, and whose lives intersected in history, in a profound and dramatic moment in 1209.

INNOCENT

Innocent III's real name was Lotario de' Conti di Segni. (Aren't you glad they shortened his name?) In 1198, at age thirty-seven, he was unanimously elected pope. He brought the papacy to the zenith of power, intimidating even princes and kings. Anyone who challenged his supremacy lost. Challengers were met with the force of his commands or even excommunication (banishment from the church).

In 1213, Innocent III humiliated King John of England by declaring him to be a vassal, which would have forced him to yield the whole country of England to the pope. (As a side note, this action was undone when some barons compelled King John to sign the Magna Carta in 1215, a document that has great significance for American liberties.) In addition, the ruthless Pope Innocent III called for a bloody campaign against the Albigensi, a small religious group in northern Italy and southern France.

Innocent III believed that he was the "vicar [representative] of Christ," and as such, he was to rule all mankind. He believed that he had the right to appoint all earthly rulers, including the emperor. Innocent took literally Jeremiah 1:10, which was preached at his ordination sermon: "See, today I appoint you over nations and kingdoms to uproot and tear down, to destroy and overthrow, to build and to plant." In Innocent's mind, his position gave him the authority to declare, in effect, "I'm the boss, so follow me!" He mistakenly thought that leadership flows from position.

Admittedly, he did leave a legacy. He convened a major church conference, known as the Fourth Lateran Council, in which it was decided that Catholics should be required to go to confession and partake of Communion at least annually.

But in spite of the fact that he was the most powerful pope, and even more powerful than any secular rulers, he is little known today. One of his greatest accomplishments was his positive response to St. Francis of Assisi in 1209 (after a very negative response a few days earlier), the other man in this historical illustration of the *true* nature of leadership: influence.

FRANCIS

Francis, delineated simply by his hometown—"of Assisi"—was born into a wealthy family in Assisi, in what is now northern Italy. His father was a wealthy cloth merchant. Francis was a flippant youth, without a serious thought. If one were to predict his future based on his earliest years, one would presume that his life would be quite lackluster.

Two events radically altered Francis's life: a severe sickness and a military expedition at age twenty that resulted in his becoming a prisoner of war for one year. He became repulsed at his love for things and thus rejected materialism. He left the potential of his father's wealth and pursued a life of prayer.

Another event would rock the world of Francis. In 1205 he made a trip to Rome. Outside St. Peter's Basilica, the world's largest church, he conducted an odd experiment. For a full day, he exchanged places with a beggar. What he experienced transformed his understanding of life.

Equally unusual was his response to a person who had leprosy. Most people would have absolutely nothing to do with someone plagued with this horrific disease. But Francis violated all known protocol. He not only embraced the person; he actually kissed the person's sores, a repulsive thought to most. In contrast to his contemporary Innocent III, who chose Jeremiah 1:10 as a Bible verse that was self-exalting, Francis, in 1209, chose Matthew 10:7–10 as his scripture of choice. These Bible verses instruct followers of Christ to go out and preach and heal persons, but not to take any financial provision for the journey. He chose to live in poverty and to practice forgiveness and brotherly love.

He chose the lowly life of a beggar, asking for funds not for himself, but for the purpose of repairing church buildings that had fallen into disrepair. His passion for a simple life and his zeal for Christ quickly attracted followers.

FRANCIS MEETS INNOCENT III

However, this following created a problem. In order to have a recognized religious group, one had to have permission from the pope. And the intrigue of the story enters at this point. Francis, the man who chose to have nothing, had to gain permission from Pope Innocent III, the man who wielded all power. The two figures met. What a sight that must have been: one lowly beggar standing before the most powerful earthly leader.

The year was 1209. Francis and his motley-appearing group traveled to Rome in order to get permission from Innocent III to continue to minister. Quite by accident, they encountered the pope in a hallway. It was a moment of drama. Francis, surprised to see the world's most powerful person, inarticulately blurted out his request. There was a moment of silence as the all-powerful Innocent looked at the lowly Francis. Finally, the stunned and angry pope told the strange-appearing man from Assisi "to go roll in the mud with the pigs." And how did Francis respond? Did he retaliate for Innocent's thoughtless command? No. Francis, obedient as he was, sought out a nearby pigpen and did exactly as he had been ordered. He rolled in the mud with the pigs!

Had Bishop Guido, who was also from Assisi, not been in Rome at that time, our story might have ended with Francis in the pigpen. But it doesn't end there. Bishop Guido persuaded Francis to leave the hogs behind and meet with a well-placed cardinal who would be able to arrange a more appropriate and formal meeting with the pope.

At the second meeting, Pope Innocent III was quite intrigued with Francis, particularly the fact that Francis had taken his words literally (which Innocent likely never meant) and had rolled around in the mud with the pigs. The world's most powerful person was charmed by Francis's life and zeal, and the pope granted him and his followers official recognition. Francis and his followers became known as the Preachers of Penance, a title which was later changed to Franciscans.

POSITION VS. TRUE INFLUENCE

No one there could have conceived the strange twist of history that would occur. Who could have guessed that the all-powerful Innocent III would become largely unknown, and that St. Francis of Assisi, the man who had nothing, would, centuries later, become one of the most celebrated persons on earth? Who would have thought that Francis would be called "the world's favorite saint, [the] gentle lover of everyone and everything in God's creation"?[3]

Let me ask you a question. How many persons today recognize the name Innocent III? What did you know about him before you read this chapter? How many know that in the Middle Ages, he was the most authoritative pope, wielding power over kings and princes? Very few, if any.

PRINCIPLE OF INFLUENTIAL LEADERSHIP # 5:
People Who Leave Positions Leave Openings;
Influencers Leave Legacies

How many persons today would recognize the name St. Francis of Assisi? Many. Very many. And equally amazing, the Franciscans, named after this powerless, positionless wandering preacher, blanket the entire earth with a massive network of hospitals, schools, and numerous other ministries.

Let me ask you the question one more time. Pope Innocent III and St. Francis met in 1209. One had position. One did not. Which has had more influence? Francis, of course. And Francis, not Innocent, was the strongest leader because leadership *is* influence.

※

ROBERT STEPHENSON SMYTH BADEN-POWELL

Perhaps you were a young man who was fortunate enough to be in the Boy Scouts. Or maybe one of your brothers or cousins was in the Boy Scouts. If so, have you ever wondered how it all began? Or have you ever wondered why 3.3 million young men are part of the Boy Scouts of America (including all BSA groups), led by more than 1.2 million volunteers? How did the organization begin? Who was the person who sparked such a concept? What was he like? How did he have such influence? You already know the answer: leadership.

The founder of the Boy Scouts surely holds a record for having one of the longest names. Robert Stephenson Smyth Baden-Powell (1857–1941) was the eighth of ten children born to the Reverend Baden-Powell, a professor at Oxford University. Robert became one of the most highly acclaimed military men of his generation. But he is known today not as a military hero but as the founder of the Boy Scouts.

As a youngster, he did not enjoy the classroom. One of his instructors even labeled him lazy. Such was not the case. The instructor simply did not know how to direct the enormous potential within young Robert.

FIND YOUR NICHE

Baden-Powell was, quite simply, an outdoorsman! Ever ready for adventure, he and his brothers sailed a yacht around England's south coast and paddled canoes up the Thames to its source. He joined the army, was commissioned to the Thirteenth Hussars, beginning the career for which he was eminently suited. He subsequently served with distinction in India, Afghanistan, South Africa, and Malta. Routinely promoted, by the age of forty, he was given command of the Fifth Dragoon Guards in 1897.

Robert was quickly becoming one of the most famous figures in the British Empire. The press celebrated his exploits. Youngsters idolized him much as they do today's superstar athletes. During a 217-day siege during the Boar War (1899–1900), Baden-Powell wrote a military text, *Aids to Scouting*, which is a distillation of what he learned working with young soldiers. He described the games and contests that helped train effective cavalrymen.

PRINCIPLE OF INFLUENTIAL LEADERSHIP # 6:
Jettison Anything That Takes You Away from Your Major Calling

---

In the midst of it all, General Baden-Powell pondered his military career. As inspector general of cavalry, he had truly "made it" in the military. An even higher honor, becoming a field marshal, could conceivably have been his. But in 1910, at age fifty-three, he retired from the army to devote himself to the organization he had inspired. Doing so, he apparently accepted the advice of King Edward VII, who suggested he could help the world more through the Scouts than the army!

Originally intended for boys aged eleven to fifteen, the Boy Scouts soon took on added dimensions. The year Baden-Powell retired, he and his sister, Agnes, founded the Girl Guides, an organization known in the United States from 1912 on as the Girl Scouts. In 1916 he organized the Wolf Clubs for younger boys in Great Britain—transformed into the Cub Scouts in the U.S. In 1910 an American publisher incorporated the Boy Scouts of America, which soon became a distinctively American organization. In other nations the same pattern followed. Within a century of its founding, there were troops in 110 nations.

> ### PRINCIPLE OF INFLUENTIAL LEADERSHIP # 7:
> *Titles Follow Influence*

Following WWI, the first international Scout Jamboree was held in London. The assembled Scouts named Baden-Powell "Chief Scout of the World." With the same energy he had invested in his military career, the general presided over the expansion of his organization. He lived out the precept that every minute was "sixty seconds worth of distance run."[4] He also continued to participate in the outdoor activities he had loved since he was a boy—fishing, hunting, and playing polo.

> ### PRINCIPLE OF INFLUENTIAL LEADERSHIP # 8:
> *A Leader's Influence Is Ultimately Determined by the Legacy He or She Leaves*

In 1938, his strength waning, Baden-Powell retired to Kenya, where he died three years later. Toward the end of his life, he wrote a farewell message to his beloved Scouts:

Remember, it is the last time you will ever hear from me, so think it over. I have had a most happy life and I want each one of you to have a happy life too.

I believe that God put us in this jolly world to be happy and enjoy life. Happiness does not come from being rich, nor merely being successful in your career, nor by self-indulgence. One step towards happiness is to make yourself healthy and strong while you are a boy, so that you can be useful and so you can enjoy life when you are a man. Nature study will show you how full of beautiful and wonderful things God has made the world for you to enjoy. Be contented with what you have got and make the best of it. Look on the bright side of things instead of the gloomy one. But the real way to get happiness is by giving out happiness to other people. Try and leave this world a little better than you found it and when your turn comes to die, you can die happy in feeling that at any rate you have not wasted your time but have done your best. "Be Prepared" in this way, to live happy and to die happy—stick to your Scout Promise always—even after you have ceased to be a boy—and God help you do it.[5]

Three million young men. One million adult volunteers. That's influence. And that is the true measure of leadership.

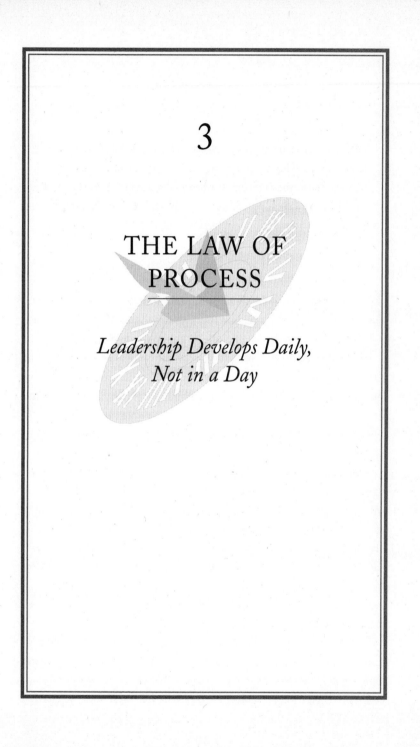

3

THE LAW OF
PROCESS

*Leadership Develops Daily,
Not in a Day*

PRINCIPLES OF THE
PROCESS OF LEADERSHIP

I am uniquely qualified to write this book. Of the six billion persons on earth, I am the only one who had to follow John Maxwell in a leadership position since he has become so knowledgeable on leadership.

For fourteen years, John served as the senior pastor of Skyline Wesleyan Church in the San Diego area. In 1995, he announced his resignation so that he could follow his calling to teach leadership globally.

FOLLOWING THE LEADER

The church began to look for a new pastor. I was one of those who was contacted. I remember the day very well! It was May 1, 1995. I (along with other potential pastoral candidates) was asked if I would be open to consider coming to Skyline as the new senior pastor. I immediately declined, saying, "Anyone who tries to follow John Maxwell is a fool." (Several years have passed since I made that comment. I think the statement might *still* be true!) But four months later, I found myself accepting the senior pastoral role at Skyline Church. I *did* follow—or attempted to follow—Maxwell. And it has been a challenge.

It was not a challenge because of anything that John did. He did everything within his power to help me succeed. During my first two years as senior pastor, he still lived in San Diego, so he was frequently in the congregation when I was preaching. He could not have been more supportive.

What made it so difficult following him as a leader? The answer is probably obvious to every reader—his incredible leadership skills. Frankly, I needed to grow a lot in my leadership skills. People were amazingly patient with me. Most stayed. Some left. But overwhelmingly, they stayed. The church has grown and prospered in many ways.

This chapter is extremely important to me, for it focuses on the one area that I have most lacked in my leadership skills—process. I understood process in other arenas of my life: academics, spirituality, and parenting. But when it came to developing leaders, I underestimated the importance of process.

On occasion, someone would say, "Jim, you're too 'event-driven.'" That would sting! But I knew the speaker was right. I was an "event king." In fact, I can "out-event" anybody. At "eventing," I'm good! But leaders are not produced in events. They are made in process. So I have been on a huge learning curve for the past few years. I wish I could say that I have changed and that I have conquered the process concept. I haven't. But I'm growing. I'm not where I want to be. But I'm not where I used to be. And while I see how far I have to go, I am thankful for the progress.

I felt that this brief autobiographical insight might be valuable to you. You can see why I value the precepts of this chapter so much. I am on a journey. I am a learner. And if it's not too late for me, it's not too late for you. I am not only a writer of this chapter. I am a reader too. I want to learn everything I can from those who have gone before us. Some understood process. Others, to their detriment, did not.

GEORGE WHITEFIELD'S FOLLOWERS VS. JOHN WESLEY'S FOLLOWERS

History provides some spectacular examples of this, but none so impressive as the difference between two men—both living in England in the 1700s. George Whitefield and John Wesley were phenomenal leaders, who were both exceptionally gifted. Both commanded enormous respect. Tens of thousands followed them. And they were friends (except for a period of time in which they had little contact due to a theological conflict). Wesley even preached the sermon at Whitefield's funeral.

ONE STRIKING DIFFERENCE: PROCESS

Whitefield and Wesley shared many things in common, but they had one noticeable difference. As the years went by, Whitefield's followers dissipated. His organization faltered. Wesley's did not. What was the difference? Both men were brilliant. Both were winsome and compelling communicators. Both experienced phenomenal success in their lives. But Wesley understood process. Whitefield, it would appear, did not.

WHITEFIELD

George Whitefield (1714–70) was one of the most effective public communicators of the eighteenth century. As a preacher, he moved the crowds. The son of a poor innkeeper in Gloucestershire, England, Whitefield experienced a meteoric preaching career beginning at age twenty-one when he was ordained by the Church of England (which in the U.S. was called the Episcopal Church). He became a household name on both sides of the Atlantic, making more than seven exhausting trips to the American colonies, the first in 1738. He traveled in all thirteen of the American colonies, from Maine to Georgia. He preached more than eighteen thousand times! His sermons were so inspiring that they touched off what has been called the Great Awakening in America.

George Whitefield preached not merely in the safety of church buildings, but in the less safe open air where he could be heckled or pelted with stones from unruly critics. But he was undaunted. He was bold and courageous. Thousands responded to his booming voice, which could be heard by a crowd of 20,000 (some have even dared to say 40,000) *without* present-day public address systems. Many gave of their finances to help support the orphanage that his wife operated in the Georgia Colony. His British followers organized into a denomination known as the Calvinist Methodists in 1743. It is at this point that the Law of Process begins to play a part in our story. But before we talk about Whitefield's understanding (or lack of understanding) regarding the Law of Process, let's visit the life of Whitefield's friend, John Wesley (1703–91).

WESLEY

Susanna Wesley (1669–1742) gave birth to nineteen children, eleven of whom died in infancy. The fifteenth child was a baby boy named John. Susanna's husband, Samuel, was a Church of England pastor in the small community of Epworth in 1709 when an angry parishioner decided to torch the parsonage. Fortunately, the flames and smoke awakened Samuel and Susanna from their sleep in time to get their children out of the house—or so they thought. Tragically, they had miscounted. Young John, age five, was still in the house, standing at a second story window, looking helplessly down at his panicked parents.

The neighbors, seizing the moment, formed a human ladder, standing on each other's shoulders, until one could reach in and rescue young John, only seconds before the house collapsed in the flames. The grateful mother clutched her five-year-old in her arms and exclaimed, "Truly, you are a brand plucked from the burning," a statement of destiny that foreshadowed the enormous legacy that Wesley would someday leave.

Like the other Wesley boys, John attended Oxford. Eventually, he became a notably unsuccessful missionary to the Native Americans in Governor Oglethorpe's Georgia Colony. As one historian wryly observed, if John Wesley had died before his thirty-sixth birthday, he would not have rated even a footnote in anyone's history book.[1] Instead thousands of books have been written about him, hundreds of doctoral dissertations have pondered his life and thought, and millions of persons globally, from scores of denominations, point to him as the father of their faith. How could this be? What happened? And what can present-day leaders learn from him regarding the Law of Process?

On May 24, 1738, Wesley wrote, his "heart was strangely warmed." That phrase depicts a profound change in his life—from one who lacked a deeply Christian experience with God to one who was willing to travel every day for the rest of his life to share with others what had happened to him. He was challenged by his friend George Whitefield to stop preaching to the small civil crowds who gathered in church buildings, but to be willing to stand in open fields before thousands and preach. That is the last thing Wesley, a very orderly, proper Oxford graduate, wanted to do. But he accepted the challenge, and his field (outdoor) preaching touched off a half-century spiritual explosion that is referred to as the Wesleyan Revival, or Evangelical Awakening, which altered the course of English history.

Wesley's traveling and speaking schedule was impressive, even by today's standards. He operated out of three headquarters—London, Oxford, and Bristol—traveling constantly. His energy level was amazing. He arose every morning at four o'clock, working eighteen-hour days. He rode on horseback a quarter of a million miles. He stopped riding a horse when he reached about seventy years of age, but he continued the rigorous travel schedule by horse and buggy. He traveled 4,000 to 5,000 miles a year, as many as 80 miles a day! It is believed that Wesley may have spent more time in the saddle that any other man who ever lived, including Bonaparte and Caesar.[2] Equally amazing was his ability to convert the saddle to a library chair, reading literally hundreds of books while riding on horseback.

He preached 40,000 times, often up to 5 times a day! On September 21, 1773, his crowd at Gwennap Pit, a natural amphitheater, was estimated at 32,000. He authored (and in some cases edited) an estimated 233 books. At the time of his death in 1791, he led an enormous organization: 120,000 members in the Methodist movement,[3] with some suggesting that the total adherents numbered one million.[4]

What happened to the organization that he founded—the people called Methodists (or the Wesleyan Methodists, as they were later called)—after his death? Did it disappear? Did it flourish? What occurred?

STRUCTURES THAT EMBRACE PROCESS

Wesley's Methodist movement flourished globally after Wesley's death. Today there are scores of denominations that point to Wesley as their inspiration. There are millions of believers who see him as the father of their denominations. In contrast, George Whitefield's denomination, the Calvinist Methodists, had insignificant impact, eventually ceasing to even exist. Why? What was the difference between Wesley's and Whitefield's leadership style?

> **PRINCIPLE OF THE PROCESS OF LEADERSHIP # 1:**
> *Gathering People Is Easier Than Keeping People*

Wesley understood the Law of Process. He quickly saw that *gaining* followers was not the key issue; *sustaining them* was the real challenge. To that end, Wesley began to organize his new converts. He understood process.

> **PRINCIPLE OF THE PROCESS OF LEADERSHIP # 2:**
> *People Grow Best When There Is*
> *Relationally Based Accountability*

Throughout England, with very little clergy support (some say as few as forty Anglican clergy were sympathetic to his movement), Wesley and his army of lay leaders organized. "Class leaders," as they were called, had oversight over a dozen or so believers, monitoring their growth toward spiritual maturity. Class members were expected to candidly report their personal spiritual progress (or lack of it) in their weekly meetings.

Within the class (about a dozen persons) was a smaller organizational structure. "Bands" were small groups of four or five persons, with even more in-your-face accountability. Persons were organized in bands according to their gender and marital status. Married men in one; single men in another; married women in another; and single women in yet another band.

> **PRINCIPLE OF THE PROCESS OF LEADERSHIP # 3:**
> *Multiply Yourself*

Wesley had the capacity to multiply himself. To oversee the burgeoning organizational structure that proliferated throughout England, a multitude of traveling "lay preachers" watched over the class leaders. And if one could not travel full time, one could still assist in leadership in Wesley's massive army of volunteers as a "local preacher." The entire organizational scheme had one crystal clear goal: to provide a structure whereby persons could grow from one level to the next. And it worked! In fact, it worked brilliantly.

> **PRINCIPLE OF THE PROCESS OF LEADERSHIP # 4:**
> *Crowds Dissipate; Disciples Follow*

Whitefield's followers had no such structure to assist them in their personal growth. Once converted, they were simply to gather in churches. But that did not happen. What was lacking was a process, a system or device by which a person would be enabled to go to the next level of growth.

> **PRINCIPLE OF THE PROCESS OF LEADERSHIP # 5:**
> *Understand the Difference Between Programs and Movements*

What is the difference between a movement and a program? Programs begin big and end small. Movements begin small and end big. Wesley led a movement—it started small, but kept growing. Whitefield's church might be called a "program," in that it enjoyed early success, but ended small. It lacked the durability of a "movement." Process thinking helps you make certain what you are leading is a movement, not a program.

Two men. Two leaders. Both were outstanding. But only one understood process. The other didn't.

GEORGE WASHINGTON

Few historic figures have enjoyed the sustained support and nearly unanimous adulation given the father of the United States of America, George Washington. Having distinguished himself in his native Virginia during the French and Indian War, he was appointed by the First

Continental Congress to lead the colonial army during the War of Independence. He did so successfully—so successfully that some of his supporters even suggested he be proclaimed king of the new country. Generally self-effacing, however, he retired to his home at Mount Vernon following the war, only to be brought back to service as president of the new nation, unanimously elected by the electoral college in 1789.

> **PRINCIPLE OF THE PROCESS OF LEADERSHIP # 6:**
> *Personal Integrity Is Foundational in the
> Leadership Development Journey*

Washington's public success stood rooted in his solid character. A man who knew him well, Gouverneur Morris, rightly wrote that the nation depended on Washington's personal character, "your cool, steady temper is *indispensably necessary* to give firm . . . tone to the new Government."[5] Washington overstated his limitations, claiming to have inherited "inferiour endowments from nature." However, he rightly acknowledged that he lacked the intellectual brilliance of luminaries such as John Adams, Thomas Jefferson, and Alexander Hamilton, who served him in his first administration.

To Samuel Eliot Morison, one of our greatest historians, Washington's "superiority lay in character, not talents. He had the power of inspiring respect, but no gift of popularity. He was direct, not adroit; stubborn rather than flexible; slow to reach a decision rather than a man of quick perception. [His] dignity . . . that concealed his inner life came from humility, and . . . self-control."[6]

> **PRINCIPLE OF THE PROCESS OF LEADERSHIP # 7:**
> *Prioritize Principles Over Popularity or Preferences*

As a general and a president, Washington could make tough decisions, often displeasing people in order to do what he judged to be right.

"Disinterested and courageous, far-sighted and patient, aloof yet direct in manner, inflexible once his mind was made up," Winston Churchill wrote, "Washington possessed the gifts of character for which the situation called."[7]

WASHINGTON'S PROCESS FOR DEVELOPING CHARACTER

Here is a key question for us all: How did Washington become the great leader he was? How did he get that way? The answer is exactly what you are already thinking: process. All of us are the sum total of the tiny decisions we make daily.

If you don't like who you have become, it is because of the thousands of small, seemingly insignificant decisions that you have made each day over the course of the years. If you like what you have become and are becoming, it is because you have made several hundred thousand seemingly small, moment-by-moment decisions in a very wise manner. You are the sum total of your life's decisions.

Most people do not realize that life is comprised of lots of little decisions—all with a huge cumulative, collective impact. Most of life is not determined by big decisions, although they are important. It is the sum total of the so-called small decisions that builds character. And our leadership is built on that foundation: our character. George Washington was no exception.

Washington's character didn't suddenly appear when he was called to a position of leadership. Rather, he began early on to cultivate characteristics he deemed worthy to emulate. Just as one develops a strong physique through constant, rigorous exercise, so, too, one forges a character through disciplined patterns of behavior.

PRINCIPLE OF THE PROCESS OF LEADERSHIP # 8:
To Go to the Next Level, Have a Plan

As a youngster, Washington wrote down a list, 110 "Rules of Civility & Decent Behaviour in Company and Conversation," which is most revealing. It is believed that he found the rules in an English translation of a

1595 French Jesuit treatise, *Bienseance de la Conversation entre les Hommes.* But wherever he found them, he clearly sought to follow them in the process of becoming a man. A sampling of the precepts (spelled in the English of the day) proves illuminating:

1st   Every Action done in Company, ought to be with Some Sign of Respect, to those that are Present.

22d   Show not yourself glad at the misfortune of another though he were your enemy.

44th When a man does all he can though it Succeeds not well blame not him that did it.

65th Speak not injurious Words neither in Jest nor Earnest; Scoff at none although they give Occasion.

73d   Think before you Speak pronounce not imperfectly nor bring out your Words too hastily but orderly & distinctly.

89th Speak not Evil of the absent for it is unjust.

PRINCIPLE OF THE PROCESS OF LEADERSHIP # 9:
The Power of Process Is the Cumulative Impact of Many Small, Correct Decisions

---

The fascinating aspect of this list of rules is their general triviality. Now and then one finds deeply moral issues stressed. But overall, the rules simply urge one to live carefully, considerately, and consistently. The little things one does—speaking correctly, dressing appropriately, greeting others courteously—all add up. They, in fact, build strong character. And they add up, as Washington demonstrated, to strong character.

In and of themselves, one might be amused at the seeming unimportance of these rules. But these are much more than a list of rules. They reveal the inner workings of a person who was willing to pay the price of going to the next level. He was not above a form of self-accountability in order to become all that he could be. Washington understood the Law of Process. And all of America benefited.

THE PROCESSORS OF THE MIDDLE AGES

A group of persons in the Middle Ages were geniuses in understanding process. They knew that one did not become a mature Christian in an instant. They knew it was a deliberate, intentional process. Due to their "mystical" closeness to God, they are, not surprisingly, called the Mystics.

Let's assume for a moment that I have invited you to my home for dinner, and nine guests from the Middle Ages are to join us. All of them, I explain, have something to teach us about leadership.

We enjoy lively conversation during the meal and afterward. When the guests have gone, you and I take a moment to revisit the unique contributions of each one. Here is our overview of the nine dinner guests:

1. Bernard of Clairvaux (1090–1153) was one of the most influential French spiritual leaders of the Middle Ages. He consistently turned down opportunities for career advancement, instead focusing his energies on cultivating love of God in others.

2. Bonaventure (1221–74) was a strong administrator and profound thinker. But he understood process and learned the value of making a little progress each day. He never tired of teaching others how to grow in intimacy with God.

3. Johannes Eckhart (1260–1327) was trained at the prestigious University of Paris. He inspired students for generations to pursue God daily with all one's heart.

4. John Ruysbroeck (1293–1381) was so influential in his writings and teaching about daily spiritual growth that he became known as a "director of souls," impacting such students as John Tauler.

5. John Tauler (1300–1361) became one of the "Friends of God," a loosely knit fellowship of students of Meister Eckhart. He, too, understood how to grow daily in one's love for God and others.

6. Catherine of Siena (1347–80) was an articulate activist and cultural critic, ready to challenge both persons and institutions to take the steps toward growth and maturity. She urged political leaders to stop wars. She challenged clergy who were greedy and apathetic.

7. Thomas à Kempis (1380–1471) wrote what may well be the world's most popular book outside the Bible. It is titled *The Imitation of Christ*, a manual on how to spend your life learning to act like Jesus.

8. John of the Cross (1542–91) reflected on how to survive moment by moment and overcome the difficult times in life in a widely heralded work, *The Dark Night of the Soul*.

9. Teresa of Avila (1515–82) was an aristocratic socialite who chose to leave high position and privilege in order to heal theological divisions between Catholics and Protestants, and to ignite reform in her homeland of Spain. She believed in the ability of a person to grow increasingly in the love of God.

All nine of them were successful influencers, who recognized these process leadership principles:

> **PRINCIPLE OF THE PROCESS OF LEADERSHIP # 10:**
> *Growth Occurs Gradually and Is Experienced Daily*

> **PRINCIPLE OF THE PROCESS OF LEADERSHIP # 11:**
> *Process Leadership Means Believing That People Can Be Better Than They Currently Are*

PRINCIPLE OF THE PROCESS OF LEADERSHIP # 12:
The Leadership Journey Is to Be Traveled in a Relationship Between the Mentor and the One Being Mentored

---

In the same way that we have just learned some of the great lessons from the Mystics of the Middle Ages, there are many other eras, many other persons to meet in the pages of this book. And they, too, will teach us much about leadership.

⚓

JEREMY'S STORY

Allow me to bring the story line closer to home and to contemporary times. There was a baseball pitcher named Jeremy. He pitched for several farm teams: the St. Louis Cardinals, the Colorado Rockies, and the Duluth Dukes. Like most professional pitchers, he experienced both encouraging and discouraging moments in his career.

No moment was more jolting than his first day of spring training for the Texas Rangers in March of 1998. Since he held many records for the Duluth Dukes from the previous season, he felt he was ready for the big break that would put him into the majors. After ten years in the minors, this was his chance, it seemed, to make it. But on the first day of spring training, pain shot through his shoulder. Cortisone failed to ease the pain. Eventually, surgery was required to repair the shoulder, but it never regained its strength. At age twenty-seven, Jeremy, who had dreamed of being a major-league pitcher since age eight, could pitch no more.

Within three years Jeremy was standing before crowds as a public speaker. As the associate pastor of one of America's largest churches, he occasionally fills in for the senior pastor, speaking to nearly six thousand people a weekend. How did he go—so quickly—from a baseball pitcher to an outstanding preacher/communicator? The answer: he didn't. That is, he didn't get that way *quickly*. It all occurred slowly, painstakingly slowly. So slow and so invisible was the transformation that most never noticed. That's because it was a process drawn out over many years.

> **PRINCIPLE OF THE PROCESS OF LEADERSHIP #13:**
> *Persons Who Want to Grow to the Next Level*
> *Always Find a Way to Seize the Moment*

During the off-season, while other pitchers enjoyed a well-deserved rest, Jeremy was cramming in as much college education as he could. When he had to leave for spring training each March, he went to his professors and worked out directed study programs so he could complete each course.

While other students took off Christmas break, Jeremy used the three weeks to read every book that John Maxwell had written on leadership. And every time he got in his truck to drive to an appointment, he made sure that he had a John Maxwell leadership tape to listen to. Once he completed his bachelor's degree, he immediately poured himself into a master's degree, which he promptly completed. And on a continual basis, he interviewed his father-in-law on numerous historical and theological matters.

By age twenty-nine, Jeremy, who had never read the Bible before age twenty, had become a superb Bible teacher and now preaches every couple of months to the nearly six thousand people who attend High Desert Church in Victorville, California. Other pitchers were cast aside from the farm system, only to struggle to find a new sense of identity. But Jeremy cruised to his new role. The reason is obvious: he understood process.

While others watched TV reruns between games, Jeremy read textbooks and wrote papers. While others spent Christmas vacation sleeping in late, Jeremy read several dozen leadership books. While others hummed along with their favorite rock tunes on the radio, Jeremy used each driving mile to listen to America's top leadership guru. While others sat and talked trivia, Jeremy interrogated his relatives regarding theology and history.

> **PRINCIPLE OF THE PROCESS OF LEADERSHIP #14:**
> *People Who Are Willing to Stay in Process*
> *Seem to Have More Luck*

To the uninformed, it looked as if Jeremy had a lucky break. It seemed that High Desert Church's Senior Pastor Tom Mercer just picked Jeremy out of the blue. It appeared that he was an overnight success. If he was an overnight success, he was a *nine-year* overnight success. Jeremy understood process, and it paid huge dividends.

How do I know this story? I watched it unfold firsthand. Jeremy— Jeremy McGarity, that is—is my son-in-law. He understood the Law of Process.

4

THE LAW OF
NAVIGATION

*Anyone Can Steer the Ship,
But It Takes a Leader to
Chart the Course*

PRINCIPLES OF NAVIGATIONAL LEADERSHIP

Failure to care about the numbers of your organization is simply another way of saying that you do not care whether your organization—be it a school, factory, company, church, or civic group—lives or dies. Leaders *do* care about the numbers of their organization, in the same way that a conscientious parent cares about the vital signs of his child.

Numbers *are* important! The importance of numbers was recently demonstrated in college basketball. In the 2001–2 University of Kansas basketball program, an amazing thing happened. The men's team became the first team to sweep through the Big 12 with a 16-0 record. The women's team, the same year, likewise broke a record, going 0-16 in the Big 12. Some people say numbers aren't important. Really? Are 16-0 and 0-16 unimportant? Not if you're on the men's team! Numbers, in and of themselves, matter little. But *what numbers represent* means everything, especially if you were playing basketball for the University of Kansas in the 2001–2 school year.

Jesus talked about numbers. He said that if ninety-nine sheep were safe, but one was lost, He would go looking for the lost sheep. Numbers *do* matter, especially if you are the one lost sheep!

The bottom line: numbers do matter; at least what they *represent* matters. Always. And they certainly matter when it comes to strategizing, plotting the course for the organization that one leads.

CHARTING

Leaders don't merely plot the course and then walk away. They monitor progress or the lack of it. They look for early indicators that might demonstrate the potential for success or failure. Leaders anticipate early enough to make midcourse or, preferably, *early*-course corrections. But as we shall learn in the following stories, that is no easy task.

⚓

THE *EXXON VALDEZ*:
A LESSON IN NAVIGATIONAL FAILURE

Several years ago, my wife, Carol, and I were taken fishing in Valdez Harbor in Alaska by our good friends Al and Donna Woods. When we arrived at a particular area of the harbor, they pointed out where a major oil tanker had failed to make a sharp right turn, a dogleg turn that should have led it safely out into the ocean.

PRINCIPLE OF NAVIGATIONAL LEADERSHIP # 1:
Leaders Pay Attention and Anticipate
What Might Shipwreck Their Organization

On March 23, 1989, at 9:12 P.M., the old tanker *Exxon Valdez* left the Trans Alaska Pipeline Terminal. William Murphy, the ship's pilot, attempted to maneuver the 986-foot vessel through the Valdez Narrows. Helmsman Harry Claar was steering. Joe Hazelwood, the captain, was nearby. Murphy left Hazelwood in charge.

When the *Valdez* encountered an iceberg, Claar was ordered to take the ship out of the normal shipping lanes in hopes of avoiding the icebergs. Claar then handed the wheel over to Third Mate Gregory Cousins with instructions to turn back into the shipping lanes at a specified point. Claar left and was replaced by Helmsman Robert Kagan. Cousins and Kagan were at the helm.

Slightly past midnight, early in the morning on March 24, 1989,

Cousins and Kagan failed to read the numbers and did not navigate back into the normal shipping lanes. At 12:04 A.M., the oil tanker struck Bligh Reef in Prince William Sound. The result? More than eleven million gallons of crude oil were released in the ocean, the largest spill in U.S. history.

FOUR BAD DECISIONS

What went wrong? There were at least four obvious causes for the disaster.

PRINCIPLE OF NAVIGATIONAL LEADERSHIP # 2:
Fatigue, Incompetence, Alcohol (and a Host of Other Things) Can Impair the Leader's Ability to Read the Numbers

---

Several bad judgments forebode the disaster.

- First, where was the captain? In the wrong place! He was in his quarters at the time. He should have been navigating his ship through this treacherous area.
- Second, there is ample evidence that the crew was fatigued.
- Third, there was the failure to have proper escort, the lack of badly needed competency.
- Fourth, and most offensive, the clearly impaired judgment skills were caused by alcohol. Simply stated, it was a preventable disaster!

But it is equally catastrophic when present-day leaders fail to navigate *their* "ships" through the treacherous "waters" of contemporary culture. It might be caused by fatigue. It might be caused by incompetence. And the use of alcohol has destroyed many an organization. Wise is the man or woman who reads the numbers and charts the course carefully. There is a name for that. It is called leadership.

This chapter is about navigation. It is about knowing the course. It is about keeping the ship on course, whatever that ship might be.

History can be a profoundly revealing instructor. Some succeeded at navigation. Some didn't. Some succeeded for a time, then failed to *continue* to read the navigational charts. Here are some looming examples.

⚓

CHRISTOPHER COLUMBUS: CHARTING THE COURSE

Charting the course can be extremely difficult. Sometimes, even with the brightest minds and most daring dreams, things can veer off course. Christopher Columbus was one man who understood that more than most. Although he is credited with charting the course successfully in many ways, he also knew the bitter disappointment of being unable to *continue* to chart the course.

PRINCIPLE OF NAVIGATIONAL LEADERSHIP # 3:
Ask for God's Help (You'll Need It)

Few men have dreamed so grandly as Christopher Columbus. Following his dreams, he accidentally discovered the New World—the Western Hemisphere. He believed himself called to greatness, confident that God "gave me the spirit and the intelligence for the task . . . It was the Lord who put into my mind (I could feel His hand upon me) to sail to the Indies . . . There is no question that the inspiration was from the Holy Spirit, because he comforted me with rays of marvelous illumination from the Holy Scriptures."[1] Consequently, a new epoch dawned on October 12, 1492, when Columbus landed in the New World.

THE SIGNIFICANCE OF COLUMBUS'S DISCOVERY

His landfall prompted, sixty years later, the Spanish historian Francisco Lopez de Gomara to state: "The discovery of the Indies, what we call the New World, is, excepting only the Incarnation and death of our Lord,

55

the most important event since the creation of the world."[2] Lopez de Gomara saw clearly, for the New World discovery helped create the modern world.

No territorial conquest in world history compares with Europe's penetration of four of the world's seven continents within four centuries. No economic development rivals the prosperity enjoyed by Europeans as a consequence of their conquest and its attendant technological development. Two centuries later, the English political philosopher Adam Smith would concur with Lopez de Gomara, writing in *The Wealth of Nations* (1776) that the discovery of the New World and the rounding of the Cape of Good Hope to India were "the two greatest and most important events in the history of mankind."[3]

THE MAN DESTINED TO CHART A COURSE

Born in Genoa, Italy, in 1451, the boy christened Cristoforo Colombo (Christopher Columbus is a Latinized version of his name) rather naturally took to the sea as a teenager. He learned the art of navigation and, sailing under various flags, spent several years in Portugal, the center of navigation in his day. He may have ventured as far north as Iceland, where he could have heard of Leif Ericson's settlement on Vineland four centuries earlier, and he knew the Atlantic from Iceland to the Cape Verde Islands off the coast of Africa.

> PRINCIPLE OF NAVIGATIONAL LEADERSHIP # 4:
> *Ask Competent Persons Lots of Questions*

Columbus was notably well informed, having read such works as Marco Polo's account of his trip to China, and he sought to improve his social standing through maritime adventures. Toward the end of his life, he wrote,

> I have had dealings and conversations with learned men, priests and laymen, Latins and Greeks, Jews and Moors, and many others of other sects. I found my Lord very favorable to this my desire, and to further

it, He granted me the gift of knowledge. He made me skilled in seamanship, equipped me with the sciences of astronomy, geometry and arithmetic, and taught my mind and hand to draw this sphere, and upon it the cities, rivers, mountains, islands and ports.[4]

To which he added, with some exaggeration: "I made it my business to read all that has been written on geography, history, philosophy and other sciences."

PRINCIPLE OF NAVIGATIONAL LEADERSHIP # 5:
If You Dream Big, Calculate Accordingly

Early on he envisioned sailing due west across the Atlantic Ocean by way of the Canary Islands, then west along the twenty-eighth parallel, rather than rounding the southern tip of Africa (a feat accomplished by Bartholomew Diaz in 1487), in order to reach Japan and China. Few folks doubted that the earth was spherical, so the proposal made sense. But Columbus miscalculated the distance from the Canaries to Japan. He thought it was 2,400 miles, roughly the distance to Haiti, whereas it is, in fact, 10,600!

PRINCIPLE OF NAVIGATIONAL LEADERSHIP # 6:
People Must Believe in the Navigator
Before They Will Climb Aboard the Ship

In the late 1480s Columbus took his proposals to the rulers of Portugal, Spain, France, and England, but he found no one willing to support him. Rejected, he nevertheless wrote, "I plow ahead, no matter how the winds might lash me." Propitiously, in 1492, Spain's monarchs Ferdinand and Isabella ("the Catholic") drove the last Moors from Spain. Free of that concern, Queen Isabella felt attracted to Columbus's fervent faith and to his vision.

Isabella prevailed upon her husband, King Ferdinand, and they called Columbus to the court and agreed to subsidize him. He secured three ships (the *Niña*, the *Pinta*, and the *Santa Maria*), the title "Admiral of the Ocean Sea," and handsome financial dividends should his mission succeed. He quickly assembled crews (totaling about one hundred sailors) to man the three vessels, and the expedition set forth a few months later on August 3, 1492.

PRINCIPLE OF NAVIGATIONAL LEADERSHIP # 7:
There Is No Such Thing As Luck;
Good Things Happen When Opportunity and Preparedness Meet

They sailed from Palos, Spain, to the Canary Islands, a well-known route. Then they struck out for regions unknown. The voyage went quite well. "The sea was like a river," and the ships moved steadily westward. Conditions could hardly have been better. The admiral carefully set the course and confidently persevered. On October 12, the expedition landed in the Bahamas, naming the island San Salvador, claiming it for Spain. They then sailed around Cuba and established a settlement on the island now divided between Haiti and the Dominican Republic, which Columbus named Hispaniola.

PRINCIPLE OF NAVIGATIONAL LEADERSHIP # 8:
Don't Take Yourself Too Seriously, But Take
Your Mission Seriously

Columbus stands forever memorialized by his epoch journey—a journey that literally changed the world! He was, without doubt, a brilliant visionary, a marvelous mariner, a man of courage and perseverance. He had the power to persuade others, most importantly the Spanish monarchs, to support him as he followed his dream. Despite a variety of manifest flaws, he was a deeply religious man who devoutly worshiped and sought to serve his Lord.

In 1502 Columbus compiled *The Book of Prophecies,* tying together Scripture, important quotations, and some of his own reflections, providing a perspective on his role in the history of the world. Important to him was the prospect of world evangelism as a result of his voyages. He saw himself as God's chosen one, entrusted with opening the world to the gospel. How correct he was! The great expansion of the Christian faith followed Columbus's epochal journey.

GEORGE ARMSTRONG CUSTER: THE NAVIGATIONAL GENIUS

Almost everyone has heard of Custer's Last Stand. Few know now that at one time George Armstong Custer was one of the most famous soldiers in American history. Ironically, however, he's better known for his defeat at the Battle of the Little Bighorn than for his military exploits.

In truth, Custer could be memorialized as a great soldier. A soldier he was, and that was all he ever wanted to be. His paternal grandfather was a Hessian mercenary who was part of British General John Burgoyne's force, defeated in 1778 during the Revolutionary War. Subsequent to surrendering, he settled in Pennsylvania and became a loyal American. His grandson, George Armstrong Custer, was born in 1839 in New Rumley, Ohio. Aspiring to a military career, he obtained an appointment to West Point Military Academy in 1857, where he was remembered as a "big jolly boy" rather than a good student. Unsurprisingly, he graduated in 1861, academically last in his class of thirty-four! However, he turned out to be a better soldier than student.

CHARTING THE COURSE IN THE CIVIL WAR

Custer's military exploits were awesome:

- The Civil War had just begun, so he went from West Point to Washington, D.C., and took part in the First Battle of Bull Run.

- Various engagements allowed him to prove his mettle as a cavalryman.

- In 1862, during the Peninsular Campaign, General George McClellan appointed him one of his aides.

- In 1863, he was recommended for a brigadier generalship, and he played a significant role in the Gettysburg and Virginia Campaigns.

- His energy and boldness on the battlefields attracted much attention and acclaim.

- He had eleven horses shot out from under him but suffered no serious injuries.

- In 1864, he served under General Philip Sheridan, one of the most important Union officers, and fought effectively in the Shenandoah Campaign.

- At age twenty-five, he became a major general of volunteers and took part in the final campaign against Lee's Army of Northern Virginia in 1865.

- Leading the Third Division of the Cavalry Corps, he pursued the collapsing Confederate forces.

He proved relentless in attack, bold in battle, striking effectively at several crucial points. When Lee finally surrendered, Sheridan gave Custer the small table that Lee and Grant used to formalize the accord. "I know of no one," Sheridan said, "whose efforts have contributed more to this happy result than those of Custer."[5]

PRINCIPLE OF NAVIGATIONAL LEADERSHIP # 9:
*Don't Believe Your Own Press Releases; If You Do,
You Will Be the Only One*

Hugely popular, the "boy general" paraded his glory, wearing yards of gold braid on a black velveteen uniform. Tall, slender, strong, with long blond hair, he looked like the romantic hero he envisioned himself to be.

Some of his fellow officers, however, were less than impressed! One of them said Custer looked "like a circus rider gone mad."[6]

CHARTING THE COURSE ON THE FRONTIER

Following the Civil War, the army was radically reduced. Accordingly, Custer's rank was reduced to a captain, and he was ultimately assigned to the Seventh Cavalry, stationed in Kansas, where he served once again under General Philip ("Little Phil") Sheridan. The U.S. Army, following the Treaty of Medicine Lodge Creek in 1868, determined to restrict the Cheyenne-Arapaho and other Native Americans of the southern plains to their reservations. Renegades who refused to follow orders were to be pursued and destroyed. Custer was thus authorized to lead troops against some Cheyenne-Arapaho camped on the banks of the Washita River (near the Texas border in western Oklahoma) in the fall of 1868. Surrounding the village of Black Kettle, Custer's soldiers destroyed the village, returning in triumph to Sheridan's accolades.

PRINCIPLE OF NAVIGATIONAL LEADERSHIP # 10:
Yesterday's Successful Charting Won't Get You Through Today's Storm

---

Now a hero of the frontier wars with Native Americans as well as the Civil War, Custer loomed large in the public mind. Some suspected that Custer even began to fancy himself a potential presidential candidate. Assigned to duty in the Dakota Territory, he engaged in many campaigns, enjoying unending success. In the summer of 1874, he led a twelve-hundred-man exploring party through the Black Hills, where gold was discovered. The Sioux revered the Black Hills as their holy lands, and treaties had promised they would be protected. Once gold was discovered, of course, miners poured into Sioux country. Tensions mounted. Small groups of Native Americans, such as those following Sitting Bull, refused to comply with the treaty of 1868, leaving assigned reservations to hunt buffalo.

Consequently, a plan was drafted in 1876 to punish the renegade Sioux and Northern Cheyenne. Three large army columns were to move, in concert, to trap and destroy the warriors. Colonel Custer was supposed to lead the column marching west from Fort Abraham Lincoln, across the Missouri River from Bismarck. In March of that year, however, Custer was called to Washington to testify concerning fraud in the Department of Indian Affairs. When he testified, he criticized Grant's former secretary of war, William Belknap, and some of the president's own family. The president, outraged, relieved Custer of his command, placing General Terry in charge.

Popular outcries forced Grant to relent somewhat, and he sent Custer back to Dakota to serve as head of his regiment, but under Terry's command. As the column neared its objective, Terry divided his corps of nine hundred, sending Custer with half the men on ahead. Terry expected Custer to locate the Native Americans and then wait for the rest of the troops. Having received his instructions, Custer shook hands with Terry and rode to the head of his regiment. An experienced officer, Gibbon, warned, "Now, Custer, don't be greedy. Wait for us." To which Custer curtly replied: "No. I won't."

PRINCIPLE OF NAVIGATIONAL LEADERSHIP # 11:
Failure to Read the Indicators Will Cost You Everything

But Custer's navigational instincts were off.

- He underestimated the rough terrain.

- He misjudged the difficulty of communication.

- He failed to grasp the size of the encampment he intended to annihilate.

- He was blinded by his own arrogance.

- He miscalculated the valor of resolute warriors led by chiefs such as Gall and Crazy Horse.

Those navigational errors cost him dearly. Custer was killed on the afternoon of June 25, 1876. Surrounded by hundreds of angry Native

Americans, Custer and his men died quickly, within an hour; 231 men perished. Custer himself fell with a bullet through his head and a second in his chest.

PRINCIPLE OF NAVIGATIONAL LEADERSHIP # 12:
If You Are a Leader, Avid Learning and Study of the "Terrain" Are Parts of an Ongoing Lifestyle

---

Custer's famed courage veered into recklessness during his final days. Rather than carefully plan, gather information, and then move wisely, he allowed his resentments and pride to guide him. Knowing where to go and understanding how to get there, the basics of navigation, were visibly absent at Custer's Last Stand. Just because someone has been successful at reading the navigational numbers in previous times does not excuse him from the need to *continue* reading the numbers.

JOHN CALVIN: A "CITY" NAVIGATOR

Have you ever tried to navigate a ship? Many have. But have you ever tried to "navigate" a city? Not very many have. But one tried. And for a time he succeeded.

John Calvin (1509–64) was destined to be one of the greatest systematic thinkers ever produced by Christianity. By age twenty-seven, Calvin released the first of what would be many editions of his famous *Institutes of the Christian Religion*. Not only did he outline many doctrines of Christian belief, but he laid out his biblical understanding for how society is supposed to function.

THE "NAVIGATOR" NOT WANTED

In 1536, Guillaume Farel persuaded Calvin to come to Geneva, Switzerland, as a pastor and civic leader for the purpose of structuring the city the way it should be. Calvin consented. But his prescription for the city was not well received. Two years later, he was run out of town!

> **PRINCIPLE OF NAVIGATIONAL LEADERSHIP # 13:**
> *Captaining a Ship Means Being Willing to Face Storms*

Calvin continued thinking and writing in Strasbourg, France, from 1538–1541. Meanwhile, unrest was increasing in Geneva. The appeal went to Calvin again: please come to Geneva. And he did. Calvin arrived in Geneva in 1541 and once again took the "wheel" of the city. He remained there until his death in 1564. But Calvin's twenty-three-year "reign" in Geneva was anything but easy. His aggressive vision for moral reform within the city was met with periodic strong resistance.

> **PRINCIPLE OF NAVIGATIONAL LEADERSHIP # 14:**
> *Articulate the Course Often*

Although John Calvin was a strong-willed man, he regarded himself as a "poor timid scholar." In reality he was a brilliant thinker, skilled administrator, and loving pastor. He was forceful, and he fully expected everyone to live their lives according to the Bible. He had a vision for the city of Geneva to become the city of God, and he preached of it daily in Saint Pierre Church.

> **PRINCIPLE OF NAVIGATIONAL LEADERSHIP # 15:**
> *Leaders Are, by Definition,*
> *Those Who Are Willing to Chart New Courses*

But this vision did not set well with everyone. He reported that he was shot at some fifty or sixty times. Yet he made the city of Geneva considerably better than it would have been without his guiding hand. He navigated, in this case, an entire city. And Geneva was a great city (in spite of what some of Calvin's present-day critics say), in part, because of Calvin's ability to chart the course. With the exception of Martin Luther and John Wesley, John Calvin is cited more than any other figure in church history. His theological treatises, including those on the nature of civic and community life, are still read to this day—nearly five hundred years after they were written—as aids to navigate turbulent theological waters.

※

DEVELOPING LEADERSHIP "THRUST"

There is a powerful "navigational verse" in the Bible, in Daniel chapter 11, the last part of verse 32: "But the people who know their God will display strength and take action" (NASB). The verse contains two significant principles for navigating life in general—and leadership specifically.

PRINCIPLE OF NAVIGATIONAL LEADERSHIP # 16:
Knowing God Gives You Strength

Leadership is sometimes defined as "the ability to withstand pressure." Simply stated, leaders need help—divine help. God never designed you to carry the load that so many of you are carrying alone. He wants to help. Knowing Him—that is, *really* knowing Him—gives you strength for the journey.

Most people really do want to *know* God. Yet most people don't realize that God wants to be known by them! That is the very reason He came in the form of human flesh (Jesus)—to be known by us! Putting it bluntly, God really does like you! He likes being with you! He is the key for giving you strength for the leadership load you carry or desire to carry.

PRINCIPLE OF NAVIGATIONAL LEADERSHIP # 17:
With Your God-Given Strength, You Can Take Action

Leaders who understand navigation are not passive. They are active. When a rocket lifts off from Cape Kennedy, it needs thrust. That is the ability to go against the gravitational pull and propel the rocket into space.

When I am interviewing persons for positions at the church that I pastor, I look for "thrust." I look for activists. I look for people who take action. I look for persons who are drawing fully on the strength that God can give them, that helps them to "activate."

Steering the ship is not the big deal. Having the courage, fortitude, and knowledge to chart the course is! It requires creativity and energy. And that is called "thrust." Navigationally minded leaders have it!

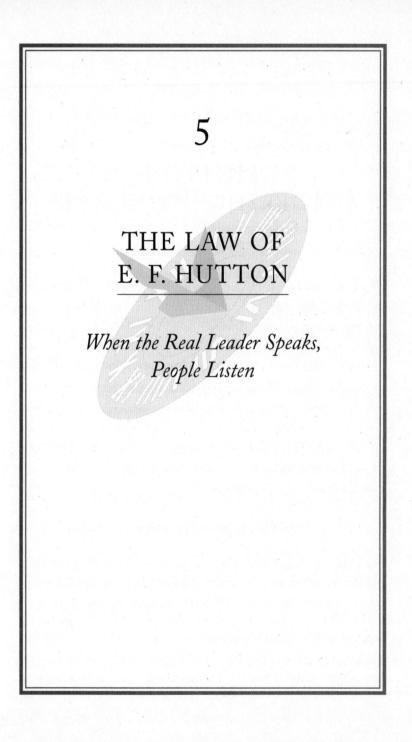

5

THE LAW OF
E. F. HUTTON

*When the Real Leader Speaks,
People Listen*

HUTTON
LEADERSHIP PRINCIPLES

Nearly five thousand of us were in the auditorium. The speaker slowly climbed the steps to the podium. Two young men assisted him, one carrying his oxygen tank. It seemed strange to see a speaker standing before a crowd with an oxygen tube leading to his nose. He took his time in beginning his speech. No one seemed to mind. All was quiet. All eyes were on the speaker, who had celebrated his eightieth birthday a couple of months earlier. As the speaker positioned his notes, John Maxwell, who was seated to my left on the second row of the large auditorium, leaned over and said, "This is probably the last time you'll ever hear Bill Bright speak." I nodded back with an "I-think-you're-right" kind of look. And then Dr. Bright started speaking.

THE DAY WE LISTENED

My mind raced back thirty-three years to my senior year of college. Only three years earlier, as a freshman, I had first heard about this young, creative businessman named Bill Bright who was making his presence felt on the UCLA campus. As a college senior in 1968, I heard he was going to be in the same city where I was in school—Oklahoma City— speaking to a group of businessmen and women. I tried to convince my two college buddies, Dave Harrison and Alden Laird, to go with me to hear him. At first they were perplexed about why they should want to go.

And after I got them there, they were even more perplexed that I would insist that we should stand in a line—all businesspersons, except for us three college guys—to shake his hand and say "hi." But after meeting him, they thanked me for insisting we go and stand in line. Why? Because they saw that Bill Bright was a leader. And when he spoke, we listened.

Coming out of my nostalgic journey from a third of a century ago, I was jolted back to present tense by Bill Bright's opening words before the attentive listeners in Orlando in January of 2002. He didn't say anything that day that I had not heard him say many times before. In fact, the frequent coughing caused by a serious lung disease prevented him from saying it as strongly and as forcefully as he used to say it. But it didn't make any difference because we were listening to Bill Bright, a leader par excellence. And when Bill Bright speaks, everyone listens.

In the event that you don't know who Bill Bright is, you need to understand that the organization that Bill and his wife, Vonette, started in 1951 has turned into a massive global ministry called Campus Crusade for Christ, with tens of thousands of staff in virtually every nation in the world. In addition, the Campus Crusade–sponsored film titled *Jesus* has been seen by nearly four billion of the world's six billion inhabitants, a staggering figure. This film is responsible for more Christian conversions than any one tool in all of Christian history. But my focus here is not on what Bill Bright has done. It is on who he is. He is a leader. And even E. F. Hutton would listen to Bill Bright!

JAMES MADISON:
AN UNIMPRESSIVE PRESIDENT

Almost every year, I receive a postcard inviting me to the Madison Reunion. Although I don't remember Great-grandfather Madison, I have vivid memories of Great-grandmother Madison. We always claimed that we were related to President James Madison, even though I don't think anyone successfully linked us genealogically to America's fourth president. But if one of my relatives somehow proved that we were, in fact, related to James Madison, I would choose to say that I was related to the father of the U.S. Constitution *rather than* the fourth president. Why? Because that was Madison's finest moment. His presidency was not.

James Madison followed Thomas Jefferson in the presidency and, as such, inherited challenges and predicaments left over from the Jefferson presidency. Madison's leadership was unable to overcome the difficulties, which doomed his two terms to mediocrity at best. Here is a glimpse of America's fourth president. "Jemmy" Madison was:

- a poor politician in a position that demands great political gifts.

- short and physically unimpressive.

- weak-voiced.

- regarded as being a bit puzzled and overwhelmed by events.

- unable to evoke little enthusiasm or affection from even those who considered themselves friends.

- "negative in his dealings with Congress."[1]

- noted for allowing "Jefferson's personal 'strings' for influencing House and Senate to rot from disuse."[2]

- "stubborn to the point of stupidity."[3]

- unable to avoid conflict with England, immersing the nation in the War of 1812.

- incapable of providing strong wartime leadership.

HUTTON LEADERSHIP PRINCIPLE # 1:
You Are Not a Leader
If People Don't Listen to You

Madison's inability to lead was tragically demonstrated in 1814. The British army, under General Robert Ross, marched from the Chesapeake Bay to Washington, D.C. Madison called for 95,000 militia to assemble and defend the capital. And what happened? Only 7,000 responded!

Madison had talked. Very few listened. This was a major sign of his lack of leadership.

The Americans met the British near Bladensburg, five miles from the city. Madison's militia fired a few shots, suffered a few casualties, and promptly fled the battlefield. British troops poured into Washington the evening of August 24, reaching the White House in time to eat the evening meal prepared for the First Family, who barely escaped capture.

MADISON IN HIS EARLY LEADERSHIP DAYS

Madison hardly stands out as a president. There was a time when people *did* listen to him, however. If you examine his life in the late 1700s, rather than the early 1800s, his "Hutton Leadership Skills" were remarkably evident. This same man, who seemed so inept at the presidency, was profoundly listened to in his political thinking and writing.

> HUTTON LEADERSHIP PRINCIPLE # 2:
> *When People Listen to You,*
> *You Are the Leader*

James Madison, prior to becoming president, was:

- the father of the Constitution.
- "the constitutionalist of the Revolution."[4]
- the one who did "more than Jefferson or even Hamilton to ensure that the United States got a workable system of government."[5]
- the primary architect of the Constitution's first ten amendments, the Bill of Rights.
- a great statesman.
- noted for his quiet, studious approach, ever listening to others (both living and dead).
- skilled at mediating agreements between factions, which set the course for the new republic.

71

HUTTON LEADERSHIP PRINCIPLE # 3:
*People Listen Better to a Few Well-Chosen Words
Than They Do to Incessant Talking*

James Madison shone, even when next to some of our nation's greatest luminaries. George Washington, for one, chaired the Constitutional
Convention meeting in Philadelphia in the summer of 1787. Other
prominent representatives made powerful speeches. But Madison's input
was strikingly significant. He worked quietly in committees. He kept
notes of the sessions. He offered important suggestions. James Madison
left his signature upon some of the greatest documents designed by
mankind. When he spoke (or wrote), other listened. And they followed.
Madison, in the late 1700s, was a Hutton leader.

HUTTON LEADERSHIP PRINCIPLE # 4:
*Before You Speak and Expect Others to Listen to You,
Listen to Others—Lots*

To help construct a new government, James Madison read widely in
ancient and modern sources, taking note of confederacies' strengths and
weaknesses. He became a student of Athens, Sparta, Carthage, Rome,
Switzerland, and the Netherlands.

There were no perfect models, for in many ways Americans were set
on designing what had never been tried before. That is why it is called
the great American experiment.

Madison traveled and discussed the nation's needs with various leaders. His studies led him to publish a memorandum exploring the "Vices
of the Political System of the United States." His thorough thinking and
research earned him his listening audience.

> ## HUTTON LEADERSHIP PRINCIPLE # 5:
> *People May Hear You, But in Order for Them to Follow,*
> *You Must Speak Convincingly and Compellingly*

James Madison's influence was felt in the conflict that immediately ensued. Along with other Virginians, he had put together the proposal that would serve as the basis for discussion. It was known as the Virginia or Large State Plan. Not everyone was happy about that plan. Delegates from small states, such as New Jersey, responded with a plan of their own.

Vigorous discussions occurred, and a compromise resulted, allowing for population to determine the numbers of representatives in the House and each of the states to have equal representation in the Senate. Other adjustments and compromises followed. But the basic model, the Virginia Plan, written by Madison and others, remained intact.

> ## HUTTON LEADERSHIP PRINCIPLE # 6:
> *People Listen Better When They Feel They Are*
> *Part of a Common Community with You*

The Constitution's important initial phrase, "We the People of the United States," is Madison's. Much of the wording, worked out in small sessions devoted to accurate phrasing, reflects his oversight.

> ## HUTTON LEADERSHIP PRINCIPLE # 7:
> *Leaders Are As Sensitive to the Timing of Their Speaking*
> *As They Are to the Content of Their Remarks*

In it all, he made his contribution less by setting forth novel notions than by listening carefully, then writing and speaking with sufficient skill to win others to his views. He did not proclaim loudly, but when he quietly spoke, others listened. And as a result of this skill, he deservedly is acclaimed as the Father of the Constitution.

> HUTTON LEADERSHIP PRINCIPLE # 8:
> *Speak—and People Present Will Hear You;*
> *Write—and People Yet Unborn Will Listen to You*

When the document was submitted to the several states for ratification, Madison took up his pen and, along with Alexander Hamilton and John Jay, composed one-third of the eighty-five newspaper articles subsequently compiled as the Federalist Papers, arguably the finest work of political philosophy ever written by Americans. In Virginia he struggled to counter the powerful anti-Federalist forces led by Patrick Henry, ultimately leading his state to ratify the Constitution.

> HUTTON LEADERSHIP PRINCIPLE # 9:
> *When Leaders Speak, They Keep Their Word; If Not,*
> *They Lose Their Right to Be Listened To*

While ratifying the Constitution, some states, such as North Carolina, assented only with the understanding that a Bill of Rights would be added to protect their liberties and interests. So when the first Congress gathered in New York City, James Madison took the lead in drafting the first ten amendments to the Constitution, the famed Bill of Rights.

BILL OF RIGHTS

To securely grant to the people the freedom of religion, speech, press, and assembly; to protect the people from tyrannical rule by securing their rights to property and fair trial; to reserve to the states all powers not expressly given the federal government by the written Constitution—all such provisions have proved significant to the uniquely American way of life. To James Madison, "we the people" owe a debt of gratitude! By living under the precepts that Madison advocated, we are still, in one sense, "listening" to him. He was an "E. F. Hutton" leader.

𝕳

CREDIBILITY—A KEY TO LEADERSHIP

> **HUTTON LEADERSHIP PRINCIPLE # 10:**
> *People Listen to People They Trust*

My friend Gavin Raath earned his Ph.D. at the University of Oklahoma. His graduate studies involved oratory and public communication. The key question with which he dealt was "What makes some speakers so persuasive when others are not?" The answer was surprisingly simple. Persuasive speakers are *not* those who have the greatest command of the language. They are *not* those who are most flamboyant and expressive. Dr. Raath's studies demonstrated that the greatest influencers are those who have credibility—genuine authenticity.

As a pastor of a large and growing congregation, I am always reading about what kind of speakers/preachers are successfully reaching the postmodern generation, what has occasionally been referred to as Generation X, those born between 1970 and 1984. The answer once again is amazingly simple. Those in this generational bracket listen to persons they feel are "for real"—authentic.

Some things never change. Leaders are those to whom we listen. And our desire to listen to them flows out of a sense of "realness," an authenticity that lends credibility to who they are. We are not drawn, long term, to the loudest or the most sensational. We look for authentic leaders.

And when they enter a room, we listen.

6

THE LAW OF
SOLID GROUND

Trust Is the Foundation of Leadership

Principles of Solid-Ground Leadership

When I was a child, we used to sing a little chorus in Sunday school in the fifteen-by-twenty-foot musty basement of our one-room country church in north-central Kansas. The song contrasted the decisions of two men: a "wise man" and a "foolish man." In this musical ditty, the wise man built his house on the rock. The foolish man built his house on the sand. One verse of the song ended with the words (after describing the foolish man's sandy foundation) "and the house on the sand went"—and at that point we clapped our hands together, attempting to make the sound of a house crashing down.

ON ROCK OR ON SAND?

Then the song continued, " . . . so build your house on the rock." But the song was really not about house construction. It was about one's life. The song's message was (and still is) simple, yet forceful. Build your life on principles that matter. To fail to do that means that your life is built on sand, and it will—as we used to say as children—"crash!"

FROM SOLID GROUND TO SINKING SAND

For thirteen years, I lived in one of America's great cities, with one of America's greatest football teams. I lived in the heart of the Dallas-Ft. Worth metropolitan area. And as you have guessed, the team I am referring to is the Dallas Cowboys. Although I moved away from the Dallas area several years ago, my heart still skips a beat at the sight of the blue-and-silver uniforms with the star! It is a special sight to me, indeed.

But it isn't quite as moving as it once was. Is it because I moved from Texas to California? No. Is it because the team started losing more games? No. It is because "America's team" started acting up.

When I first moved to the Dallas area in the early 1980s, the team was not doing too well. But everyone had respect for the team and had enormous respect for Tom Landry, Dallas's head coach for twenty-nine years, from 1960 to 1988. During that time, he led the team in twenty consecutive winning seasons, to five NFC titles and two Super Bowl wins (1972 and 1978). His career record of 270-178-6 meant that he had the third most wins in NFL history. He was elected to the Pro Football Hall of Fame in 1990. He was a bigger-than-life familiar figure. He became a national icon with his gentlemanly demeanor along the sidelines, where he always wore his distinctive hat. So great was the aura of integrity that surrounded this leader that there was an uproar when he was fired in an extremely sloppy way—via a press leak.

Landry's departure seemed to signal the loss of integrity for the team. Jimmy Johnson coached the Cowboys from 1989 to 1994 and compiled an impressive record with four players going to the 1991 Pro Bowl (the first since 1979). Most impressive were back-to-back Super Bowl victories in 1993 and 1994, the first Dallas Super Bowl wins since 1978.

I remember the last quarter of the 1993 Super Bowl very well. Failing to remember the date of the Super Bowl, I had months before agreed to speak at a church on Sunday night, January 31, 1993, which turned out to be the night of the Dallas win. As I left my home in the mid-cities region of the Dallas-Ft. Worth metroplex during the fourth quarter, I drove on Highway 183—a major eight-lane freeway—toward Ft. Worth. *But I was the only car on the entire freeway!* I could not see one single car either ahead of me or in my rearview mirror. I was the only one of some four million Dallas-Ft. Worth residents who was missing the game, or so I felt!

But there were problems. Accompanying the victories on the field was turmoil off the field. Sometimes the conflict was with the owner, Jerry Jones, who seemed to have qualities virtually opposite of the famous coach (Tom Landry) whom he had fired. Eventually, the tension was so great that Johnson left the Cowboys and Barry Switzer took his place.

Barry Switzer became the head coach of the Cowboys in 1994. He came to Dallas in 1989 from the University of Oklahoma where he had coached his team to three national titles (1974, 1975, 1985). But OU's impressive wins were often overshadowed by the rumors regarding the morals of the coaching staff, including Switzer.

Switzer, as a coach, had compiled a staggering record: 157-29-4. But his resignation at OU came as the university was placed on three years' NCAA probation and five of his players had criminal charges filed against them. That was an omen of things to come in Dallas.

Switzer's coaching skills earned the Cowboys another Super Bowl victory (1996), the third in only four years! It was a spectacular accomplishment. But the activities of several of the players were scandalous at best and illegal at worst. Switzer's brilliance in coaching did not make up for the moral free fall that seemed to characterize the organization.

When I moved to San Diego in late 1995, I was very proud of the Cowboys. As one might expect, I took lots of teasing for my support of the Cowboys since I was in San Diego Charger territory. But I was unprepared for the avalanche of Dallas Cowboy jokes that began to circulate. They made fun of the lack of integrity of many of the players, who seemed plagued with moral and ethical deficiencies, some of which resulted in several serious legal charges. The Cowboys ceased being America's team. The reasons are many. But the most obvious one was the brash immaturity reflected through so much of the organization. In the years that followed the 1996 Super Bowl Championship, Dallas neither looked like nor acted like America's team. And they stopped playing like it as well.

What tarnished the Cowboys' image? Was it their losses? No. It was their behavior. What did they not understand? The Law of Solid Ground. How you conduct yourself counts. They could have benefited from the little Sunday school chorus that I was taught as a child: build your house (life) on the rock, not on the sand!

> ## PRINCIPLE OF SOLID-GROUND LEADERSHIP # 1:
> *Talent Is Not a Substitute for Good Character*

It was electric to live in a city with a team that won three Super Bowls in rapid succession. But it was disappointing to see a much-loved team become a made-fun-of team! The Law of Solid Ground is important. In the words of Edwin Louis Cole, "A man's talent can take him where his character cannot sustain him." That, in essence, is the hidden warning in the Law of Solid Ground.

ROBERT E. LEE

There are good *soldiers* . . . and then there are *good* soldiers. There is an enormous difference between leaders like William Tecumseh Sherman and Robert E. Lee. Military men like Sherman certainly leave their marks with their exploits. Sherman's brutal March to the Sea through Georgia during the Civil War, burning and pillaging as he went, seared his name in the memories of southerners. A bit later, at a great gathering of Native Americans of the southern plains at Medicine Lodge Creek in Kansas in 1868, a Kiowa warrior sought to placate Sherman by declaring he was a "good Indian," to which the general declared, "The only good Indian is a dead Indian." As a soldier, Sherman left a legacy. But even his friends and followers rarely admired him.

> ## PRINCIPLE OF SOLID-GROUND LEADERSHIP # 2:
> *To Be a Good Leader,*
> *Focus on Being Good Before You Focus on Being a Leader*

On the other hand, Robert E. Lee was universally acclaimed as a good man as well as a great soldier. Friend and foe rarely failed to express their admiration for his courtly courtesies, his routine honesty, his sincere piety. Samuel Johnson once said that we should carefully study a man highly regarded by both friends and foes, for he exemplifies "authenticity," which "is the rarest of all human traits." Johnson lived an ocean away and a century before Lee, but his words accurately describe him. His military exploits—outfighting a variety of Union generals in northern Virginia—impress us. Even more impressive are the accolades concerning his character. Genuine silver, or true silver, is often called sterling. And Lee's character, for its integrity and authenticity, is often called the same: sterling.

PRINCIPLE OF SOLID-GROUND LEADERSHIP # 3:
Character Is Best Learned Early.
If You Don't Learn It Early, at Least Learn It Late—
Just Make Certain You Learn It

Robert E. Lee was born in 1807, the son of Henry "Light-Horse Harry" Lee, a Revolutionary War hero. He grew up just across the Potomac from Washington, D.C., near Alexandria, Virginia, where he was constantly reminded of George Washington, the recently deceased father of the country. Washington's residence, Mount Vernon, was just a few miles down the river.

His mother, Anne Carter Lee, deeply influenced young Robert. She conducted daily prayers and insisted on Sunday church attendance at the Episcopal Church of Alexandria. From her he learned "to practice self-denial and self-control."[1] He received a good classical education in the Alexandria Academy and was appointed, in 1824, to the United States Military Academy at West Point.

While still in his teens, Lee impressed his elders with his punctilious obedience. "Obedience to lawful authority is the foundation of manly character," he said.[2] He deeply believed that "you cannot be a true man until you learn to obey,"[3] and he was, when admitted to West Point, a true man in most every way.

> **PRINCIPLE OF SOLID-GROUND LEADERSHIP # 4:**
> *To the Leader, Intellect Is Important—*
> *But Integrity Is More Important*

Though not intellectually precocious, Lee studied diligently and well. He mastered his subjects through hard work. Consequently, he finished second in his class. He also kept all the rules! Indeed, he graduated without a single demerit in his four years at West Point, a nearly impossible attainment.

> **PRINCIPLE OF SOLID-GROUND LEADERSHIP # 5:**
> *Character Shows . . . So Does the Lack of Character*

Despite his rigorous self-discipline, however, Lee was gregarious, kind, and fully able to engage in spirited conversations. There was a dignity to him, but not of the off-putting variety. Subsequently, as he moved up through the ranks of the army's officer corps, as he married and fathered seven children, the character traits so evident in his younger years deepened and strengthened. He served capably in the Mexican War, earning the attention of his superiors, and during the 1850s, he served as the ninth superintendent of the United States Military Academy.

> **PRINCIPLE OF SOLID-GROUND LEADERSHIP # 6:**
> *Character Shines in Decision Making*

Then came the secession of the South. Though Lee loved the Union, he refused President Lincoln's offer to grant him command of the North's army. Winfield Scott, who advised Lincoln, regarded Robert E. Lee as "the greatest military genius in America." But his home state, Virginia, took first place in his heart. When she seceded, he resigned his commission as a colonel in the United States Army.

To Lee, the issue was constitutional. Writing to Chauncey Burr in 1866, Lee said, "All that the South has ever desired was that the union, as established by our forefathers, should be preserved; and that the government, as originally organized, should be administered in purity and truth."[4]

The South seceded to restore the Founding Founders' intent. Slavery deserved no defense. "If the slaves of the South were mine," Lee said, "I would surrender them all without a struggle, to avert this war."[5] But the original thirteen states predated and brought into being the Union, so states' rights superseded the Union's. And Lee supported his state.

PRINCIPLE OF SOLID-GROUND LEADERSHIP # 7:
Trust Evokes Endearment

Through all the battles of the Civil War, Lee led his outnumbered soldiers to many victories. He earned the label "the Gray Fox," outmaneuvering and outwitting his foes. But more important than his military success was the devotion he elicited from his men. Indeed, his men fought so heroically because they loved their leader. As one of his generals, Henry Wise, told him: "Ah, General Lee, these men are not fighting for the Confederacy; they are fighting for you." They fought for him because he fought alongside them.

PRINCIPLE OF SOLID-GROUND LEADERSHIP # 8:
"Finer Metal" Leaders Establish a Foundation of Trust with Those They Would Lead

Field Marshal Viscount Wolseley, commander in chief of the British army, interviewed Lee and wrote,

> I have met many great men of my time, but Lee alone impressed me with the feeling that I was in the presence of a man who was cast in a grander mold and made of different and *finer metal* than all other

men . . . When Americans can review the history of the War Between the States with calm impartiality, . . . I believe he will be regarded not only as the most prominent figure of the Confederacy, but as the greatest American of the 19th century.[6] [italics mine]

Historians may differ with Wolseley's verdict, but the men who fought for Lee would not. He was, in every way, a man worth following. He was the solid rock on which they stood. He lived the Law of Solid Ground.

THE LOSS OF TRUST

Tragically, there is a general loss of trust in contemporary culture. Ironically, Americans don't even feel they can trust the very people who supply them with information—journalists. According to an October 19, 1998, *New York Times* article, 67 percent of Americans believe that journalists invent stories, 76 percent believe they plagiarize, 87 percent believe they use unethical or illegal techniques to get stories, and 86 percent of Americans believe the articles they read contain factual errors.[7]

WILLIAM JEFFERSON CLINTON

Everyone knows the name of Bill Clinton. He came from modest beginnings. His father died before he was born in Hope, Arkansas. His family was poor. Yet he rose to become an attorney general of a state, a governor, and finally the president of the United States.

Clinton was one of the most compelling communicators in modern times. The only recent presidents who could move a crowd as powerfully as Bill Clinton were Jack Kennedy and Ronald Reagan. Clinton was a master communicator. He held audiences in the palm of his hand. In fact, he could "wow" people even more profoundly in person. He had a winsomeness. He was profoundly charismatic in personality. And he worked hard! (This quality of Clinton will be discussed further in

Chapter 16.) And it should be acknowledged that he had some significant accomplishments during his presidency.

PRINCIPLE OF SOLID-GROUND LEADERSHIP # 9:
Mistrust Overshadows Accomplishments

But even his closest friends begrudgingly acknowledged that he squandered his legacy. Few administrations were more scandal plagued.
Simply put, he failed to understand that integrity matters. In the final
days of his presidency, Bill Clinton "acknowledged that he had testified
falsely under oath about his relations with Monica Lewinsky, agreed to
a suspension of his law license for five years." The string of allegations
against Clinton includes "the Whitewater land deals, the mishandling of
FBI files, the firings at the White House travel office."[8]

The list of alleged improprieties is lengthy: "Chinagate"; "Cattlegate"
(questions regarding Hillary); his behavior with Gennifer Flowers, Paula
Jones, Juanita Broaddrick, Kathleen Willey, Elizabeth Ward Grayson,
Sally Perdue, and Dolly Kyle Browning; the conduct of political adviser
Dick Morris (prostitution related); the Marc Rich pardon; and the questionable conduct, in Clinton's final days, of his brother (Roger Clinton)
and his brother-in-law (Hugh Rodham). And the list goes on and on.
Most significantly, he is labeled as only one of two presidents to have
been impeached.

Some may feel that I have done a disservice to former President
Clinton for even mentioning these issues. And some will contend that
he was never successfully charged with illegalities in several of the scandals mentioned. That is true; he was not.

PRINCIPLE OF SOLID-GROUND LEADERSHIP # 10:
Mistrust Overshadows Ability

But the list has caused many a political pundit, who was otherwise sympathetic to Clinton's policies, and who may have been enamored with his

political brilliance, to label his presidential conduct as "tawdry," a description that seems to emerge again and again.

PRINCIPLE OF SOLID-GROUND LEADERSHIP # 11:
If You Have to Choose Between Charisma and Character,
Choose Character

Was Bill Clinton a brilliant politician? Yes. He captivated people. He captured the hearts of many. But he failed to grasp that the Law of Solid Ground (trust) was a leadership law that had not been repealed. And that lack of discernment can be costly to even the most skillful politician. Charisma, although very valuable, is not a "must" when leading. But character is!

JR

COLIN POWELL

Let's shift our attention from the office of the president to that of the secretary of state. Born to Jamaican immigrants who came to the South Bronx, Colin Powell rose rapidly through the rank of the military. From 1989 to 1993, he served as the chairman of the joint chiefs of staff, Department of Defense, under both President George Bush and President Bill Clinton. In January 2001, he was selected by President George W. Bush to be the secretary of state, the first African American to hold this office.

PRINCIPLE OF SOLID-GROUND LEADERSHIP # 12
Candor Builds Trust

Powell's "laws of power," which guide him in his decision making, have helped him to become a trusted man. "Dare to be the skunk" is Powell's way of saying to dare to ask the tough, unpopular questions. "Head for the trenches" reveals the value Powell places on the "common person," an important source of information. He warns that "experts often possess more data than judgment."

His ruthless definition of leadership causes Powell to be trusted. He contends that leadership "is not rank, privilege, titles, or money. It's responsibility." But he refuses to take the responsibility so seriously that it costs him his family. In one of his laws of power entitled "come up for air," he is fiercely committed to his wife of thirty-nine years, their children and grandchildren.

PRINCIPLE OF SOLID-GROUND LEADERSHIP # 13:
Establish Your Identity By Who You Are Rather Than What You Do

---

One final feature of Colin Powell's laws of power reveals why people trust him. He states, with typical Powell bluntness, "Never let ego get so close to your position that when your position goes, your ego goes with it." Holding onto life's honors and positions with "an open hand" enhances trust.[9]

TALENT VS. TRUST

How many of the following names do you know?

Group A: Wilbur Mills, Bob Packwood, Marion Berry, Bill Clinton, Gary Condit

Group B: Rudolph Valentino, Marilyn Monroe, John Belushi, River Phoenix, John Candy, Chris Farley, Hugh Carey, Robert Downey Jr., Dana Plato, Robert Blake

Group C: Jimi Hendrix, Janis Joplin, Jim Morrison, Eddie Mercury, Brian Wilson, Elvis Presley, Milli Vanilli, Michael Jackson, Kurt Cobain, Michael Hutchence

Group D: A. A. Allen, Peter Popoff, Jimmy Swaggart, Jim Bakker, W. V. Grant, Robert Tilton

Group E: Len Bias, Pete Rose, O. J. Simpson, Michael Irvin, Wilt Chamberlain, Dennis Rodman, Todd Marinovich, Ryan Leaf, Jason Williams

How many of these do you know? Some of them? All of them? What do they have in common? Answer: they were (are, in some cases) talented—in fact, *very* talented! But talent does *not* mean trust.

PRINCIPLE OF SOLID-GROUND LEADERSHIP # 14:
Talent Is No Substitute for Trust

All of the persons listed have more in common than talent. They demonstrated a lack of understanding of the Law of Solid Ground and, as a result, squandered the trust and opportunities they once had. "Solid ground" is a euphemism for trust, and trust flows from integrity.

What the persons listed have in common with each other is that they tarnished or destroyed their influence (and in some cases their lives) by abuse or overdose of alcohol or illegal drugs, sexual misconduct and improprieties, profoundly immature and egomaniacal behavior, deceit, and/or mismanagement of finances (sometimes including tax evasion). They were generally self-destructive. Group A, as you probably figured out, consisted of politicians; Group B, movie stars; Group C, musicians; Group D, religious leaders; and Group E, athletes. And the list could have gone on. There could have been categories for businesspersons, scientists, writers, and others. All talented. But all flawed. All failing to understand that authentic leadership must be founded on the rock, not on the sand.

THE "SOLID GROUND" QUESTION
You are a leader, or at least you desire to be. You have talent and are gaining skills. You are a "grower." But above all, acquire integrity. Live the Law of Solid Ground.

PRINCIPLE OF SOLID-GROUND LEADERSHIP # 15:
Get a Piece of the Rock

Are you focusing, as a leader, on basic integrity and honesty? Are you committed to leading from solid ground, from a rock? Or are you going to establish your leadership on sand? This is the most important question you can answer. And your answer will determine your success as a leader.

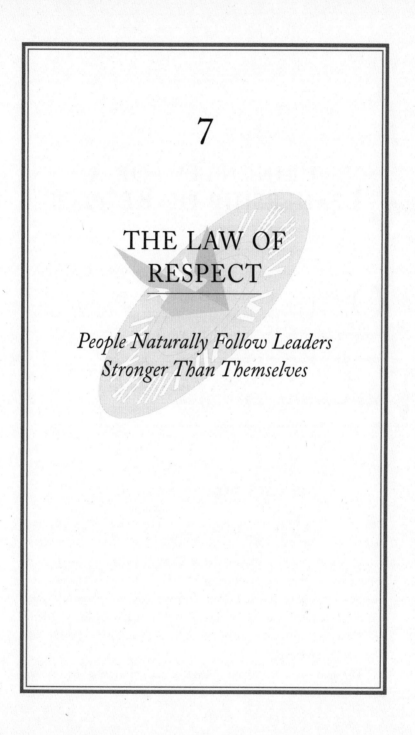

7

THE LAW OF
RESPECT

*People Naturally Follow Leaders
Stronger Than Themselves*

Principles for a Leadership of Respect

Of course, every person *wants* respect, But leaders don't *ask* for it. They already *have* it. Why? Because people naturally, and non-coercively, follow leaders stronger than themselves.

Principle for a Leadership of Respect # 1:
People Naturally Follow Leaders They Respect

THE RESPECTED THOMAS AQUINAS

Let your mind go back for a moment to the playground of your elementary school. Think back to your grade-school years. Can you ever recall a time when you were given a nickname—a pejorative nickname—something very negative? Perhaps you were called some bad names. Fortunately, most of those names don't stay with us throughout life. Such was not the case for one man named Tom. His nickname was the "dumb ox." (Now *your* nickname doesn't seem so bad, does it?) Unfortunately, Tom's nickname stuck.

The dumb ox wasn't simply called that in elementary school. He was called that in college, a season of life when names can certainly stick for one's life. The ox portion of his name, as you might expect, came from the fact that he was severely overweight. But even beyond that, he would never have won a modeling contract. One of his eyes was larger than the other. On top of that he was an introvert. And as if that weren't enough, we are told that when he *did* speak, his comments were often unrelated to what was being said. Thus, he was called the dumb ox. History has a long memory, for it has preserved that nickname now some eight hundred years after his birth.

But Tom's nickname eventually changed. What did they call an overweight, strikingly unattractive man when they stopped calling him a dumb ox? They called him the "Angelic Doctor"—quite a change from the previous name! Why did the name change? The reason is simple: people respected Tom. He became so respected that he has been an intellectual Mount Everest in his academic discipline for the last eight hundred years.

PRINCIPLE FOR A LEADERSHIP OF RESPECT # 2:
Leaders Who Are Genuinely Respected Are Not "For Sale"

Tom was born in 1225 near Aquinas, Italy, thus, the name Thomas Aquinas. By age fourteen, he was a student at the University of Naples. From there he decided to become a Catholic priest, a Dominican. His family was not happy about his plan and developed a strategy to dissuade him. They had hoped he would have much greater financial security than taking a vow to live in poverty! His brother had a creative but unsuccessful plan. They kidnapped him and held him for fifteen months, in hopes that he would change his mind. But the dumb ox was also a stubborn ox! He did not change his mind.

"Plan B" was launched in an effort to dissuade young Thomas. The family became more daring in their attempts. They arranged for him to be with a prostitute. That attempt likewise failed.

Finally, they came up with one more technique of dissuasion: they offered to purchase for him the position of archbishop of Naples. Such practices were not uncommon for the wealthy in the Middle Ages.[1] It was known as *investiture,* a profoundly offensive procedure in which religious positions were sold like franchises. But the dumb ox would not change his mind. Away to the University of Paris he went, from 1245 to 1248.

How, you may be wondering, did he go from being called the dumb ox to the Angelic Doctor? He was profoundly respected. The reason? His brilliant mind and voluminous writing. Aquinas attempted to reconcile two large bodies of thought: the writings of Aristotle (and other philosophers) and the Bible. So influential was he that his thinking was given a name (based on his name). It is called Thomism.

PRINCIPLE FOR A LEADERSHIP OF RESPECT # 3:
People Will Respect a Leader with a Vision
That Is Compelling and Makes Sense to Them

Now, we may ask, where were all the people who had called him the dumb ox? Answer: many of them were right behind him, following him, embracing his teaching. Why? Because his intellectual prowess and theological acumen commanded respect, and he got it! People tended to line up behind one of two persons during the next three hundred years: Thomas Aquinas or Duns Scotus. The debate between the Thomists and the Scotists continued until the early 1500s.

If you are a Roman Catholic reading this book, you owe a huge debt of gratitude to Thomas Aquinas. He was the most influential thinker within the Roman Catholic Church until the 1960s![2] If you are a Protestant reading this book, you owe him much as well. Aquinas knew the Bible extremely well, writing some of the finest commentaries on Scripture, helping to preserve some of the truths you value most.[3]

𝕸

WINSTON CHURCHILL:
A WORLD SYMBOL FOR RESPECT

We leave Europe in the Middle Ages to go to England before WWII.

Not everyone liked Winston Churchill. He and Lady Astor, a prominent English socialite, had a running feud most of their lives.

Once Lady Astor, provoked to anger, said, "Sir Winston, if I were your wife, I'd put poison in your coffee!" To which Churchill retorted, "Lady Astor, if I were your husband, I'd drink it!"

> ### PRINCIPLE FOR A LEADERSHIP OF RESPECT # 4:
> *In Turbulent Times That Call for Difficult Decisions,*
> *a Principle-Driven Leader Can Still Be Respected,*
> *Even If Not Particularly Liked*

Nor did everyone always agree with Churchill. All his life he suffered intense criticism, opposition, and rejection. But most everyone respected him. For one thing, he had great ability. For another thing, he usually sought to do what was right for his country. He lived in accord with his own words: "What is the use of living, if it be not to strive for noble causes and to make this muddled world a better place to live in after we are gone?"

Born to one of England's most prestigious families, Winston Churchill showed little promise (other than creative mischief) as an undersized child. Disinterested in schooling, he learned what pleased him rather than what schoolmasters desired. After twice failing entrance exams, he finally gained admission to the Military Academy of Sandhurst, where he found his true milieu. He did well and, following graduation, briefly followed an army career in India and Africa.

In 1900, at the age of twenty-six, however, Churchill was home and successfully campaigned for a seat in Parliament, where he would remain for decades to come. A few years later he became a member of the cabinet. He was something of a boy wonder.

During WWI, he successfully served his country in various capacities, including first lord of the Admiralty. He proposed the use of aircraft in the war and funded the production of landships—the first tanks used in modern warfare. Following the war, in the 1920s, he served as chancellor of the Exchequer. By that time he had been involved in five wars, held nine cabinet offices, and delivered eight thousand speeches. But he was also at times out of favor with both the people and the leaders of

Great Britain because he defied party leadership, changed parties, and had made some controversial decisions as head of the Royal Navy during WWI. From 1929 to 1939, though still a member of Parliament, he stood far from positions of power.

PRINCIPLE FOR A LEADERSHIP OF RESPECT # 5:
Never Confuse Long-Term Respect with Short-Term Popularity

Churchill tried to alert Europe to the dangers embedded in triumphant dictatorships. In 1933 he told the House of Commons about Germany's increasing military power. His strident criticism of Fascist Italy and Nazi Germany, his opposition to Britain's policies in the 1930s, left him with time to write and paint, but little national influence. His conservative bent just was not popular during a time when socialism and liberalism reigned in Britain.

On September 1, 1939, however, things changed. The policies of appeasement that characterized Prime Minister Neville Chamberlain stood exposed as bankrupt. That very night Churchill was recalled to his position as first lord of the Admiralty. News of his return quickly spread throughout the fleet: "Winston is back."

PRINCIPLE FOR A LEADERSHIP OF RESPECT # 6:
Speak Truthfully, Plainly, and Simply

A few months later, when Norway fell to the Nazis, Churchill was named prime minister, the position he had long desired. His first address to the nation, one of the finest ever uttered, declared, "I have nothing to offer but blood, toil, tears, and sweat." Acknowledging the challenges they faced, the prospects of desperate conflict, he continued, "You ask, what is our policy? I will say: It is to wage war, by sea, land, and air, with all our might and with all the strength God can give us: to wage war against a monstrous tyranny, never surpassed in the dark, lamentable catalogue of human crime."[4]

He also quoted from 1 Maccabees: "Arm yourselves, and be ye men of valour, and be in readiness for the conflict; for it is better for us to perish in battle than to look upon the outrage of our nation. As the will of God is in heaven, even so let it be" (3:58–60 KJV). Quoting Scripture came naturally to Churchill, for he drank deeply of its message. The King James Bible, he once declared, was a "lasting monument . . . to the genius of the English-speaking peoples." The Word of God, Churchill believed, had power.

PRINCIPLE FOR A LEADERSHIP OF RESPECT # 7:
Availability Increases the Chances for Respect

And Churchill's powerful words rallied his people to battle for their very existence. After the war, Clement Atlee explained how Churchill helped the Allies win the war by simply saying he talked about it! Words weighed much when Churchill spoke. Equally important, his bulldog mannerisms, his defiance of danger (walking without a helmet, his wife, Clementine, on his arm, through London's streets while bombs were bursting all around him), his jaunty "V for Victory" gestures, his sense of humor, his confidence that the English would prevail—all gave hope to the world.

He worked sixteen to eighteen hours a day and seemed daily energized by his task. He joined arms with Stalin and Roosevelt, the Allies who ultimately defeated Hitler. And in victory, he stood as one of the twentieth century's most revered heroes, a man universally respected for his wisdom, his deeply Christian vision, his courage and commitment.

⚘

ALEXANDER THE GREAT

Few people in human history have earned the appellation "great." Two popes in two thousand years—Leo I and Gregory I—are referred to as "great." Two Russian czars—Peter and Catherine—are also called "great." A Prussian despot, Frederick, and a French dictator, Napoleon, also have the title of "great" added to their names. Bestowed not for reasons of character or goodness, the name "great" generally indicates unusual attainments, standing far above others. Of all the "greats" the most ancient may well be the most impressive: Alexander of Macedon, who literally conquered most of the known world. Equally important, he succeeded, as have few others, by maintaining the respect and loyalty of his followers.

Born in 356 B.C. to the powerful warrior King Philip II of Macedon, who brought Greece under his control, and Olympias, who claimed descent from the legendary Achilles, young Alexander enjoyed both the ancestry and the education fit for nobility. A famed physical trainer, Leonidas, worked to develop his pupil's strength. He excelled in most every arena: running, fencing, archery, hunting, and horsemanship.

When a giant horse named Bucephalus was about to be rejected as intractable, Alexander lamented, "What an excellent horse do they lose for [lack] of . . . boldness to manage him!" His father, Philip, rebuked him for criticizing his elders. But Alexander retorted: "I could manage this horse better than others do."[5] Given the opportunity, Alexander succeeded by facing the horse toward the sun, so he would not fear his own shadow, then talking softly to him, gently stroking him, and leaping abruptly on his back for a successful ride. King Philip then gave Bucephalus to his son, and the horse became his most trusted warhorse. Impressed by his audacity and skill, Philip told Alexander, Plutarch records: "My son, Macedonia is too small for you; seek out a larger empire, worthier of you."[6]

Philip also desired for Alexander to have the finest teachers and trainers. What the physical trainer Leonidas did for his body, the great philosopher Aristotle tried to do for his mind. Philip employed Aristotle, noted for his ethics of the golden mean, at his court because he hoped to help his son avoid "a great many things of the sort that I am sorry to have done."

PRINCIPLE FOR A LEADERSHIP OF RESPECT # 8:
If You Want to Lead Others, Master Yourself First

Alexander's self-control, Plutarch records, enabled him to control his desires for physical pleasures: "He was so very temperate in his eating that when any rare fish or fruits were sent him, he would distribute them among his friends and often reserve nothing for himself." Equally important: "He was much less addicted to wine than was generally believed; that which gave people occasion to think so of him, was, that when he had nothing else to do, he loved to sit long and talk, rather than drink, and over every cup hold a long conversation."[7]

PRINCIPLE FOR A LEADERSHIP OF RESPECT # 9:
Model What You Want from Others

Alexander realized that his men would accept his discipline as their leader only when they saw discipline in his personal life. Thus "to strengthen his precepts by example, he applied himself" to "hunting and warlike expeditions, embracing all opportunities of hardship and danger."[8] He "exposed his person to danger in this manner, with the object both of inuring himself and inciting others to the performance of brave and virtuous actions," wrote Plutarch.[9]

When his father was killed, Alexander determined, at the age of twenty, to launch his world conquests, "the most daring and romantic enterprise in the history of kings."[10] Quelling some outbreaks in Greece, he crossed the Hellespont, with his 30,000 footmen and 5,000 cavalrymen—loyal Macedonian soldiers—and marched through Turkey, conclusively routing Darius III's 600,000 troops. From there he went to Palestine, and on to Egypt, where he laid the foundation for Alexandria, one of many cities he founded throughout his growing empire. He then marched back through Palestine to Babylon, taking control of Persia's millions of subjects.

PRINCIPLE FOR A LEADERSHIP OF RESPECT # 10:
Respect Flows Toward Authentic Greatness

In the many battles, Alexander led more by inspiration and bravery than strategy. In Will Durant's opinion, he led his troops by the "brilliance of his imagination, the fire of his unstudied oratory, and the readiness and sincerity with which he shared their hardships and griefs."[11]

Without question he was a good administrator:

- He ruled with kindness and firmness the wide domain that his arms had won.

- He was loyal to the agreements that he signed with commanders and cities.

- He tolerated no oppression of his subjects by his appointees.[12]

PRINCIPLE FOR A LEADERSHIP OF RESPECT # 11:
Vacillation Repels Followers;
Singularity of Focus Increases Followers

Amid all the excitement and chaos of his campaigns, Alexander kept clearly at the center of his thoughts the great purpose that even his death would not defeat: "the unification of all the eastern Mediterranean world into one cultural whole, dominated and elevated by the expanding civilization of Greece."[13]

PRINCIPLE FOR A LEADERSHIP OF RESPECT # 12:
Doing Precedes Leading—Talk Is Cheap

On the march, he routinely risked himself, racing chariots, hunting in dangerous terrain, and facing and killing fierce animals such as lions. He also lived a highly disciplined life in his early years, eating and drinking with restraint, thus enjoying good health and physical vigor.

PRINCIPLE FOR A LEADERSHIP OF RESPECT # 13:
Deal with Problems Early and in a Straightforward Manner

Given human nature, of course, success breeds complacency. As Alexander and his men enjoyed the dividends of their conquests, particularly the pleasures of Persia, the men began to lose some of their military ardor. At times they even grumbled and gossiped about their commander in chief. So he spoke to his men, promising to make them "masters of the world" if they chose to follow him. If not, they could freely return home with their booty. Thus challenged, however, "they all cried out, they would go along with him whithersoever it was his pleasure to lead them."[14] He wrote many letters, filled with friendly affection, and he treated his men with generosity and kindness. And follow him they did as he marched east out of Persia through the Himalayas into India! Battles and more battles! More lands added to Alexander's domain!

PRINCIPLE FOR A LEADERSHIP OF RESPECT # 14:
Wise Leaders Know That Trust Is the
Most Valuable Leadership Commodity

But earthly empires rarely last, and Alexander's began to crumble at the moment of its grandest extent. And it all began when his faithful Macedonian soldiers, who had followed him so resolutely for nearly a decade, lost their respect for him. He'd begun to adopt some of the customs of the conquered "barbarians." He even encouraged some Egyptians to worship him as a god. His famed self-restraint began to crumble. He married not only a beautiful Bactrian princess, Roxana, but he also took one of Darius's daughters as a wife, consummating a political pact. His men interpreted this as a rejection of Greek culture for Oriental luxury. He even announced, in 324 B.C., that he was the son of

Zeus-Ammon and required his subjects to prostrate themselves in his presence!

PRINCIPLE FOR A LEADERSHIP OF RESPECT # 15:
Alcohol Kills—People, Dreams, and Empires

He drank more and more. One of his closest friends died after drinking some twelve quarts of wine in a drinking contest! Alexander killed another one as a result of a drunken brawl, though subsequently he wept through the night at his loss. One of his bravest officers, Philotas, orchestrated an unsuccessful conspiracy to assassinate him. The once faithful army was, it seemed, nearly mutinous. Then Alexander, having conquered the world, fell ill of a fever (after drinking a goblet filled with six quarts of wine) and died in his thirty-third year. He never lost a battle with an enemy, and he changed the face of the ancient world. But he lost a battle with himself. The qualities that had drawn so much respect dissipated. Respect slowly ebbed to disdain.

While he succeeded, he succeeded. He did so by maintaining the sturdy loyalty of his peerless Macedonian warriors. And he did that through personal example.

PRINCIPLE FOR A LEADERSHIP OF RESPECT # 16:
If You Are Not Respected, You Cannot Lead—
At Least, Not for Very Long

But when that loyalty began to crack, the empire he'd acquired did too. The man who was once a *positive* example of the Law of Respect became a *negative* example of that same law. Laws are not guidelines. They are not merely principles. They are *laws*. If you break them, they will break you. Alexander broke this leadership law. It broke him.

⟨⟨⟩⟩

SAUL:
THE MAN WHO HAD IT ALL

Alexander was not the first to understand the Law of Respect and then violate it. No more graphic and painful example exists than Saul, the king of Israel in the Old Testament who ruled approximately one thousand years before Christ. Saul was the proverbial "tall, dark, and handsome man." He was immensely popular—sort of a homecoming king, football team captain, and Student Council president all wrapped up in one! He was profoundly talented.

PRINCIPLE FOR A LEADERSHIP OF RESPECT # 17:
Talent and Humility Are a Winning Combination

But in the beginning Saul was also very humble. He was gracious and generous. He knew that he was just a common dirt-farmer. When he was selected as king, he was so bashful that he was actually in hiding! But the people who selected him had observed his exceptional talent. So skilled was Saul that he was drafted without his knowledge to be the very first king in the history of Israel.

PRINCIPLE FOR A LEADERSHIP OF RESPECT # 18:
Time Is a Friend of Those with Character,
But an Enemy of Those with Flaws

As a new leader, Saul seemed fit for the job. He was off to a good start (see 1 Sam. 9–11). But during his forty-year tenure as king, serious flaws began to show. In the midst of military successes, spiritual and integrity failures became more obvious. He began lying and inventing excuses.

When young David routed the giant Goliath in the world's best-known military feat, David became immensely popular. King Saul responded to David's popularity with jealousy and paranoia regarding the popular teenager. In an attempt to stamp out David, Saul ordered the murder of the residents of an entire city. The failure to immediately kill David led Saul on a cat-and-mouse pursuit through the mountainous areas of Israel.

A once right-acting Saul began to violate his own religious convictions. No longer was he principled and convictional. Saul soon ceased praying to the God of the Bible and began consulting the witch of Endor. He refused to follow what God had told him. He became presumptive regarding those in positions of religious authority.

Saul died disrespected and disgraced. His enemies decapitated him, placing his body on the city wall, his head in the temple of Dagon (1 Chron. 10:10), and his armor in the temple of the Ashtoreths (1 Sam. 31:10). One can tour the city of Beth Shan (in Israel) to this day and see the site where Saul's desecrated body hung.

How can someone go from a humble, profoundly popular, remarkably skilled leader to a disgraced, disrespected failure? By failing to follow the very law that caused people to once respect him. Saul, once strong, drew followers. As an increasingly weak leader, his leadership base eroded. He failed to understand the Law of Respect.

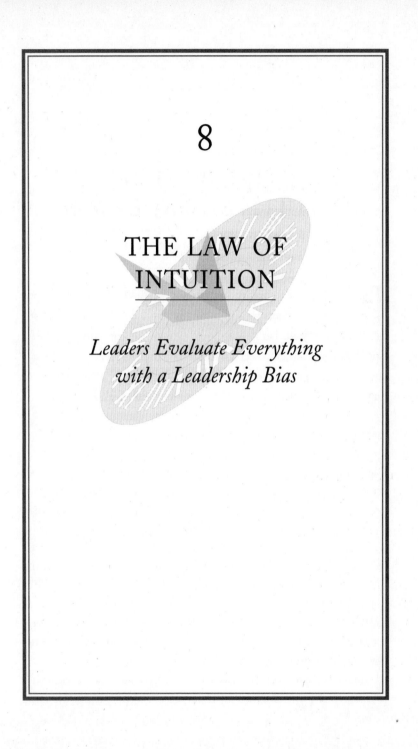

8

THE LAW OF
INTUITION

*Leaders Evaluate Everything
with a Leadership Bias*

PRINCIPLES OF
INTUITIVE LEADERSHIP

I am fascinated with history. Not everyone shares my view. Contemporary musician Sting's view of history is revealed in this quote: "I once asked my history teacher how we were expected to learn anything useful from his subject, when it seemed to me to be nothing but a monotonous and sordid succession of robber baron scumbags devoid of any admirable human qualities. I failed history." How do you really feel, Sting?

INTUITIVE LEADERS

I agree much more with Thomas Carlyle's understanding of history: "No great man lives in vain. The history of the world is but the biography of great men." And women, I might add. But history is much more than that. It is the story of great (and some not so great) men and women who were "made" for a certain moment. Admittedly, not all of them realized their significance at that time; all of them might not have realized the uniqueness or profoundness of their contributions at that time. But many did. Many seemed aware that they were alive at a time when history could be *made*, not merely read. They realized that history swings on hinges, and *they were one of those hinges*. In other words, they could actually change the way things were. It is a type of instinct.

There is a name for this instinct. In this chapter, I call it leadership intuition. My fascination with the history of Christianity causes me to see this intuitive component evident in church leaders again and again: persons who seemed to be at the right place at the right time. This inexplicable convergence results in, what is later recognized as, a movement, a major turning point of history. As a Christian, I am not diminishing the belief that God has certain people placed in certain places or certain times. He does. But God also blesses some persons with an uncanny capacity to see the moment and then to seize it. Here are some examples:

- The conversion of Emperor Constantine in 313 significantly altered the Roman Empire. Christianity went from a persecuted subculture to the point where it was the official religion (A.D. 380) of the entire Roman Empire.

- Jerome completed the translation of the Vulgate Bible in 405, which was the beginning of a journey that would eventually make the Bible the most read book in the world.

- Gregory I, the skilled administrator and leader, became pope in 590, and massively overhauled Christianity as it was then known, launching what was truly the *Roman* (Rome-based) Catholic Church.

- The Battle of Tours, won by Charles Martel in 732, totally altered the history of Western civilization, causing Europe to be Christian and not Muslim.

- The founding of the first universities in 1150 had a huge impact on learning.

- In 1617, Martin Luther overthrew the entire established church order, launching the most cataclysmic change in all of church history.

- In the year 1738, the Wesleyan Revival in England was led by John Wesley, and the Great Awakening in America was progressing under the leadership of Jonathan Edwards, whose "awakenings" would alter history.

- W. J. Seymour led the famous Azusa Street Revival in Los Angeles in 1906, which launched Pentecostalism, the fastest-growing movement in the history of Christianity.

These are only a few of the hinge points of Christian history. Even if you do not recognize a single name in this list, let me assure you that you have been altered in some very significant ways by many of the persons and movements mentioned. What do these hinge points of history have in common? Someone had leadership intuition. Someone knew, instinctively, what needed to happen and how to do it.

CHIEF JOSEPH'S EPIC EXODUS

Our study of leadership intuition now takes us to a Native American in the late nineteenth century. This backdrop provides an intriguing story as well as a demonstration of intuitive leadership.

In 1877 a small band of Nez Perces, led by Chief Joseph, fled thirteen hundred miles, from their homeland on the Oregon-Idaho border, through Yellowstone National Park, to the Canadian border in Montana. As they fled, they engaged and defeated several army detachments, commanded by experienced, decorated Civil War veterans. It was one of history's most epic flights, an exodus like that of Moses—though the Native Americans failed to enter their promised land!

Forty years earlier, the Nez Perces had welcomed Christian missionaries to their homeland. Two Presbyterians, Henry H. Spalding and his wife, opened a mission near present-day Lewiston, Idaho. Many, including Chief Joseph's father ("Old Joseph" as he was known to his white neighbors), befriended the Spaldings, embraced the Christian faith, and sought to live peacefully with the swelling wave of pioneers who came to the great Northwest.

In the 1860s, however, the wave became a flood as gold was found on the Nez Perces' land, and miners invaded the region. Federal commissioners appeared in 1863 and successfully pressured the Native Americans to cede some of their lands and accept a significantly smaller reservation, one-fourth the size of their earlier holding.

Some Nez Perces refused to sign the 1863 treaty. Old Joseph, for one, angrily stalked away from the meeting and is said to have returned home and torn to shreds the Bible that the Spaldings had given him twenty years earlier. In 1871 Old Joseph died, leaving his son a legacy of these words:

> When I am gone, think of your country. You are the chief of these people. They look to you to guide them. Always remember that your father never sold the country. You must stop your ears whenever you are asked to sign a treaty selling your home. A few years more, and the white man will be all around you. They have their eyes on this land. My son, never forget my dying words. This country holds your father's body. Never sell the bones of your father and your mother.[1]

During the next few years, tensions mounted as more and more settlers looked enviously at what was left of the Nez Perces' lands. Young Joseph, now chief, counseled patience and peace. When yet another federal commission, including General O. O. Howard, the one-armed Civil War hero, arrived in 1876 to call for still more "negotiations," they "found Joseph a disquieting figure," says Alvin Josephy, a distinguished historian. "Thirty-six years old now, straight and towering, he seemed strangely amicable and gentle; yet he bore himself with the quiet strength and dignity of one who stood in awe of no man. And when he spoke, it was with an eloquent logic that nettled the whites, who found themselves resenting their inability to dominate him."[2] And he would absolutely cede no more land! "We love the land," he said. "It is our home."

Home or not, the land was coveted by white settlers. Arguments ensued. A small dispute prompted General Howard to send 100 cavalry to keep the peace. They encountered 150 hostile Nez Perces, not under Chief Joseph's authority, and a battle broke out. At the most there were 50 armed warriors, and they routed the soldiers within a few minutes! Thirty-four troopers died. No Nez Perces perished, and only two were wounded. The United States Army, its pride on the line, could not allow such an event to go unpunished, so General Howard took the field with a force of more than 200 soldiers.

ATTEMPTING TO SURVIVE

Though Chief Joseph and most of the Nez Perces wanted anything but war, they knew the soldiers would treat them all as hostiles. So some

550 Native Americans gathered together and fled eastward during the summer of 1877. Chief Joseph, ever a "peace chief," left the military strategy to "war chiefs" such as Looking Glass, but he provided inspiration and general guidance for his people, giving special attention to the women and children who accompanied them.

Through rugged terrain, scored by deep canyons and marked by lofty mountains, the Native Americans fled. Soldiers pursued, and battles were waged. Always outnumbered, using weapons captured from the soldiers themselves, facing artillery with rifles, the Nez Perces fought their way toward freedom. They outfought and outfoxed Howard's troops, crossing Idaho into Montana. Along the way they never harmed white civilians. Encountering some surprised tourists in Yellowstone, they allowed them to leave unscathed. Desperately poor, the Nez Perces actually purchased coffee, flour, and sugar from white merchants rather than taking what they needed by force.

PRINCIPLE OF INTUITIVE LEADERSHIP # 1:
Intuition Is to Brute Force What David Was to Goliath

Having escaped Howard, however, they soon encountered another army corps, led by Colonel John Gibbon. With daring and strategy, the Nez Perces routed Gibbon's men, killing 33 and injuring 38 out of 200, and captured a pack train with 2,000 rounds of ammunition. The Nez Perces suffered twice the casualties, and Chief Joseph knew he had to escape as quickly as possible to Canada. So his diminished band struggled north, seeking the same sanctuary as Sitting Bull and his Sioux followers would find in Canada. They eluded a trap set for them by the Seventh Cavalry in the upper Yellowstone Valley, and then they hurried on. Several more engagements, some running battles, took place. Each time, Joseph seemed to choose the right place to fight, and his people effectively defended themselves.

Finally, thirty miles from Canada, the Nez Perces relaxed. They failed to detect yet another army column, this one composed of six hundred men led by Colonel Nelson Miles. The soldiers attacked, dispersing the

Nez Perces' horses and killing several prominent warriors. But the Native Americans fought fiercely, and Miles suffered severe casualties. Chief Joseph was thoroughly and constantly outnumbered, yet eluded capture for a long time and dealt severe losses to the superior army. Colonel Miles thus looked favorably upon Chief Joseph when he proposed to surrender.

> ### PRINCIPLE OF INTUITIVE LEADERSHIP # 2:
> *Leadership Intuition Discerns the Difference Between Premature Quitting and Appropriate Stopping*

After three months and thirteen hundred miles, the tattered little band of Nez Perces bowed to the will of the United States. The chief gave his rifle to Miles, faced the colonel, and gave one of the most powerful surrender speeches ever uttered:

> I am tired of fighting. Our chiefs are killed. Looking Glass is dead. Toohoolhoolzote is dead. The old men are all dead. It is the young men who say yes or no. He who led the young men is dead. It is cold and we have no blankets. The little children are freezing to death. My people, some of them, have run away to the hills, and have no blankets, no food; no one knows where they are—perhaps freezing to death. I want to have time to look for my children and see how many I can find. Maybe I shall find them among the dead. Hear me, my chiefs. I am tired; my heart is sick and sad. From where the sun now stands, I will fight no more forever.[3]

> ### PRINCIPLE OF INTUITIVE LEADERSHIP # 3:
> *Leaders Have a Unique "Get It" Factor*

In defeat, Chief Joseph became a legend. During that epic journey he demonstrated great courage and amazing acumen. Again and again he seemed to envision the moves that were needed to inspire the right kind of resistance, to bolster the will of his people. The ability is what I call the "get it" factor. Leaders with this ability internally "know" what to do next. And their followers, sensing that ability, join their causes. Chief Joseph lacked formal military training, but he outmaneuvered some of the best-trained frontier army officers. He sincerely sought peace, but when attacked, he proved a worthy warrior. He represented what many called a "savage" people, but he led his people with exemplary attention to civilized canons of conduct.

Admittedly, he failed, in the final analysis, to lead his people to freedom. But he illustrated,while struggling against overwhelming odds, the characteristics of a great leader. The fact that the Nez Perces miraculously survived as long as they did was a tribute to a leader—an *intuitive* leader. Without that gifting in Chief Joseph, the Nez Perces would have lost their lives on the Oregon-Idaho border.

THE "GET-IT" FACTOR

John Maxwell states that when it comes to leadership "intuitive skills," people fall into three categories: (1) those who naturally see it, (2) those who are nurtured into it, and (3) those who never see it. We all know many wonderful people. But some persons have the "get it" factor. And some persons don't. It's one thing to lack this gift. Many do. But it is inexcusable to wander through life without trying to improve.

WE ALL HAVE TWO CHOICES

It is not wrong *not* to have strong leadership intuition. But it is wrong *not* to take steps to develop it when you become aware that you either don't have it or need much more of it. Here is my question: What steps are you taking to develop the "get it" factor and to live by the Law of Intuition?

9

THE LAW OF
MAGNETISM

Who You Are Is Who You Attract

PRINCIPLES OF
MAGNETIC LEADERSHIP

Leaders attract. There is an old axiom: "like" attracts "like." Whoever you *are* is who you are going to get! In contrast, leaders do not attract persons radically different from themselves. And nonleaders do not attract at all. If you have no followers, you are not a leader. If you are attracting a following, you are a leader. Simple enough. But our focus here is not on the *fact* of attraction. It is on *whom* we attract. Or rather the *what* of attraction.

HENRIETTA MEARS:
THE WOMAN WHO ALTERED HER WORLD

A few years ago, I was invited to a dinner with Bill Greig II and Bill Greig III, the father-and-son publishing team. The result of that evening dinner was an invitation for me to author a book, which they published. But there was another highlight to that evening. I knew that Bill II was the nephew of the great Henrietta Mears. I had heard about her for years.

What amazed me about Henrietta Mears was not simply her incredible abilities and accomplishments. Many persons have great abilities and do great things. What really intrigued me was her ability to draw others to her and to inspire greatness in *them*. You see, Henrietta Mears influenced some of the greatest leaders of the late twentieth century.

When she was born in 1890 in Fargo, North Dakota, no one could have imagined that she would produce some of the greatest influencers in Washington, D.C., Los Angeles, and other major cities of the world. At dinner that night, I asked many questions, trying to understand the key to Mears's ability to enthuse and motivate others. Here is a portion of what I learned that day.

Henrietta Mears was always a teacher. She began by teaching Sunday school classes when she was only eleven years of age. Upon graduating from the University of Minnesota, she became a chemistry—you guessed it—teacher. First Baptist Church of Minneapolis needed someone who could teach five eighteen-year-old girls who called themselves "The Snob." An omen of things to come, "The Snob" grew from five to five hundred!

In 1928, Mears moved to California and became the director of education at Hollywood's First Presbyterian Church. Disgusted with available Sunday school materials, she wrote her own. Sunday school teachers around the country began clamoring to get her materials. Her teaching theory is revealed in this statement: "Learning is more than the ability to repeat the ideas or writings of another. The purpose of the teacher is to 'draw out,' not to 'cram in.' We must create an interest in the heart and mind that will make the learner reach out and take hold upon the things that he is taught."

The requests for her teaching materials caused Henrietta Mears to form a publishing company, Gospel Light Publications, in 1930. Her publications went from national to global status with the founding of GLINT (Gospel Light International) in 1961, two years before her death. Decades later, Gospel Light curriculum is translated in more than 100 languages by a network of 200 publishers worldwide. Regal Books, a division of Gospel Light, has published more than 800 book titles in more than 100 languages. Mears's book, *What the Bible Is All About,* although published in the 1930s, is still popular today and has sold more than 4 million copies.

She was much more than an unusually successful author and publisher, however. She was a "magnet." Eager students flocked to her classes at First Presbyterian Church in Hollywood. In less than two years, her Sunday school class increased from four hundred to four thousand! Hollywood celebrities, such as Roy Rogers and Dale Evans, listened to her weekly. She was characterized by unending energy, vivacious laughter, and profoundly colorful hats.

PRINCIPLE OF MAGNETIC LEADERSHIP # 1:
Leaders Recognize, Gather, and Empower Others with Comparable Levels of Effectiveness

---

Henrietta Mears was much more than a teacher who gathered students. She was a leader who magnetically attracted other leaders. One who felt her influence was Richard Halverson. In 1942, he became director of Forest Home, a popular retreat center that the charismatic Mears had founded in the San Bernardino Mountains in 1938. Through her profound influence, he became one of America's most respected pastors, serving as the chaplain of the United States Senate from 1981 to 1995.

Another to come under her mentoring was a young man named Bill Bright and his wife, Vonette. After leaving the extension faculty of Oklahoma State University, Bright moved to Los Angeles, launched a successful business career, and began attending Hollywood First Presbyterian Church. There, in 1944, he was impacted by the teaching of Henrietta Mears, which caused him to embrace the claims of Christ as being true. This launched him on a five-year journey of studying the Bible at the theological seminaries at both Princeton (New Jersey) and Fuller (Pasadena).

Bill Bright, along with his equally talented wife, began sharing the Christian faith with students at UCLA. So magnetic were both the Brights that people wanted to join their newly founded organization, Campus Crusade for Christ. Beginning in 1951, the organization they started (and still direct) now has more than 22,000 full-time staff and 489,000 trained volunteers in 186 countries.

PRINCIPLE OF MAGNETIC LEADERSHIP # 2:
Leaders Who Attract Also Impact

Mears influenced others, such as the world's most famous evangelist—Billy Graham. In the mid-twentieth century, a teaching swept through many American churches and seminaries, stating that the Bible was not reliable and Jesus was not divine. Two very young, yet widely known evangelists—Charles Templeton and Billy Graham—reacted to the teaching in very different ways. Charles Templeton (1915–2001), one of North America's most popular preachers (from Canada), promptly left the ministry and pursued other interests.

Templeton's close friend, Billy Graham, likewise wrestled with the teaching that attacked the Bible. To resolve his intellectual struggle, the young Graham went to Forest Home, the retreat center that Henrietta Mears had established. There, alone in the mountains, the young preacher laid his open Bible on a tree stump. He prayed, admitting to God that he did not understand everything in the Bible, but that he would simply preach it as God's Word. The result? He began to pepper his sermons with the now well-known phrase, "The Bible says . . ."

At that retreat center, there is a plaque commemorating that moment with these words:

> In Honor of Billy Graham, who had a life changing encounter with God here at Forest Home when, as a young preacher, he knelt with a Bible in his hands and promised God he would . . . take the Bible by faith and preach it without reservation. From that time, his preaching was marked by a new and God-given authority. Preaching the Scriptures in the power of the Holy Spirit he has seen multiplied thousands turn to Jesus Christ in repentance and faith.

Once again, another world leader was tied to the name of Henrietta Mears.

Henrietta Mears was a brilliant writer, successful publisher, and skilled businesswoman. She was one of the finest teachers ever. But she was a leader not just of followers, but of other leaders. Like "begets" like. That is a fancy way of saying, "What you are is what you will attract." Mears was a visionary. And as one would expect, she attracted some of America's greatest visionaries.

※

C. S. LEWIS'S MAGNETISM AS A THINKER, WRITER, AND PERSON

Just as the magnetic power of the poles affects compass needles, so in every generation the power of certain minds attracts the thinkers who shape their culture. Few twentieth-century thinkers have more deeply shaped Christendom than C. S. Lewis, a studious Oxford instructor.

In one of the end-of-the-century pieces published in 1999, *Christianity Today* reported a poll indicating that America's evangelicals ranked C. S. Lewis as the most influential writer of the century. Lists of the century's one hundred best books, whether compiled by Christian magazines such as *World Magazine* or secular journals such as the *National Review*, placed books by Lewis (especially *Mere Christianity*) near the top. His books still sell well forty years after his death. His children's books, *The Chronicles of Narnia*, remain so popular that the publisher plans to issue more of them, written by other authors.

Chuck Colson, the founder of Prison Fellowship, became a Christian, in part, through reading Lewis's *Mere Christianity*, finding its arguments cogent and persuasive. In the essay "The Oxford Prophet," he portrayed Lewis as "a true prophet for our postmodern age."[1]

PRINCIPLE OF MAGNETIC LEADERSHIP # 3:
Speak Simply;
People Are Not Drawn to a Leader They Do Not Understand

In 1939 a publisher asked Lewis to write a treatise on "the problem of pain." Discussing the project with his brother, Warnie, Lewis said, "I must convince the reader that I advocate Christianity not because I like it or that I think it is good for society, but because it is true. It happened. It is the central fact of our existence! And the apology [defense] must be in the common language of the people, just as the Gospel was."[2] A bit later he said much the same in a conversation with his friend J. R .R. Tolkien: "Nothing can be done unless we move completely away from this language of the scholars and the clergy. Apologetics has to be driven by the simplest words in the English language."[3]

> ## PRINCIPLE OF MAGNETIC LEADERSHIP # 4:
> *Think, Then Speak*

So this erudite Oxford scholar decided to address the common man. When World War II broke out, he found ample opportunities to do so. His book, *The Problem of Pain,* was largely ignored by university scholars but widely read by thoughtful Christian laymen. That success led the British Broadcasting Company to ask him to give some radio talks, explaining the essence of the Christian faith. Those talks, attracting millions of listeners, would eventually be published as *Mere Christianity,* probably the greatest of Lewis's apologetic works.

At the same time, Lewis wrote a series of imaginary letters that were published in the *Guardian,* a Church of England newsletter. These were put together in *The Screwtape Letters,* an enormously successful publication. Such success brought invitations for him to speak, especially at military installations.

Meanwhile at Oxford, Lewis helped organize and orchestrate the Socratic Club, a debating society that challenged skeptics to present their best case against Christianity. Lewis routinely analyzed, dissected, and refuted the skeptics in these sessions.

Within a half decade Lewis became world acclaimed—the "apostle to the agnostics" as some called him. Readers began to write him, and he daily had to devote himself to correspondence. He even conducted a sustained correspondence with an Italian priest in Latin!

Lewis and some literary friends, the Inklings, met regularly to discuss their writings. J. R. R. Tolkien was creating his imaginary world, later fleshed out in *The Hobbit* and *The Lord of the Rings.* Lewis himself was writing his space fiction trilogy. They mixed camaraderie and criticism—

quite a brew! But it was invigorating, and through his circle of friends, Lewis reached out, influencing ever more people.

PRINCIPLE OF MAGNETIC LEADERSHIP # 5:
Childishness Is Immaturity, and It Repels; Childlikeness Is a Virtue

---

To escape the dangers of London during the war, some children stayed with Lewis in his residence near Oxford, the Kilns, which is still a private residence today. Talking with them, he began thinking about writing children's stories. With regularity, during the 1950s, he published *The Lion, the Witch, and the Wardrobe* and five other volumes in *The Chronicles of Narnia*. He had come to believe that folks might understand and embrace Christ more readily through reading imaginative fiction than reasoned defenses. Children, as well as adults, joined his fan club, writing letters to which Lewis patiently responded.

Few men have written so well in a variety of genres, appealing to a multitude of readers. Consequently, thousands of people who never met the man were drawn to him. And those who journeyed to Oxford to meet him in person generally found their appreciation for him intensified. Though he never sought power of any sort, the power of his ideas rippled across the globe, a gentle tidal flow that made the world more like the Christ he so humbly served.

He has been deceased a long time. In fact, he died the same day as John Kennedy's assassination—November 22, 1963. Yet references to C. S. Lewis's writings are frequent. When I took a group of persons on a historical tour of five European nations in 1995 and again in 2002, the entire busload wanted to remain in Oxford until we had located Lewis's beloved home, the Kilns. Although it is marked only by a small, nondescript sign and is a private residence, the people on my tours simply wanted to stand on the street in front of the house for a few moments, even though it had not been occupied by Lewis for more than three decades. Leaders are, by definition, magnetic. And they tend to draw persons like themselves. The Law of Magnetism states that who you are is who you attract.

CRAZY HORSE:
THE MAGNETIC WARRIOR

We are now making a small chronological change, but a large cultural shift. We need to move the hands of time back fifty to seventy-five years. And we will leave the erudite and sophisticated Oxford University for the adventuresome environs of frontier America.

One of my favorite parts of the country is the Black Hills. I have actually not been there much. I have generally seen them from the airport when flying into and out of Rapid City, South Dakota. But I have many friends in the Dakotas and Montana, and I have vicariously caught their infectious love for these beautiful mountains. The following story will have much more meaning to you if you can picture that mountain range and somehow take your mind back through the years to a story with a painful ending, but one that powerfully depicts the awe of a magnetic leader.

Of all the mystic warriors of the plains, Crazy Horse remains most deeply entrenched in the minds of his people, the Lakota Sioux of South Dakota. Tourists traveling through the Black Hills frequently pause to see the giant faces of four American presidents etched in the granite at Mount Rushmore. A few of them may take a side trip to an even larger visage, being carved in stone, to commemorate the Native Americans of that region, Crazy Horse. Ironically, no picture was ever taken of Crazy Horse, so no one knows exactly what he looked like! But his image, his memory, remains: he is the penultimate warrior, the man who gave his life fighting to defend his people.

THE PREPARATION OF A LEADER

Crazy Horse was born (ca. 1842–45) not far from Rapid City, South Dakota, near *Pa Sapa*, the Black Hills, the holy lands of the Sioux. Even as a child he was unusual, for he had light hair and a fair complexion. He was called "the fair-haired boy," or "Curly," by his Oglala kinsmen. As he matured, however, he proved himself a fine horseman, hunter, and warrior. Though slender and only five feet nine inches tall, he was lithe, strong, tough, and durable.

PRINCIPLE OF MAGNETIC LEADERSHIP # 6:
To Nurture Others, Nurture Your Own Soul First

Crazy Horse was also unusually thoughtful, given to spending much time alone, praying and thinking, pondering his visions. Late in life he said, "A very great vision is needed and the man who has it must follow it as the eagle seeks the deepest blue of the sky."[4] He rarely took part in childish pranks or games, often listening instead to adults discussing more serious things. To Mari Sandoz, his finest biographer, he was "the strange man of the Oglalas."[5]

During the 1850s, as he entered adolescence, Crazy Horse began to understand some of his elders' concerns. White people, immigrants following the Oregon Trail westward, brought changes to Lakota land. A conference held in 1851 at Fort Laramie resulted in a treaty that sought to establish peace between the races. However, it failed. Minor incidents blossomed into major resentments. In 1855, for example, General W. S. Harney, determined to punish the Sioux for an earlier incident, slaughtered one hundred Sioux at Blue Water Creek. Young Crazy Horse was away from the village when the attack came, but he witnessed the carnage and talked with the survivors. He decided early on never to trust the white man and always resist his incursions.

EMERGING AS A LEADER

In the 1860s, Crazy Horse proved himself a great warrior. He studied carefully with an acclaimed master named Hump. Men called them "the grizzly and his cub." His father, at an appropriate time, gave him his own name, Crazy Horse. He led raids against the Lakotas' traditional enemies, the Crows, Shoshones, Pawnees, Gros Ventres, and parties of white men. Following the Civil War, he helped the great chief Red Cloud win a prolonged war with the United States Army, closing the Bozeman Trail, which had been cut through the heart of Sioux hunting grounds.

In scores of engagements, Crazy Horse demonstrated his courage, serving as a decoy, leading soldiers into deadly ambush, riding his horse amidst danger with daring aplomb. In the hit-and-run fighting that characterized these conflicts, he demonstrated unusual skill. He won battle after battle.

Following Red Cloud's success, the Sioux signed a treaty with the United States in 1868. Violations of that treaty almost immediately ensued, however, and conflicts broke out in the 1870s. In 1874, Lieutenant George Armstrong Custer led a force of twelve hundred men into the very heart of the Black Hills, violating the 1868 agreement. In the process, gold was discovered, and hoards of prospectors tramped through the Sioux's holy mountains.

Native Americans like Crazy Horse knew much about Custer— "Yellow Hair," as they often called him. Then the Lakotas started to call him "the Chief of all the Thieves" who had opened "the Thieves' Trail" into the Black Hills. Hostile bands, led by Sitting Bull and Crazy Horse, refused to abide by restrictions of the 1868 treaty, leaving the reservations to hunt buffalo, to live as they always had—freely. Crazy Horse later explained: "I was hostile to the white man . . . we preferred hunting to a life of idleness on our reservations. At times we did not get enough to eat and were not allowed to hunt. All we wanted was to be left alone." That was not to be, however.

PRINCIPLE OF MAGNETIC LEADERSHIP # 7:
*Leaders Attract Followers to Themselves,
But It Is "the Cause" That Inspires Sacrifice*

In 1876 the army determined to corral the Sioux, to force them to stay on the reservation. Three detachments were mobilized and were to act like pincers to crush the Sioux in their hunting grounds in eastern Montana. One of the columns, led by General George Crook, marched north from Fort Laramie in Wyoming. Forty miles south of the Little Bighorn, at Rosebud Creek on June 17, Crook met Crazy Horse. Crook had 1,300 soldiers. Crazy House had 1,000. A furious fight transpired, involving hand-to-hand fighting and spectacular battles on horseback.

Crazy Horse was everywhere, inspiring his men. The battle ended in a draw. But Crook retreated, and the Sioux claimed victory. Everyone knew that more battles would follow.

No one had to wait long. Seven days later, Crazy Horse was camped along the Little Bighorn, along with 10,000 to 15,000 Sioux and Cheyenne, when Custer and the Seventh Cavalry attacked. Mounting his war pony, Crazy Horse led hundreds of warriors to a ford across the river. He was heard shouting his trademark war cry: "Come on Lakotas! It's a good day to die." Within an hour, he and others had slaughtered the soldiers.

Shortly before he died a year later, Crazy Horse explained, "Soldiers came and destroyed our villages. Then Long Hair [Custer] came . . . They say we massacred him, but he would have done the same to us. Our first impulse was to escape, but we were so hemmed in we had to fight." And fight they did—successfully.

PRINCIPLE OF MAGNETIC LEADERSHIP # 8:
Leaders Inspire in Life and in Death

It was the last success, however. Subsequently, the army chased down the hostiles, burning their villages, keeping them from finding the food needed for survival. Eventually, even Crazy Horse surrendered in 1877. He was asked to come to Fort Robinson, Nebraska, to talk. He accepted.

When Crazy Horse arrived, he was taken to the guard house. He then realized he was to be arrested. "Another white man's trick!" he exclaimed. "Let me go! Let me die fighting!"[6] He resisted, and a guard plunged a bayonet into his back, fatally wounding the warrior who had never been seriously wounded in battle! He died on September 6, 1877.

In death, as in life, however, Crazy Horse stood as a symbol for his people: a strong warrior, ever defiant, defending his people unto death. He was and still is a symbol of courage. He was a leader above leaders. He inspired. And he still inspires many today. He is *still* talked about, extolled as a model of courage, more than one hundred years after his death.

BERNARD OF CLAIRVAUX

Like most people in the Middle Ages, Bernard had no last name. Thus, he was called Bernard of Clairvaux (1090–1153), named after a town in France where he lived much of his life. His life was so contagious that he is still remembered and admired centuries after his death. Like many leaders, he had a magnetism that has drawn others to him century after century.

Bernard was profoundly affected by his mother's death in 1107. Her death marked Bernard's "long path" toward God. He was an ascetic. An ascetic is one who practices severe personal disciplines, including fasting and even sleep deprivation.

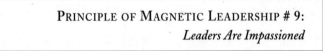

PRINCIPLE OF MAGNETIC LEADERSHIP # 9:
Leaders Are Impassioned

But Bernard's life was much more than self-denial. He had passion for living, for others, and for God. And that passion infected others. In fact, when he originally decided to join the Cistercians (an order or group of monks) in Citeaux, France, in 1112, his enthusiasm caused his brothers and twenty-five other people to join at the same time!

But the cadre that joined with Bernard was only an omen of what was to come. His monastery prospered profoundly. Others wanted in. They were attracted to Bernard's personal commitment to righteous and holy living. The result? He founded seventy more monasteries filled with persons who wanted to be like him. Remember, the Law of Magnetism states that you not only *attract*, but you attract persons who are *the same as you*. And in Bernard's case, that meant people who were fiercely committed to loving God and loving others.

PRINCIPLE OF MAGNETIC LEADERSHIP # 10:
The Intensity of Magnetism Impacts the Breadth of Influence

But the multiplication of leaders did not stop there. The seventy monasteries that he founded were equally magnetic. (Remember the law?) Those seventy monasteries founded an additional one hundred monasteries.

The most influential leaders of his day, especially the popes, sought his counsel. Pope Eugenius III once complained to Bernard of his immense influence and popularity, saying, "They say that it is you who are pope and not I."[7] And Eugenius was, in a very real sense, correct. As we discovered in the second law of leadership—the Law of Influence—position, by itself, does not equate leadership. Leadership—not titles and positions—is influence.

MARTIN LUTHER KING JR.

What recent American has had the *most* streets, avenues, boulevards, or bridges named after him? It is not Elvis Presley, Ronald Reagan, John Kennedy, or Babe Ruth.

Martin Luther King Jr. has had more than five hundred streets, roads, or bridges named after him. The church that I pastor is Skyline Church, located in La Mesa, California, on Highway 94, the major freeway that runs from San Diego's downtown to the eastern portion of San Diego County. And what is Highway 94's official name? You already guessed it. It is the Martin Luther King Jr. Highway.

Nearly forty of the fifty states have at least one street named in King's honor. Some states have many: Georgia with 72; Mississippi with 65; Texas with 54. Representative John Lewis (D-Ga.) claims that "no other American of our time has . . . so many streets named after him."[8] This is not an accident. John Maxwell believes that Martin Luther King Jr. is likely the single greatest leader in the twentieth century.

But Martin Luther King Jr. is known for more than streets and bridges. On December 5, 1955, Rosa Parks refused to adhere to Montgomery, Alabama's bus segregation policy. Others quickly joined the cause, launching a boycott of buses by blacks. King was elected president of the Montgomery Improvement Association, which encouraged the boycott. By

December 1956, Alabama's segregation laws were declared unconstitutional by the U.S. Supreme Court. Blacks could ride freely on Montgomery buses.

The Montgomery victory was only the beginning. In 1957, King and several other black pastors formed the Southern Christian Leadership Conference. Two years later, King resigned the pastorate of the Dexter Avenue Baptist Church and became copastor, with his father, of Ebenezer Baptist Church in Atlanta.

But Martin Luther King Jr.'s advocacy of civil rights was far from easy. He and his followers were occasionally jailed, sometimes beaten. Influenced in 1959 by Mahatma Gandhi in India, King advocated social change through nonviolent protest, which was best typified by his "Letter from Birmingham Jail," written on April 16, 1963. Although small at first, the movement quickly expanded across the southern states.

PRINCIPLE OF MAGNETIC LEADERSHIP # 11:
Leaders Give People Hope

The most riveting moment of the movement did not occur in the South, however. It unfolded in our nation's capital. In August 1963 hundreds of thousands thronged to Washington, D.C., for a civil rights rally, where they heard one of the world's most compelling and effective speeches. Who has not heard that resonating voice compellingly declaring, "I have a dream. I have a dream"? Virtually every reader of those words can hear—literally hear in their minds—the prophetic voice of Martin Luther King Jr.

The dream—that people would be judged by "the content of their character," not the "color of their skin"—riveted a nation on August 28, 1963. The power of those words still echoes through the national collective conscience four decades later.

And if that speech is not enough, consider the ominous words of Martin Luther King Jr.'s famous "I've Been to the Mountaintop" speech, in Memphis, Tennessee, on April 3, 1968: God has "allowed me to go up to the mountain. I've looked over and I've seen the Promised Land . . .

I'm not worried about anything; I'm not fearing any man. Mine eyes have seen the glory of the coming of the Lord." The next day—April 4, 1968—King was shot and killed while standing on the balcony of the Lorraine Motel in Memphis.

PRINCIPLE OF MAGNETIC LEADERSHIP # 12:
Noble Causes Outlive Their Leaders

But the dream did not end with the man. King's magnetism could not be stopped by a bullet. His voice was not silenced by death. Almost hauntingly, we can all *still* hear, "I have a dream. I have a dream."

The effort for civil rights for blacks moved aggressively forward in the days following King's death. Although racism is far from eradicated, King's life and message did more to bring racial justice than did the life of any other twentieth-century American. The reason? For starters, *truth* was on King's side. All humans, regardless of race, are made in God's image.

But added to that is the sheer magnetism of the man and the message. America was significantly changed by a man who never even reached his fortieth birthday! He is one of the most spectacular examples of a leader who lived the Law of Magnetism. He attracted. And he attracted others who were (or quickly became) like him in the struggle for justice.

10

THE LAW OF CONNECTION

Leaders Touch a Heart
Before They Ask for a Hand

PRINCIPLES OF
CONNECTED LEADERSHIP

D o you remember when you were a child—say, in the fourth grade? You had a crush on the person who sat next to you. Your parents allowed you to "like" him or her. But you couldn't say you "loved" the person because you were just a kid. The implication was that "to like" someone is several notches below "loving someone." And that is the way it should be when you are a child.

LIKE vs. LOVE

But as an adult, I sometimes wonder if the mature use of those words causes them to be reversed. Let me explain. As a Christian, I am expected to obey the biblical command to love others. That does not mean I must like them. But I love them, that is, I reach out to them in loving ways, with loving acts of kindness. Or as Christians might say to one another, "I love you with the love of the Lord."

But to like is, it seems to me, a notch above love in this case, just the reverse of our elementary school days. I, as a Christian, must love everyone, that is, desire the very best for others. But I don't have to be *with* a person just because I love (biblically speaking, "care for") him. In contrast, I spend time—in some cases, lots of time—with persons I like.

I even think that the phrase "God loves you" has lost its zing, its potency. People have become immune to it. But when I stand before a crowd and say, "Your heavenly Father really *likes* you. He *likes* being with you. He really enjoys His time with you. And you really *like* being with Him," it gets very quiet. The notion that a person is really *liked* by God, not just loved by Him, seems to carry greater weight.

PRINCIPLE OF CONNECTED LEADERSHIP #1:
People Will Follow a Leader They Dislike,
But They Will Joyfully Follow a Leader They Like

I recently discovered something. When you are interviewing a potential employee, one of the most important qualities necessary for hiring them is that you like the person. Yet in the times in which I have read guidelines for interviewing and hiring, I have only seen that statement made once! That truly amazes me. Liking the person is an important component for being able to work together. In fact, it may be one of the single most important components, particularly if you have to work together very closely.

Many years ago, I hired a very qualified person. His résumé was impeccable. His past experience was impressive. But it didn't work out. He worked for me for a very short time. After he left the position, I realized that I had seen one major "warning light" during the hiring process. I really didn't like him. Don't get me wrong. We never had one second of conflict. And we never had a tense moment or a cross word during his brief employment. But to put it bluntly, I had no desire to be with him, and I think he felt the same about me.

That does *not* mean that something was wrong with him. In reality, there was nothing wrong with him. And it doesn't mean that something was wrong with me. We loved each other as Christians. I wanted the very best for him; he wanted the very best for me. We would have done acts of kindness for each other without hesitation—and *we actually did*. But we did not particularly enjoy being with each other. Because we did not like each other, that feeling definitely affected our ability to work together long term.

There are people who are drawn to Skyline Church (where I am the pastor), and they don't know why. They simply like me or they like the church or they like some of the people in the church—and they don't know why. There are others who have left the church and really can't figure out why. Simply and straightforwardly put, they didn't like me or the church in general or some part of the church. And nothing was wrong with that feeling of liking or dislike. It is hard to explain (and probably doesn't need to be). It just exists.

PRINCIPLE OF CONNECTED LEADERSHIP # 2:
Connection of the Heart Overrides Differences of the Mind

In my denomination, pastors, like myself, are under the oversight of district superintendents. Many years ago, my wife, Carol, and I pastored a church in the heart of the Dallas-Ft. Worth area. Our district superintendent was Gene Fuller. We really liked him. We had many differences both in age and in church methodology. But we just liked him. We had no problem following his leadership, even when we disagreed with him because, you guessed it, we liked him. There were times when he disagreed with me, and he even asked me to do things I did not want to do. And I did them. Why? You already know. I liked him.

❧

JOHN MAXWELL'S CONNECTION: LIKEABILITY

In his book *The 21 Irrefutable Laws of Leadership,* John Maxwell states that the Law of Connection is the ability of a leader to touch a heart before asking someone to follow you. Connection is one of the areas in which John is a genius. His ability to connect with a person or a crowd is one of his strongest, if not *the* strongest, assets. Everyone knows that John Maxwell is an incredible leader. But there is another point that is often missed. People *like* John. They want to be with him. They want to be around him. Succinctly stated, he connects better and more quickly to others than almost any other person I know. And that is a significant part of the genius of his leadership.

Remember, I told you in a previous chapter that I am the only person on earth who has followed John in a position of leadership since he became a nationally recognized leadership expert. I know what I am talking about. He connects profoundly. The people of Skyline Church not only loved him (they are Christians; they love everybody!). They liked him too. And that "liking quotient" is a significant part of leadership. As a result, they loved following him.

I've got bad news and good news. The bad news is that all of us (or, certainly, most of us) are not as engaging and winsome—as overwhelmingly likable—as John Maxwell. He is the best.

PRINCIPLE OF CONNECTED LEADERSHIP # 3:
The Ability to Connect Well with People Is
Less About Personality Type Than About Valuing People

But here is the good news. Likeability, or connectivity, does not depend on your being as charismatic as John Maxwell. In fact, charisma is not a prerequisite (although it sure doesn't hurt). Connectivity is about caring, about reaching out. It is about valuing people (yes, valuing them even more than yourself). It is about adding greater value to the lives of other people. In other words, if you don't have the innate winsomeness of Maxwell, you can certainly cultivate a caring, affirming manner. You may not be outgoing. You may not be gregarious. You may not be able to charm the pictures right off the wall, as John does. But you can—or you can learn to—care for other people, find ways to connect with their hearts.

Connectivity is about authenticity. People can tell when you care about them. Most people don't object to being (appropriately) used, but they do object to being misused in a way that benefits only the leader and abused by consistently being taken advantage of; being subjected to hidden agendas, etc. The aspiring leader does well to assess how he can invest himself in others, how he can add value to the lives of others.

PRINCIPLE OF CONNECTED LEADERSHIP # 4:
When a Leader Touches the Hearts of People,
They Want to Be with Him and Identify with His Cause

Here is a test of connectivity: Do the people you want to lead *want to be with you?* I call it the "with-ness quotient." If they don't want to be with you, it generally means they are not all that excited about following you.

⁂

JEROME AND JUNIPERO SERRA

Let me give two profoundly different examples from history—from vastly differently centuries and from different parts of the world. The first one is Jerome (ca. 345–ca. 419). The second is Junipero Serra (1713–84).

JEROME

In the fourth century, there were three doctors, unusually bright theologians: Augustine, Ambrose, and Jerome. Jerome was an outstanding scholar of his era. His linguistic skills allowed him to do something never accomplished before. In A.D. 405 he translated the entire Bible from Hebrew (Old Testament) and Greek (New Testament) into Latin—a twenty-three-year process.

But apparently, being a Bible translator does not guarantee that a person will have a pleasant personality, because he didn't! According to one writer, Jerome was an "unrestrained controversialist,"[1] a nice way of saying that you might not want to invite him over for dinner because he liked to argue. A less charitable writer says bluntly that he had a "crusty disposition."[2] Another one said it in such a tactful way: Jerome's "scholarship and zeal for . . . life have been allowed to outweigh the ambiguities of his character."[3] That's a subtle way of saying, "He's a real jerk, but at least the guy was smart and lived well." A compliment? Well, yes. But with an obvious disclaimer. In fact, Jerome moved to the Holy Land, specifically Bethlehem, to do his translation, due, in part, to his bitterness over not being chosen as bishop of Rome. Another legitimate motivating factor was his desire for seclusion. But with a personality like his, he needed seclusion.

PRINCIPLE OF CONNECTED LEADERSHIP # 5:
If You Touch Their Minds, You Have Their Respect;
If You Touch Their Hearts, You Have Their Lives

He was a brilliant translator and, as such, did the world a profound favor. And in all honesty, in that regard he is a type of leader or influencer. But his inability to connect most assuredly reduced the impact he might have had. Jerome, with all his wonderful and admirable abilities, lacked understanding of the Law of Connection. To connect is to touch others' hearts in such a way that they *want* to follow you; they *want* to be with you. Jerome lacked the ability to connect.

JUNIPERO

Junipero Serra was quite the opposite. He is known as the man who founded California. I live in San Diego. He is, rightfully, a hero to many in our city. Although he was born to a poor family in 1713, his academic prowess took him to the highest academic rank: the achievement of a doctorate (in the field of theology). He declined the comfort and luxuries of university life, instead asking for the rigors and suffering of the life of a missionary.

Arriving in the San Diego area in 1769, Junipero Serra defended the Native Americans from improper treatment by Spanish army officers. In 1773, he asked for a type of "bill of rights" for the Native Americans to protect them from abuse. (Note: He has been falsely accused of taking advantage of Native Americans. There is no such historical verification. These accusations are rooted in contemporary movements of historical revisionism—redoing, rewriting history—and anti-European, anti-American, anti-colonialistic political correctness, with a touch of anti-Christian bias as well.) He reached out to the Native Americans with love, desiring to teach them how to raise crops and livestock, thus making their food source more dependable. In addition, he ministered successfully to their spiritual needs through the establishment of a string of spectacular missions:

- San Diego in 1769

- San Carlos in 1770

- San Antonio and San Gabriel in 1771

- San Luis Obispo in 1772

- San Francisco de Assisi and San Juan Capistrano in 1776

- Santa Clara in 1777

- San Buenaventura in 1782

The list of missions is an unbelievable accomplishment! Few persons accomplished more in the eighteenth century. His preaching was exuberant and flamboyant. In order to attract the attention of the Native Americans, he would pound on his chest with a stone, and he even went so far as to place a lighted torch against his chest.

PRINCIPLE OF CONNECTED LEADERSHIP # 6:
Connection Is Established When People Know You Care

Serra's melodramatic preaching style moved his intended audience to embrace his God. But they first embraced Junipero. His concern and care for them were well known. They embraced his heart; then they embraced his God. He captured their hearts first; then they followed his vision. That is what the Law of Connection is all about.

By 1784, more than 5,300 California Native Americans had embraced Christianity. Records indicate that 6,000 were baptized, making a public declaration of their faith in Christ. Junipero Serra touched the hearts of the Native Americans. That is why they followed him.

WILL ROGERS

We leave the late 1770s and the West Coast, and leap forward over one hundred years to 1879. Our story still pertains to Native Americans, but it now shifts to the Indian Territory that gave birth to Will Rogers. We remember Will Rogers as:

- an entertainer

- a comedian

- a film star

- a syndicated columnist who was daily read by millions

- a radio personality who entered millions of homes each week

- a rope-throwing cowboy

He mastered all the communications media of his day!

Rogers captivated the hearts of his own generation in the 1920s and 1930s. Yet his appeal endures. His jokes, fifty years old, still amuse us, for he had a philosophical depth to his wit, which makes it perennially fresh. He always preferred to make folks *think* while they smiled rather than mindlessly roar over slapstick silliness. "A joke don't have to be near as funny if it's up to date," he said.

And Rogers spoke—and still speaks—for a certain segment of America: an America rooted in the earth, as indigenous as his Cherokee forebears, forged on the frontier, incarnated in down-to-earth common men. Rooted in the American earth, Will reflected a native, populist perspective—rural and small scale, skeptical of big money, big people, and big powers. He spoke the timeless wisdom of simplicity and clarity, discerning what was basic and true about man and his world.

Rogers was born to mixed-blood parents in 1879 in Indian Territory (now the state of Oklahoma). He later asserted, "There is nothing in my life of which I am more proud than my Indian blood. Some folks," he quipped, "are proud that their ancestors landed at Plymouth Rock—well, mine met the boat!" As a child, he briefly attended a Cherokee school, for "I had Indian blood in me," he said, "and just enough white blood to make my honesty questionable."

Will's Indian-ness, however, was more than a gimmick or a vague point of pride. He felt deeply the injustices suffered by the first Americans, and he often condemned the people and policies that caused them. He felt especially angry about the Cherokee's mistreatment. Speaking at an Old Trail Drivers Association barbecue in San Antonio in 1926, he astounded and angered some of his hosts, charging, "You old trail drivers . . . did all right. You'd start out down here with nothing, and after stealing our cattle in the Indian Nation, you'd wind up in Abilene with 2,000 head or so."

PRINCIPLE OF CONNECTED LEADERSHIP # 7:
Connection Does Not Require Abandonment of Principles

Such barbed comments may sound strange when uttered by a man who claimed he "never met a man he didn't like." But he seemed able to both laugh at and prod the consciences of folks he genuinely liked. He made a career out of gently chiding the establishment types who ran the country. Attuned to the drums of his Cherokee ancestors, he instinctively sided with the little guys who were so regularly dispossessed in America. He sympathized with the small farmers who were pushed from the land as America industrialized, so he often poked fun at the bankers who called in their mortgages.

Once speaking to a group of bankers, he actually condemned the easy credit borrowing so typical of the 1920s. "If you think it ain't a sucker game," Will asked, "why is the banker the richest man in town?"[4] He then advocated laws to stop people from borrowing money! Musing about his hearers' (the bankers') job prospects under such laws, he acknowledged most of them would be unemployed. "But," he said, "I don't care what you do. Go to work, if there is any job any of you could earn a living at. Banking and after-dinner speaking are two of the most non-essential industries we have in this country. I am ready to reform if you are."[5]

His favorite targets, of course, were politicians. He never tired of exposing the faults and failures and downright deviousness of the nation's alleged "leaders." Generally speaking, he thought congressmen were little more than "local bandits sent to Washington to raid headquarters."

Covering the 1924 political conventions, he reported that the Republicans were deadly dull. Rather than be in Cleveland with the Republicans, he'd have preferred to go to a circus or see Grant's tomb instead!

PRINCIPLE OF CONNECTED LEADERSHIP # 8:
Humor Accelerates Connection

Joining the Democrats in New York a few weeks later, Will said, "What the Democrats lack in class they will make up in noise." Delegates, he warned, should leave watches and jewelry at home.

Amazingly, politicians asked him to speak at political conventions! Bankers paid him handsomely to speak at their meetings. Folks loved him because he made them laugh. But they loved him for a deeper reason: his unique capacity for friendship.

PRINCIPLE OF CONNECTED LEADERSHIP # 9:
Listening Enhances Connection

Wherever he went in his constant travels, he talked with—and listened to—all sorts of folks. He knew and enjoyed spending time with millionaires and paupers, presidents and cab drivers, kings and farmers. Whether in Hollywood or Hong Kong, Toronto or Tokyo, he made friends.

Explaining his constant forays, he once said that the trips helped him to know "what he was talking about." The constant contact with people enabled him to understand his audience. Eddie Cantor, a noted entertainer and good friend of Will's, said he "knew what audiences were thinking and what the people of the country were thinking."

> PRINCIPLE OF CONNECTED LEADERSHIP # 10:
> *The Depth of Connection Affects the Breadth of Leadership*

Rogers enjoyed staggering influence. A *New York Times* writer in 1929 noted that Will "spoke to and for 40,000,000 Americans daily, rich and poor, stand-patters and liberals, and they all heard him gladly while statesmen and professors addressed deaf ears."

> PRINCIPLE OF CONNECTED LEADERSHIP # 11:
> *Connection Is Less About the People Liking the Leader*
> *Than About the Leader Liking the People*

With some justification H. L. Mencken called Will Rogers the most dangerous man alive because of his power. It was a power rooted in his compelling love for people. People listened to him because they knew he liked them.

During the dark days of the Great Depression, he hosted fundraisers across the nation to alleviate some of the suffering it caused. And he continually celebrated the virtues of ordinary folks—moms and dads who did their duty, local folks who made communities click.

❦

SHOW US YOUR HEART

In August 1995, I was scheduled to preach a candidating sermon at Skyline Church in San Diego where the members of the congregation were to look me over as a prospective pastor to decide whether they would like to have me as their next pastor.

Flying in from Dallas-Ft.Worth, I was having second thoughts. *Why was I going to the church where John Maxwell had been the pastor? How on earth could I follow him?* I preached the four Sunday morning services. They went well, I thought.

PRINCIPLE OF CONNECTED LEADERSHIP # 12:
A Heart Connection Gives You Permission to Lead

During the afternoon, Glen and Don, two members of the church board, pulled me aside privately and said, "Jim, what you preached this morning was fine. But tonight is different. Don't give us another sermon. Show us your heart. Show us your heart. *Show us your heart.*" After hearing it for the third time, I responded, "I am hearing you. I will show you my heart."

I will admit now that as I walked away I wasn't quite sure what they meant. But during the afternoon, I started thinking of all the *emotional* connections I had with the church. Although I had grown up in the Midwest, I had had many deep emotional ties with persons from Skyline Church. As a result of those close ties, I had developed a very deep love for the church, even when I was a high-school student on the plains of Kansas. I knew the history of the church backward and forward. And it was a history that I loved.

I realized that afternoon that Skyline Church could have found many other pastoral candidates who were better, faster, or smarter than I was. But they could not have found one who loved their church more than I did. So that night in the service, I told them of my deep emotional bonds to their church. When I finished the congregation erupted into a lengthy standing ovation.

At the end of that service, Carol and I went to a fellowship hall and greeted people for the next three and a-half hours. The line was that long! The following Sunday the congregation voted for me to be their pastor. Why? They had seen my heart. Glen and Don, conditioned by John Maxwell's Law of Connection, had given me good advice. Connectivity pays rich dividends.

THE "FORGIVEN FILE"

Our goal as leaders is to connect with people's hearts *before* we ask for their allegiance to us—their hands. But what do we do when we work alongside someone, even *for* someone, when the "heart connection" is not there? What do you do when someone has demanded your commitment, but he does not have your heart?

PRINCIPLE OF CONNECTED LEADERSHIP # 13:
The Failure to Connect Is Not a License for Estrangement

As a pastor I have occasionally received unkind letters. What does one do with such letters? Although some are truly constructive, others are downright mean-spirited. Do you tear those letters up and throw them away? Well, that is certainly one option.

My father, a profoundly wise man, suggested a different plan. "File them," he said, "but label that file the 'Forgiven' file." And that is exactly what I have done. It would have been one thing to destroy the letters, but it is much better to make a conscious choice to forgive those who attack or malign us. Remember, forgiveness is not a feeling. I didn't feel like forgiving them. I forgave them as an act of my will, intentionally. Then eventually the feelings of forgiveness followed. And I deliberately, in appropriate timing, made every attempt to make those persons my friends. Enemies can be turned into friends when you "file" their attacks in a "Forgiven" file.

Not every leader you follow will touch your heart before he asks for your hand. Some might even have the audacity to demand your allegiance without attempting to first draw you in. That is unfortunate, and it is very poor leadership.

Some of you are leaders who have tried hard to connect with persons under your leadership. Instead of responding positively to you, they have reacted harshly or negatively. And they may have tried to undercut your authority, your leadership.

But rather than react, remember to mentally, emotionally, and spiritually place their abuses in a "Forgiven" file. Then pray that they will someday connect with you.

And in the meantime, make certain that when *you* are in the position of leadership, you always connect with people emotionally before you expect them to buy into your vision.

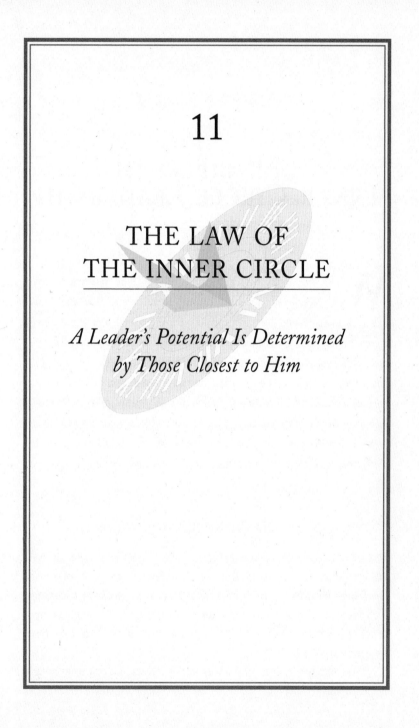

11

THE LAW OF
THE INNER CIRCLE

*A Leader's Potential Is Determined
by Those Closest to Him*

PRINCIPLES OF
INNER-CIRCLE LEADERSHIP

When I was in the fifth grade, my dad drove me to the nearest sizable town—Concordia, Kansas, population 7,000—to hear a great speaker. (Note: Just in case you are interested, the three closest towns to our Kansas farm were Ames, population 40; Rice, population 8; and Huscher, population 3, that is, until Ralph passed away and Julie went away to college, then it was down to a population of 1.) The auditorium was filled with men and their sons to hear the author of the book *Mover of Men and Mountains.*[1] The author? The famous inventor of the world's largest earth-moving equipment, R. G. LeTourneau of the LeTourneau Company. I remember it as if it were last night.

⚂

R. G. LETOURNEAU

R. G. LeTourneau dropped out of school at age fourteen and began shoveling sand and dirt by hand. But his mind begin to think of ways to do the job better. Moving from Portland, Oregon, to Stockton, California, LeTourneau eventually opened a repair shop. But due to the incompetency of his partner, he was $5,000 in debt (an enormous sum at the time) by age thirty-one.

Desperately trying to find a way to pay it back, LeTourneau bought a tractor and scraper and began an earth-moving company. His inventive mind began to think of a better way to move dirt. He designed equipment that would not merely push dirt around, but would pick it up. From his creative mind came more than three hundred novel inventions. From 1930 to 1940, Stockton, California, was the "earth-moving capital of the world," with both LeTourneau and Caterpillar companies located there.

The advent of World War II brought with it new needs in earth moving. Seventy percent of all the equipment used in the war was built by LeTourneau. If you have ever seen footage of the D-Day invasions, much of the equipment was built by this simple mechanic: transporters, missile launchers, and bridge builders.

In 1946, LeTourneau established a technical school in Longview, Texas. That school—now known as LeTourneau University—has flourished and has many satellite campuses across Texas.

But the zenith of LeTourneau's career was his invention of the electric wheel, special motors that were placed inside each wheel of his massive equipment. As a child, I was fascinated by earth-moving equipment that had tires ten feet tall and six feet wide, tires that were capable of literally walking through a forest, crushing the trees.

LeTourneau's monthly newsletter from the late 1950s titled *Now*, which reached 600,000 persons, featured pictures of this heavy equipment on the cover of each issue. As a child, I saved every one of them in a well-worn shoe box, frequently reviewing the pictures of the earth movers that he built. When it was my turn to fix the bulletin board in my one-room country school—Hillcrest School, District #6, in Cloud County, Kansas—I covered the entire surface area with pictures of LeTourneau machines. My teacher and classmates, used to frilly and colorful bulletin board displays, were likely not as enamored with a solid mass of black-and-white photos of enormous earth movers, but I sat back and gazed at the pictures with sheer delight. It was the best bulletin board I had ever seen!

Why have I told you this? Certainly not to teach you something about huge machines or my fascination with them. Or to let you know about one fifth grader's bulletin board project. The reason for the story is this: R. G. successfully lived out the Law of the Inner Circle. You see, the only comment I can recall from R. G. LeTourneau's speech when I was a fifth grader pertained to his brilliance in understanding this principle.

> **PRINCIPLE OF INNER-CIRCLE LEADERSHIP #1:**
> *A Good Inner Circle Helps You to Know Things You Do Not Know and Do Things You Cannot Do*

Based upon my childhood memory, R. G. stated the Law of the Inner Circle in the following way that night in Concordia, Kansas: "When I hire someone, I hire someone smarter than I am. Then I am quiet and listen. If I do all the talking, then I will learn nothing. I will only know what I knew before I hired him. But if I am quiet and listen, I will soon know not only what I knew before, but I will know what the other person knows too."

> **PRINCIPLE OF INNER-CIRCLE LEADERSHIP # 2:**
> *Your Inner Circle Will Write Your Future in the Present*

R. G. knew his inner circle could make him or break him. So he hired people "smarter than I am." (Note: LeTourneau was always extremely modest, saying that he was simply a "sinner saved by grace and a mechanic whom God had blessed.") You see, R. G. LeTourneau had no formal education. He had two choices: to either (1) hire persons who were weaker than he was in order to make himself look good, or (2) hire persons who knew things he did not know so they could help take him to the next level. He chose the latter. And that is what the Law of the Inner Circle is all about.

※

JOHN MAXWELL'S INNER CIRCLE

I want to give you a personal look at this principle superbly lived out. John Maxwell, who authored *The 21 Irrefutable Laws of Leadership*, did not come to an understanding about this law in a vacuum. He experienced it firsthand.

When requests began pouring in for John to teach on leadership several years ago, he wisely got permission from his church board of Skyline Wesleyan Church (where he then pastored) to travel, lecture, and be gone from the church much of the time. They approved, knowing that there was a "mantle" on him to teach leadership nationally. But there was a reason that the church board approved his frequent absences: he had an incredible inner circle to provide the necessary care and leadership for the church when he was gone.

> **PRINCIPLE OF INNER-CIRCLE LEADERSHIP # 3:**
> *A Good Team Knows How to Lead in Your Absence*
> *Just As You Would Lead If You Were Present*

I saw the evidences of this inner circle when I became the senior pastor of the church after John resigned in 1995. John had mentored three incredible leaders who were part of his pastoral staff: Dan Reiland, Sheryl Fleisher, and Tim Elmore. This team knew John's heart and mind so well, they could respond to any situation just as John would have, had he been present. Each one of the three was deeply connected (remember the Law of Connection in the last chapter) to approximately three hundred key leaders (my own estimation): Dan, to young to middle-aged married couples; Sheryl, to women; Tim, to young singles. These three could literally guide the church through their superb network, and they did it very successfully for years.

> **PRINCIPLE OF INNER-CIRCLE LEADERSHIP # 4:**
> *The Quality of Those Closest to You Will Determine the*
> *Height of Your Flight*

John constantly bragged about his inner circle—and for good reason. They were very significant in determining John's outstanding ministry at Skyline Church. John had another inner circle at INJOY, his leadership resource group. And once again, that team was stellar. That team, as John is quick to tell you, is an extremely significant part of his profound impact across America today. He certainly understood *and experienced* the Law of the Inner Circle, which states that "a leader's potential is determined by those closest to him."

𝄞

FRANKLIN DELANO ROOSEVELT'S BRAIN TRUST

Elected president in 1932, Franklin D. Roosevelt faced challenges new to the American experience. The Great Depression had sucked the nation's economy into an apparently bottomless whirlpool. From the dizzy heights of investor euphoria in 1929, the nation's fortunes had fallen into desperate straits: Farms were failing. Businesses were destroyed. Banks were closing. Jobless beggars stood on street corners, and people were fearful. They needed changes, solutions, new policies. So FDR's New Deal appealed to both their most instinctive fears and their utopian aspirations.

To chart such new directions, the new president relied upon an informal group of advisors, especially influential during his 1932 election campaign when he formulated the ideas that would be enacted during the critical first hundred days of his administration. He chose not to rely on experienced politicians—much to the despair of some within his own party. Southern Democrats, especially, quickly felt stiff-armed by FDR, whose ideas appeared contrary to many of the party's traditional positions.

FDR also chose to disregard the American tradition of the strictly limited federal government demarcated by the Bill of Rights and markedly supported by his predecessors, such as Grover Cleveland, a fiscally conservative Democrat, and Herbert Hoover, whom he defeated in 1932. Dramatic new paths were demanded, he thought. Only radically new ideas could rescue the country.

So FDR turned to an elite corps of intellectuals, recruited from the nation's premier universities, who proposed the ideas that would shape the policies of the First New Deal. Many of their proposals consisted of government-directed social reform, with its concern for the aged and infirm and the unemployed and disadvantaged.

PRINCIPLE OF INNER-CIRCLE LEADERSHIP # 5:
Your Inner Circle Will Not Merely Determine Your Height and Breadth of Influence; It Will Determine Your Direction As Well

---

FDR's team took the nation leftward. His administration was propelled by radical thinkers such as:

- Jane Addams, who developed in her work at Hull House, an inner-city settlement house. She borrowed from Adolf Berle, who envisioned the kingdom of God as a social entity established in accord with the social gospel of liberal Protestants.

- John Dewey of Columbia University, who advocated instrumentalism and secular humanism. He was noted for his experimental, pragmatic approach to knowledge, his experience-centered educational theories, his relativistic ethics, and his socialistic political agenda which deeply influenced several members of the brain trust.

- Samuel Rosenman, his legal counsel in Albany, who was asked by FDR to bring together a talented team of thinkers to supply creative ideas. Thus, he recruited the following professors:

  - Raymond Moley, who was a Barnard College professor

  - Basil O'Connor, who was a skilled lawyer

  - Rexford Guy Tugwell, who was a Columbia University professor

  - Adolf Berle Jr., who was also of Columbia

These people were part of FDR's brain trust. FDR called the last five men listed here his "privy council." They discussed and debated economic theory. They consulted experts from various fields. They wrote the papers and proposed the projects which would take shape in the New Deal.

Rosenman and O'Connor, as lawyers, represented the New Deal's commitment to institutionalize, through laws, the reforms thought necessary to save the nation from the Great Depression. In the hundred days, a glittering galaxy of laws were passed by a supportive Congress. To implement the laws, scores of new bureaucracies were mandated. To man the agencies, administrative staffs were hired, so hundreds of young lawyers and social workers flooded Washington.

Visiting the Department of Agriculture, Sherwood Anderson (a famous writer) reported: "I stood there in the office a few minutes and at least ten of my old western friends came in, old radicals, young ones, newspaper men, etc."[2] Another observer noted, "A plague of young lawyers settled on Washington. They all claimed to be friends of somebody or other."[3]

These brainy professors and lawyers drew upon a variety of radical critiques of free enterprise capitalism, the laissez-faire economic system. Free enterprise capitalism, they insisted, had laid the firewood ignited in the Great Depression.

They also "scoffed at the nineteenth-century faith in natural law and free competition," says historian William E. Leuchtenberg.[4] According to Raymond Moley, everyone in the brain trust joined in a "rejection of the traditional [Woodrow] Wilson-[Louis] Brandeis philosophy that if America could once more become a nation of small proprietors, of corner grocers and smithies [blacksmiths] under spreading chestnut trees, we should have solved the problems of American life."[5]

Professors like Tugwell especially relied upon the economic analyses and proposals of Thorstein Veblen, an eccentric, radical thinker who detested free-enterprise capitalism and championed a centrally managed economy controlled by highly educated social engineers.

Tugwell, though a blue-blooded, city-bred Columbia University professor, considered himself something of an expert on agriculture. After all, he had studied it! (One problem: he never farmed.) "Since my graduate-school days," he said, "I have always been able to excite myself more about the wrongs of farmers than those of urban workers."[6] Consequently, he proposed the vigorous agenda of price controls and farm subsidies that formed the heart of the Agricultural Adjustment Administration.

Many historians regard FDR's New Deal a "revolutionary" movement, a decided departure from the social, political, and economic policies of the nation's first 150 years. One cannot deny that today's America is significantly different, due to the course that FDR chose to follow. To the extent that judgment is correct, it reveals the power of revolutionary ideas proposed by an inner circle of radical thinkers, the brain trust and its allied intellectuals.

> **PRINCIPLE OF INNER-CIRCLE LEADERSHIP # 6:**
> *When Your Leadership Has Ended,*
> *You Will Be Remembered As Much by What Your Inner Circle*
> *Did and Said As by What You Did and Said—So Choose Carefully*

Some readers will likely view FDR's views as progressive and desperately needed, with a profoundly positive impact upon present-day American culture. They will regard the selection of his inner circle as the epitome of good leadership.

To others, FDR appears as the one who brought an end to American free enterprise, thus introducing socialism, which has had catastrophic consequences to this day. Either way—good or bad—your inner circle will chart your course. And you will be remembered according to what they did, said, or thought.

ANDREW JACKSON'S KITCHEN CABINET

When Andrew Jackson was elected president of the United States in 1828, he marked the rise of the common man. Earlier leaders of the Republic, such as Washington and Jefferson, represented the Virginia aristocracy. Others, like John Adams and John Quincy Adams, came from the educated elite of New England. But Andrew Jackson, solidly rooted in the western frontier, represented a different group of folks, ordinary folks who poured to the polls and catapulted him to the nation's highest office.

Following his second inauguration in 1833, his followers demonstrated their affection for Old Hickory. According to Justice Joseph Story, the people, "from the highest and most polished down to the most vulgar and gross in the nation," tramped into the White House to enjoy the reception.

Chaos ensued. Everyone tried to meet and greet Jackson as well as indulge in the cake, ice cream, and punch. Dishes were smashed, fights erupted, and Jackson had to flee the scene for his own safety! Aides saved the White House by taking the punch outside where the celebrants then collected. To Justice Story, "the reign of King 'Mob'" boded ill for the Republic.[7] However one appraised it, Jackson was to be a different kind of president.

Jackson not only represented a new constituency; he also ruled differently. According to his foes, he acted as arbitrarily as a king, ruthlessly imposing his will upon the nation. According to his fans, he led forcefully, tossing aside needless restrictions and implementing the will of the majority that supported him. One of Jackson's distinctive approaches was to rely upon a Kitchen Cabinet rather than the official cabinet.

THE FIRST CABINET

When President George Washington installed the first cabinet, including Thomas Jefferson as secretary of state and Alexander Hamilton as secretary of the treasury, he did so with the consent of the Senate. Thereafter he met with his cabinet officers and entrusted them with the responsibilities of government. Successive presidents followed Washington's model. Administrators were public officials, authorized by Congress to implement legislation and carry out the president's directives.

Jackson, following tradition, appointed a Senate-approved cabinet (including Martin Van Buren as secretary of state and John Eaton as secretary of war), one of the best, he claimed, to ever have been named.

PRINCIPLE OF INNER-CIRCLE LEADERSHIP # 7:
Regardless of Who You Say Your Inner Circle Is,
Who You Listen to Is Your Inner Circle

Other than Van Buren, however, it was a mediocre crew, and Jackson actually relied upon another, unofficial group of advisors, many of them old friends whom he totally trusted:

- Van Buren was a sagacious New York politician.

- Amos Kendall, a Kentucky newspaper editor, championed the rights of debtors—an issue close to Jackson's heart, since he believed bankers systematically exploited small farmers. The Bank of the United States, one of Henry Clay's pet projects, Jackson thought, was a "hydra of corruption," and he vowed to crush it! To battle-entrenched eastern financial interests, to defeat wealthy bankers, he needed help from men like Kendall. Kendall wrote many of the official papers for Jackson, giving intellectual guidance to the administration.

- Isaac Hill, a journalist, had edited a New Hampshire newspaper and was a strongly partisan Democrat. Disabled and melancholic, Hill consistently assailed the rich on behalf of the poor, inciting class envy in order to recruit supporters. Notably unprincipled, he used his pen to circulate malicious stories, including one about John Quincy Adams serving as a pimp for the Russian czar!

- Francis Preston Blair was another newspaper editor from Kentucky, a small man barely weighing one hundred pounds who came to Washington to edit the *Globe* and contribute to Jackson's cause. He proved to be a masterful polemicist, ever effective in waging political war with his words.

- Major William B. Lewis of Tennessee served Jackson for years in their home state, and Jackson asked him to accompany him to Washington. While he was paid for working as second auditor of the Treasury, he lived in the White House and mainly provided Jackson friendly counsel. He was able, and always loyal, greatly influencing the president.

PRINCIPLE OF INNER-CIRCLE LEADERSHIP # 8:
With the Passage of Time, You and Your Inner Circle Become
Virtually Indistinguishable Because You Function As One

Other persons came and went in the Kitchen Cabinet. It was clearly an inner circle of highly trusted men who advised Jackson. According to their advice he made up his mind. And when Jackson made up his mind, things happened. Few American presidents have acted more decisively than Jackson.

Although committed to the republican nature of the United States, he used his presidential powers without restraint when he believed he should. Thus, he threatened South Carolina with military action when the state dared to defy a federal mandate. When the Supreme Court upheld the Cherokee in a crucial decision, *Worcester* v. *Georgia*, he brushed it aside, allegedly saying, "John Marshall has made his decision. Now let him enforce it." He was determined to remove the Cherokee, and not even a Supreme Court decision could deter him.

Love him or hate him, Jackson strongly shaped the United States during his lifetime. Today he still stands as one of our more controversial presidents. And his informal circle of advisers, his Kitchen Cabinet, explains some of his legacy. In fact, it is a major part of his legacy.

⚜

BILLY GRAHAM'S LONG-TERM INNER CIRCLE

In 1934, an evangelist was preaching in a revival in Charlotte, North Carolina. Two fifteen-year-old boys went to the tent meeting, mainly out of curiosity caused by the evangelist's controversial charges that local high-school students were lax in their morals. As Mordecai Hamm preached, the young men—Billy Graham and Grady Wilson—were gripped by Christ. They were never the same.

By 1949, a young Billy Graham had become an evangelist in his own right. In that year, he preached a crusade in Los Angeles. That event would make him a national sensation. He never enjoyed anonymity from that moment on. His name quickly became a household name—first nationally, then globally. But few know the inner circle that guided him, helping him to make decisions that increased his effectiveness and resulted in a life of integrity:

- Grady Wilson, who found Christ the same night that Graham did, has been a lifelong friend, confidante, and associate evangelist.

- T. W. Wilson, Grady's brother, was another lifelong confidante and associate.

- Cliff Barrows was a musician who, while on his honeymoon in 1945, filled in for a no-show musician and ended up being one of Graham's closest associates for over a half century. He likely directed the singing of more persons than anyone in history.

> **PRINCIPLE OF INNER-CIRCLE LEADERSHIP # 9:**
> *Avoid Having a "Musical Chairs" Inner Circle*

What is amazing about these (and other associates who could be named) was (1) the extremely high quality of leadership skills they possessed, and (2) the longevity with which they worked with Graham—literally their whole lives! Billy Graham would have succeeded at anything he attempted because he is a profoundly gifted leader. But he went farther than he could have ever gone on his own because he followed the Law of the Inner Circle.

Your close confidantes will determine your potential. The Law of the Inner Circle has not and will never be repealed. This law can break you. But you cannot break it.

12

THE LAW OF EMPOWERMENT

*Only Secure Leaders
Give Power to Others*

Principles of
Empowering Leadership

I was in the first grade, age six. All eighteen of the students in my one-room country school—grades one through eight (we had not heard of kindergarten back then!)—took a field trip, approximately one hour from our school. The reason? A president of the United States was coming "home." President Dwight David Eisenhower was coming to visit his hometown of Abilene, Kansas.

THE FLAG AND A FUNERAL

I was standing on the south side of the street, facing the president's boyhood home. The crowd, by the standards of a six-year-old, was huge. Finally, after what seemed like two eternities, I could see the presidential motorcade to my left in the distance, eastbound. With delight, I began waving the small six-by-nine-inch flag that Dad and Mom had purchased for me, mounted on a gold-painted stick that was approximately two feet in length.

In my patriotic exuberance, I underestimated the arch of the wave and, to my horror, accidentally hit the ground with the tip of the flagpole. The little cloth flag came in contact with a tiny mud puddle in the gutter of the street, and there for all the world to see, *including the president of the United States,* was a one-inch mud splotch! *On the flag of the United States! Just as the president was arriving! Right in front of his boyhood home!*

I was horrified. Embarrassment turned to tears. I hate to leave you in the lurch, but I honestly cannot recall anything after that. Modern-day psychologists would have a field day with this one, claiming that the pain caused me to block out all memories of the rest of the event.

Leaving that story unresolved, let's run the clock ahead sixteen years, to April 2, 1969, the funeral of Dwight David Eisenhower in—you're right—Abilene, Kansas. I was no longer a first grader, but was a college senior at Southern Nazarene University in the greater Oklahoma City area. Two friends of mine—Paul and Mike—and I decided to drive six hours during the night to arrive at Abilene by 6:00 A.M. We hoped to get a good place along the same street I had been a decade and a half earlier so that we could see the Eisenhower funeral cortège and the motorcade of then President Richard Nixon.

Unfortunately, one hundred thousand other persons had the same idea, and the crowds flooded into Abilene. But Abilene's six thousand residents were prepared. They decided to bend over backward to welcome the fans of their hometown hero. And I'm glad they did. I became terribly sick just as I arrived in Abilene at 6:00 A.M. A night of too much junk food and no sleep had taken its toll. As we parked the car, I knocked on the door of the first house I could get to, telling the homeowners I was very sick and needed a bathroom. They welcomed me and took me right in as if I was their long-lost son (maybe they had forgiven me for accidentally putting a splotch of mud on the flag?) and became my badly needed haven. To this day, I am grateful to my spontaneous, but unnamed hosts.

Moments later, a much-relieved college student rejoined his buddies to try to find a place to stand. And stand we did. For six uninterrupted hours we stood waiting for the motorcade. During the last hour, the press of the crowd was so great, I could not move either foot. In fact, we were so compacted, I felt I could have lifted both feet and not slid down!

But this story is not ultimately about soiled flags and overwhelming mobs. It is about a man. Actually, it is about a phenomenal leader who commanded the respect of millions. He was Dwight Eisenhower. He accomplished what few could. His list of achievements was (and is) amazing.

As you would expect me to say, he understood the laws of leadership. I could have used him for a prime example for several laws of leadership.

But I have chosen this one. He lived it well. It is the Law of Empowerment. He was a secure leader; he gave power to others.

You see, although I didn't understand it as a first grader, and I still did not grasp it as a college senior, I was in Abilene, Kansas, on those two occasions as a tribute to Eisenhower's leadership, *including* his ability to empower those around him. And thus, he is a central figure in this chapter.

DWIGHT D. EISENHOWER EMPOWERS

Millions of Americans trooped to the polls in 1952 to elect Dwight D. Eisenhower as their president. Their reason? "I Like Ike!" campaign lapel buttons said it all. Folks cared little that Ike represented the Republican Party; he could have run for either party and won the election. They might have admired the articulate speeches of Adlai E. Stevenson, the egghead Democratic candidate, but his rhetorical flourishes failed to outshine the luster of a true American war hero, the man who led the Allies to victory over the Axis powers in World War II, General Dwight D. Eisenhower.

History's elite achieve greatness in various ways, for as Shakespeare noted, "Some are born great; some achieve greatness; and some have greatness thrust upon them." Reared in poverty in Abilene, Kansas, Eisenhower was hardly "born great." He did, however, learn from his godly parents to work hard, control his temper, fear God, and build character.

From Abilene, Eisenhower went to West Point, where he joined the class of 1915, an outstanding group that would produce 59 generals. Though only an average cadet at the academy—he ranked 61st academically and 125th in discipline out of 164 graduates—he found his life's work and diligently pursued his calling as a soldier.

During World War I, he drew duty in the United States and saw no action in Europe. Between the wars he faithfully served in various positions, attracting favorable attention from superior officers such as Douglas MacArthur. He attended the prestigious general staff school at Fort Leavenworth, graduating first in his class in 1926, an important step toward subsequent promotions. More importantly, he displayed the ability to work with others, to soothe hot tempers, and to enable others to do their best, whatever their task.

His winsome smile, his contagious optimism, and his genial humility ever impressed those he worked with. So when the volcanic Second World War erupted, he was soon made a brigadier general. And when the United States moved toward engagement in Europe, the army's chief of staff, General George C. Marshall, picked Ike over 366 senior officers to command America's troops in Europe in 1942.

The first Allied offensive response to Nazi aggression (labeled Operation Torch) was an invasion of French North Africa, and Eisenhower led it. The operation involved working with the French and the British—no easy task for an American "outsider." But Ike orchestrated a successful campaign and was elevated to the rank of full general. Then he headed the Allied invasion of Sicily and the Italian peninsula, routing the German and Italian defenders. By the summer of 1944 Rome had been captured, and Italy would soon be delivered from Axis control.

Pressured by Stalin to open a second front in Europe, the Allies planned an invasion of France. Eisenhower was intimately involved in the discussions, and on December 24, 1943, he was appointed supreme commander of the Allied Expeditionary Forces. Since it had been widely assumed that an English commander would head up the effort, some officers, such as Field Marshal Montgomery, could hardly disguise their disapproval for placing an American in charge of the invasion.

PRINCIPLE OF EMPOWERING LEADERSHIP # 1:
I Don't Have to Get the Glory

Other commanders were more dashing, more celebrated for their battlefield behavior, more renowned for their brilliance. One of Eisenhower strengths was that he could work alongside persons without needing to get all the credit for the successes. Perhaps only Eisenhower could have worked with both Montgomery and France's imperious Charles de Gaulle as well as get along with Churchill and Roosevelt, who often had their own ideas concerning military strategy!

> **PRINCIPLE OF EMPOWERING LEADERSHIP # 2:**
> *Empowering Bonds Others to You for the Journey*

Ike also assembled a corps of officers, uniting them in the formidable task of crossing the English Channel with an expeditionary force that could defeat the Nazis.

- He began by naming as his deputy supreme commander, Sir Arthur William Tedder, the British air chief marshal who had served at his side during the North African campaign. The two men truly liked each other; they trusted each other. Indeed, Ike's subordinates generally used the word *trust* when they discussed him. A quality of his character elicited trust. Montgomery himself, while holding that Ike's military abilities might be minimal, acknowledged that he had "the power of drawing the hearts of men toward him as a magnet attracts a bit of metal. He merely has to smile at you, and you trust him at once."[1]

- For his chief of staff Eisenhower selected General Walter Bedell Smith, an experienced soldier whom Ike knew well. Smith proved to be an able aide, soothing ruffled feathers when needed, rebuking delinquents as appropriate.

- To head the naval operation, so vital to the invasion of Normandy, Ike chose Admiral Sir Bertram Ramsay, a capable British sailor who had helped him plan and execute the invasion of North Africa.

- Bowing to the pressure of Prime Minister Churchill, Ike appointed Field Marshal Sir Bernard Law Montgomery as head of the Twenty-first Army Group. Montgomery was a dramatic, dominating man beloved by his troops but so set in his ways as to be difficult to command. He was assigned a secondary role in the planned invasion.

- An American who rivaled Montgomery as a testy personality was General George Patton. Because Patton was renowned as a bold battlefield leader, the Nazis expected him to play a central role in any invasion, so Ike held him, with Montgomery, in reserve during the initial phases of the invasion. Both Montgomery and Patton, however, would ultimately play significant roles as the Allied armies swept across Europe following D-Day.

• From the Mediterranean theater Ike also brought General Omar Bradley to help him conduct the war effort. Bradley proved to be one of the finest American war leaders, a brilliant strategist and effective field commander. Leading the U.S. First Army Group, he worked with Montgomery, coordinating American and British troop movements.

Once these men were selected and appointed, Ike freed them to implement his general commands. He knew he could not win the war by himself. He knew he needed to put the very best men in the right places. He recognized the importance of drawing upon military brilliance and charismatic leadership.

> ### PRINCIPLE OF EMPOWERING LEADERSHIP # 3:
> *Empowering Others Is a Risk*

But Ike's team was not always easily managed. He defended George Patton, despite Patton's tempestuous ways, because he knew how brilliantly Patton could lead men in battle. He worked patiently with disgruntled critics like Montgomery and proud politicians like Charles de Gaulle because he knew a concerted effort was absolutely necessary for the Allies to succeed.

> ### PRINCIPLE OF EMPOWERING LEADERSHIP # 4:
> *Empowering Others Is Worth the Risk*

As a result, Ike emerged from the war as one of the great heroes of that conflict. And he ultimately became a hugely popular president of the

United States because of his unique ability to possess, but never hoard, power. The power he possessed he dispersed, empowering his subordinates to do the work they needed to do.

ℜ

ROBERT E. LEE EMPOWERS STONEWALL JACKSON

Civil War historians often rank Robert E. Lee as the war's finest general. Next to Lee (and even higher, in Winston Churchill's view), they often rank his subordinate, Thomas J. (Stonewall) Jackson. Both men attended West Point, where Lee compiled a sterling record while Jackson's was nondescript. Both served in the Mexican War, wherein Lee captured his superiors' plaudits while Jackson was not particularly noticed.

THE ODD COUPLE

Clearly, they differed as individuals. Lee, the polished patrician from plantation country, ever reflected the gentility of his rearing and class. Jackson, a rugged man from western Virginia, represented the non-slave-holding yeomen—the plebeians—of the Old South. Patrician and plebeian, brought together by the exigencies of conflict, they fought and won some of the greatest Confederate victories, including Seven Days and Fredericksburg and Chancellorsville.

THE FAMOUS NICKNAME

Jackson gained attention for his role in the first significant battle of the Civil War, the First Battle of Bull Run, in 1861. There he and his detachment stood like a stone wall and repulsed the federal forces. The federal forces were fresh out of the nation's capital. Jackson provoked a rout that swept both Union troops and a crowd of Washington socialites, who had come out to watch the action, back to the Union capital. Jackson urged that the Confederate troops pursue retreating Yankees, for they could easily have occupied Washington, but his superiors demurred, preferring to follow a purely defensive strategy.

Subsequently, Jackson was assigned to Robert E. Lee's command, defending Richmond from an invading Union force under General

George McClellan. "Against the superior numbers of the enemy," writes a trusted historian, "these brilliant Confederate commanders now made a striking use of brains, audacity, and swift movement, utilizing interior lines and taking advantage of Union blunders and of McClellan's caution which they read like an open book."[2]

During this confrontation—known as the Seven Days' Battle of the Peninsular Campaign—President Davis appointed Lee commander of the Army of Northern Virginia. Lee quickly discerned Jackson's remarkable military potential and began to rely upon him to win the struggle. Jackson was more than a tenacious fighter. He was a thoughtful strategist.

Lee dealt with Jackson, as he preferred to do with his other subordinates, by delegating and empowering rather than demanding and micromanaging. For an innovative, self-reliant officer like Jackson, Lee's approach freed him to plot strategies and make battlefield decisions within the broad parameters of his superior's intent.

> ### PRINCIPLE OF EMPOWERING LEADERSHIP # 5:
> *Empowerment Implies Confidence*

"Great and good," were Lee's words describing Stonewall Jackson.[3] He so trusted Jackson that he rarely gave him specific instructions. A general outline of the battle plan was all he needed. Lee's empowering supervision unleashed Jackson's uniqueness. Victorious again at the Second Battle of Bull Run, Jackson fully earned Lee's confidence.

> ### PRINCIPLE OF EMPOWERING LEADERSHIP # 6:
> *Empowering Another Is Not an Event;*
> *It Is an Ongoing, Developing Relationship*

Their relationship, writes Lenoir Chambers in his biography of Jackson, "was rare. It was also secure. From thereon there would never be any lack of understanding or of easy, friendly adaptation to changing events, no presumption by Jackson but no lack of respect by either man. The Lee-Jackson

---

concept—an intimately co-operative partnership of two remarkably different men—was now free to rise to assured and continued development."[4]

PRINCIPLE OF EMPOWERING LEADERSHIP # 7:
If You Desire to Be Greater Empowered by a Superior, Demonstrate a Fierce Proactive Loyalty to Him

---

Jackson, reciprocating Lee's trust, totally admired and sought to serve him. He publicly stated that he would follow Lee blindfolded, wherever he led. He neither envied nor criticized his superior officer. Jackson's officers certainly admired their man, but they shared his ultimate allegiance to Lee. Lee's men, while aware that their commander was in charge, granted Jackson the respect and freedom he needed to operate with remarkable independence.

Jackson was fatally injured at Chancellorsville in 1863. His death presaged the death of the Confederate States of America, for the faint hopes for military success rested firmly upon the unusual fusion of minds and abilities that made the Lee-Jackson relationship remarkable in the annals of military history.

"Assuredly the most fatal shot of the war to the Confederates," an English newspaper declared, ". . . was that which struck down the life of 'Stonewall' Jackson."[5] Lee himself noted after the war: "If I had had Stonewall Jackson at Gettysburg, we should have won a great victory."[6]

Jackson died and Lee lost the war. But their partnership, firmed up amidst the fiery trials of the war, bears witness to the power of empowerment.

THE MODELS OF EMPOWERMENT

Throughout history, leaders who empowered have succeeded in ways that nonempowering leaders could not. Ideas are converted into movements when—and only when—the original visionary releases and entrusts the dream to others. That process is called empowerment.

A leader can have impact without empowering others, but his dream, his vision, will not outlast the life or the immediate geography of the visionary. It is in the empowering process that the dream takes wings, soaring to previously unrealized heights. Peter Waldo understood this in the late 1100s. John Wycliffe understood this in the 1300s. John Wesley understood this in the 1700s.

PETER WALDO AND THE "POOR MEN"

Peter Waldo (1150–1218) was born into wealth in Lyons, France, and could have lived his life in luxury. Interested in the Bible (which, at that time, had not been translated into the languages of common people in any country), he hired two priests to translate portions of it into French. Startled to discover a verse about giving to the poor, he disposed of much of his wealth accordingly in 1170. He began an intensive study of the Bible and then started sharing what he had learned. The response was overwhelming.

PRINCIPLE OF EMPOWERING LEADERSHIP # 8:
Empowerment Identifies You As a Follower
Inextricably Connected with the Leader and His Cause

Waldo's fresh faith, unmitigated zeal, and authentic passion to get the message out to common people created a huge following. But producing a following does not assure effectiveness, and Waldo apparently understood that. He modeled powerfully the Law of Empowerment, training and releasing the "Poor Men of Lyons," as they were called. The Poor Men memorized large portions of Scripture (remember, few people had Bibles back then), sharing them as they traveled the countryside. Crowds were drawn to the itinerant preachers, as they had been to the originator of the movement. Those who followed were called Waldensians or Waldenses. Church and civil authorities, troubled by the vitality of the movement, excommunicated them in 1184. Efforts to kill them over the next four hundred years, the thirteenth through sixteenth centuries, drove the Waldensians into the mountains.

PRINCIPLE OF EMPOWERING LEADERSHIP # 9:
Empowerment Sustains the Cause

It would have been easy to stamp out this movement if Peter Waldo had not empowered others. Opponents could have simply killed Waldo. But the movement could not be stopped because the empowered Poor Men spread the message far and wide. Waldo was secure. And as such he shared all that he knew, empowering others. The movement far outlasted him.

JOHN WYCLIFFE AND THE LOLLARDS

John Wycliffe (ca. 1329–84) was one of the most brilliant minds in England in the fourteenth century. If leadership is influence, then Wycliffe was also one of the greatest leaders, if not *the* greatest leader, of his time.

Wycliffe stood against clergy who were wicked and apathetic. Equally offensive to him was the massive accumulation of wealth by the church. He also argued against the superstitions that the church of that time used to manipulate the uneducated masses. Needless to say, Wycliffe was popular with the peasants and hated by the fraudulent church leaders who had much to lose by Wycliffe's exposés.

The basis of Wycliffe's objections was his stunning grasp of the Bible, a book that was largely unknown at the time. He proclaimed a simple, biblically based explanation of the gospel, free from the manipulations of a self-serving clergy.

Angry church officials constantly threatened him with arrest. Rumors of assassination followed him. By 1380, he was officially condemned in Oxford, England. He was taken from his loved university position and banished to an obscure preaching assignment. Ostracized and emotionally and intellectually starved (he was denied access to the university library), he died in 1384. So furious were church officials with him that forty-four years after his death, they exhumed his body, burned it, and scattered it in the Swift River. But the hateful act of throwing his ashes in the river only symbolized the distribution and promulgation of his teachings.

> **PRINCIPLE OF EMPOWERING LEADERSHIP # 10:**
> *As a Leader, Release*

Wycliffe, you see, understood the Law of Empowerment. In the final years of his life, 1380-84, right before and during his banishment, he translated the New Testament (in 1380) and the Old Testament (in 1382). He then trained and released a group of persons to travel the countryside and read the Bible to people in their own language—English. Remember, the common persons had no Bible, and if they had had one, they could not have read it.

Wycliffe's traveling preachers (or, more accurately, Bible readers) were barefoot, quite poor, and like nearly everyone at the time, uneducated. They were called Lollards, which is believed to have meant "those who stammer and stutter," in other words, persons who are noticeably inarticulate. But that did not keep Wycliffe from continuing to train them. And the result was that the freeing power of the biblical message spread throughout England. Amazingly, we don't know the name of a single one of them. But we do know that they were exceptionally effective.

Wycliffe never heard the phrase "Law of Empowerment," but he modeled it. And due to that, his message, which would have been silenced, was spread throughout a nation.

JOHN WESLEY AND THE LAY PREACHERS

Few persons, if any, have chronicled every day of their lives as did John Wesley, who lived nearly the entire eighteenth century (1703–91). That careful journaling includes his mentoring strategy. He trained 653 lay preachers, 57 percent of whom continued working with him until their deaths.

In 1979 I received my Ph.D. degree, doing an analysis of the effectiveness of John Wesley in mentoring others. I made an interesting discovery. His ability to empower others increased with time and experience.

PRINCIPLE OF EMPOWERING LEADERSHIP # 11:
Empowerment Is a Learned Art,
and Its Success Improves with Time and Experience

In the first generation of persons that he trained, some 193 individuals, 60 percent of them, either quit or were asked to quit! Admittedly, not a great success rate.

But in the second generation of 460 mentorees, the figures virtually reversed: 35 percent left him either by choice or by Wesley's request, but a whopping 65 percent served him till their deaths. That is amazing when we consider what one had to go through to be one of Wesley's lay preachers, a rigorously demanding calling.[7]

Why am I overloading you with statistics at the end of this chapter? I want you to see the heat of these stats. Just as John Wesley improved in his effectiveness of empowering persons through his lifetime, so can you. Wesley could have given up early on with a failure rate of 60 percent. But he didn't. He turned it around. And you, with time, determination, and commitment, can likewise more effectively empower others. Secure leaders release power to others. Wesley did. So can you.

13

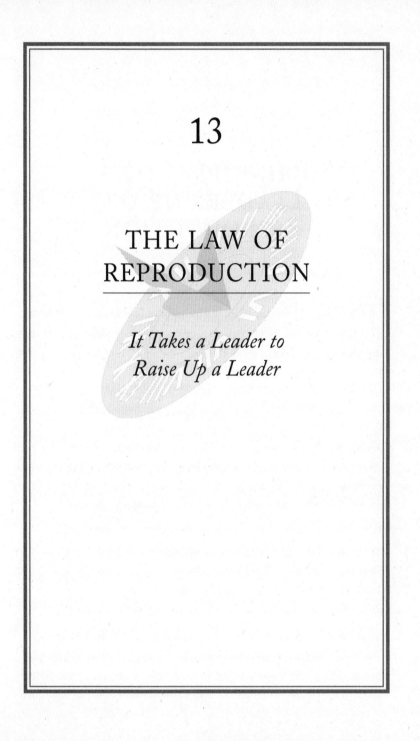

THE LAW OF
REPRODUCTION

*It Takes a Leader to
Raise Up a Leader*

PRINCIPLES OF A LEADERSHIP OF REPRODUCTION

The day was June 18, 1956. It was supposed to be another beautiful day in upstate New York. A nice day to spend some time at the lake. But the day did not go as planned.

❦

DAWSON TROTMAN

Dawson seemed as strong at age fifty as he had been at age twenty. So when he saw a swimmer in trouble, he did not hesitate to dive in, fully expecting to be able to save him. But in trying to rescue another, he lost his own life. The nation grieved the loss of Dawson Trotman.

PRINCIPLE OF A LEADERSHIP OF REPRODUCTION # 1:
Those Who Reproduce Themselves in Others
Create Movements That Long Outlive Them

What would happen to the organization he had founded in 1934? Would the Navigators continue? Would it fall apart? Everyone knew the answer. The organization, comprised of college students and young adults clustered around America's universities, would flourish. And how

172

did everyone know that? Because the Navigators specialized in reproduction—raising up leaders. Thus, the organization would prosper, even
after the founder's premature death.

Stated briefly, the purpose of the Navigators is to reproduce one's
Christlike living skills in another—thus raising up a leader who will con-
tinue the reproduction process. Although gripped in grief, the growing
Navigators organization continued resolutely with its mission.

Trotman's personal life story is amazing. In high school he was Mr.
Popularity: valedictorian, student-body president, and captain of the
basketball team. But in his post–high-school years, he followed a path-
way of drinking and gambling. Late one night he was so drunk, he could
not find his car. A policeman planted a nagging question in his heart
with the words, "Son, do you like this kind of life?" "Sir, I hate it," replied
young Trotman. The policeman encouraged him to change his ways.

Two days later, Dawson Trotman attended a church. The young
people were having a contest to memorize portions of the Bible. Always
up for competition, he memorized the assigned verses—the only youth
to follow through with the challenge. Week after week, he continued the
practice. A few weeks later, one of the verses popped up in his mind, and
he personally embraced the teachings of Christ on the spot.

In 1933, Trotman was sharing Bible verses with a sailor named Les
Spencer. Spencer, amazed at Dawson's grasp of Scripture and memo-
rization of verses, exclaimed that he wished he had Trotman's skills.
Trotman seized the moment, teaching Spencer how to understand and
memorize the Bible. Spencer, in turn, then trained another, and the
Navigators (a name intentionally chosen for its nautical status) was
born.

By the end of WWII, thousands of men on ships and bases had been
trained in Scriptural leadership and spiritual multiplication. I have been a
pastor for nearly twenty-five years. I do not believe there has ever been a
ministry that has been more successful in reproduction—one leader raising up a godly leader, who raises up a leader, who raises up a leader, and
so on—than the Navigators.

The ministry was incorporated in 1943 in California, but moved to
its present-day breathtaking Glen Eyrie Conference Center in Colorado

Springs in 1953. The Navigators have 3,600 hundred staff representing 60 nationalities working in 101 countries.

A young Billy Graham was so impressed with Trotman's skills in reproducing himself in others that he invited him to the now famous 1949 Los Angeles Crusade to train the new converts. A young Bill Bright asked Trotman to lend his influence to Bright's at-the-time brand-new Campus Crusade for Christ organization in 1951 on the UCLA campus.

Many ministries, organizations, and companies now prioritize reproduction, that is, one leader raising up another leader. But no organization has done it so consistently, so self-consciously, and with such focus, as the Navigators. The distinct Navigator imprint is so successfully passed on that even present-day mentorees have the Dawson Trotman persona or spiritual DNA, some five decades after he drowned! In reality, leaders who are "reproducers" never die. Their legacy cannot be stopped by drowning.

BILL BRIGHT'S *TRANSFERABLE CONCEPTS*

In a previous chapter, I listed the amazing accomplishments of Bill Bright, founder of the massive Campus Crusade for Christ. The key to Bright's success stems from his grasp of spiritual multiplication—or reproduction. He structured the entire organization with a bent toward reproduction, the ability of one person to replicate himself in another person.

I learned my need for help in this area in the mid-1970s. I have six academic degrees: A.A., B.A., M.A., M.Div., Th.M., and Ph.D. You would think I would know how to teach what I've learned. And I can. But I have not always known how to teach what I know *in a way so that the person learning from me could pass it on to another, who would, in turn, pass it on to another.*

> **PRINCIPLE OF A LEADERSHIP OF REPRODUCTION # 2:**
> *Successful Reproduction Depends Upon Transferability,*
> *the Capacity to Pass On Key Concepts, the Persona of the Leader,*
> *or the Ambience of the Organization*

In 1975, I was the pastor of a small inner-city church in Trenton, New Jersey, while in graduate school at Drew University. A number of persons who started attending the church had no Christian background at all. I realized that I needed help in teaching them in ways that they could take what they learned from me and pass it on to another. I simply lacked that skill. The writings of Bill Bright, whom I did not know at the time, helped me enormously in this effort. I discovered his booklets titled *Transferable Concepts.* Those little pamphlets altered how I taught.

I can remember it as if it were yesterday. I thought, *I have done all this study, but it took these little, simple booklets*—Transferable Concepts—*to show me how to share information in a way so that the person I am teaching can pass it on.*

The Law of Reproduction states, in effect: it doesn't make any difference how good a leader you are if you can't develop others, who are able to raise up another generation of leaders. The Law of Reproduction is ultimately about transferable concepts, as Bill Bright called them.

PRINCIPLE OF A LEADERSHIP OF REPRODUCTION # 3
In the Leadership "Relay,"
It Makes No Difference How Fast You Run If You Drop the Baton

---

THE FIVE GOOD EMPERORS

One of the most spectacular examples of the law of reproduction occurred from A.D. 96 to 180, during what is called the *Pax Romana,* or the "peace of Rome." Rome was not peaceful by accident. Peace was the result of the leadership of five good emperors, who had followed two terrible emperors: Nero and Domitian.

"Good emperor #1" was Nerva, who provided stability and decorum to Rome. Since he had no children, he legally adopted Trajan, who was "good emperor #2." Trajan, a skilled administrator, expanded the empire. Like Nerva, Trajan had no heirs, so he adopted Hadrian, who became "good emperor #3." Hadrian proved to be an exceptional hands-on leader, carefully examining the empire and rebuilding portions of it. Like Nerva and Trajan before him, he had no heirs, so he adopted Antoninus Pius, who became "good emperor #4." Antoninus proved to be a cautious yet compassionate leader. Amazingly, Antoninus had no children, and thus, for the fifth time, an adopted man became an emperor: Marcus Aurelius, "good emperor #5." Marcus was the philosopher-ruler. But he was also a superb leader.

Unfortunately, Marcus had a son, Commodus, who inherited the throne and who became a corrupt and capricious ruler. The relay of good emperors had ended. Rome's eight-decade period of great leadership had ended. The baton of good leadership had been handed so well, four different times. But the baton was finally dropped. Relays are not determined solely by how fast you run, but by how well you get the baton into the hands of the next runner. "Reproductive leadership" works the same way.

JOHANNES ECKHART: THE "MASTER" REPRODUCER

Some leaders in the Roman Catholic hierarchy in the Middle Ages were very corrupt. Many people reacted against the immorality of clergy during that time by attempting to be close to God. This movement is called Mysticism.

One of the Mystics—although an occasionally controversial one—was Johannes Eckhart (1260–1327) of Cologne, Germany. But he is rarely called by his first name Johannes. Usually, he is referred to as Master, or *Meister* in German. Why was he called master? In part, because he was a reproducer; he replicated himself in others, putting his stamp on them:

- John Tauler (1300–1361), one of the great influencers during the Black Plague (1347–50), as a member of the Friends of God group who merged love for God with love for others

- Henry Suso (1300–1366), skilled devotional author of *Little Book of Truth* (1329)

- Martin Luther (1483–1546), the great Reformer influenced by the Master after reading Eckhart's writings two hundred years following his death

Master Eckhart also influenced John Ruysbroeck (1293–1381), who became a "director of souls"—that's Middle Ages language for reproducer—for others. One of the persons mentored by Ruysbroeck was Gerhard Groote (1340–1384), who began reproducing himself in others through the Brethren for the Common Life across Germany and the Netherlands. Even after Groote's death, his influence continued. One of the young students who came to the school that Groote had established was Thomas à Kempis (1380–1471), who came to Deventer, in east central Netherlands, at age twelve. He would become one of the world's most famous authors.

THOMAS À KEMPIS'S BOOK OF REPRODUCTION

What is the most widely read spiritual book, outside the Bible? It is believed to be Thomas à Kempis's *The Imitation of Christ*. It has been translated into more languages than any book in history, with the exception of—once again—the Bible. Amazingly little is known about Thomas à Kempis, the world's most successful author. But there are two things we know about him, both pertaining to the Law of Reproduction.

Thomas à Kempis's life itself is a clear example of life reproduction or multiplication. His *Imitation of Christ* reflects the influence of his mentor Gerhard Groote so strongly that it has been argued at times that Groote is the real author. In other words, the mentor left his thumbprint indelibly stamped on the "mentoree." That's reproduction!

Furthermore, à Kempis (who scholars have affirmed *is* the real author of *The Imitation of Christ*) wrote one of the finest manuals on reproducing leaders. The title tells it all: Simply imitate Christ. The word *imitate*, according to the dictionary, means "to produce a copy of." That is the nature of the law of reproduction.

PRINCIPLE OF A LEADERSHIP OF REPRODUCTION # 4:
Reproduction Is the Method by Which You Can Go from
Merely Reading History to Creating History

In this brief account we walked through four generations:

- Johannes Eckhart, who influenced Ruysbroeck

- John Ruysbroeck, who influenced Groote

- Gerhard Groote, who influenced Kempis

- Thomas à Kempis, who influenced much of the world through his book.

ANOTHER FOUR GENERATIONS

In the New Testament, Jesus mentored His best friend, John (writer of the Gospel of John; three small letters: 1 John, 2 John, and 3 John; and the difficult-to-understand, final book of the Bible, Revelation), who reproduced himself in Ignatius, who helped shape the life of Polycarp.

JESUS TO JOHN

Jesus was crucified, resurrected, and ascended to heaven in approximately A.D. 30. But He had skillfully discipled John, His best friend. John, who miraculously survived an attempt on his life, died approximately A.D. 100. But not before he had reproduced his leadership in another.

JOHN TO IGNATIUS

John mentored Ignatius (ca. A.D. 35–ca. 107), who was the leader of the church in Antioch, the third-largest city in the world at the time, with a population of 500,000. Under his skillful leadership, the church grew from a small group to possibly as many as 100,000! Ignatius was tragically forced to march many miles, through many towns, as he was taken to the site where he was killed for his faith in Christ.

IGNATIUS TO POLYCARP

Ignatius, particularly through his writings, left his mark on Polycarp (ca. A.D. 69–ca. 155), church leader in Smyrna (in Asia Minor). As an old man, Polycarp was burned alive for his faith in Christ. When asked to deny Christ, he replied, "For eighty-six years . . . He has never done me wrong; how can I [deny Him]?"

This is the way reproduction is supposed to happen. Investing in others results in your influence continuing long after your name is forgotten.

※

"LITTLE CHARLIE"

You've heard of "Little Richard," the well-known rock and roller. Well, I want to tell you about "Little Charlie." As I have stated, I serve as the senior pastor at Skyline Wesleyan Church in San Diego. But I am only one of about fifteen pastors on staff at the church. One of them is named Charlie Alcock. He is our pastor to high-school students.

Charlie is an incredible reproducer. He does it naturally, yet with focused intentionality. As the years have passed, we have hired other pastors that he recommended. They were people that he had mentored when he lived in Indiana: one helps disciple our youth, another helps pastor middle-school students, and yet another assists with our student complex. It is quite apparent that these young men have been profoundly influenced by Charlie. They think like him, respond like him, tease like him, even play the piano like him! I call them "Little Charlies." And that is a high compliment to Charlie Alcock. Charlie understands the Law of Reproduction.

14

THE LAW OF
BUY-IN

*People Buy Into the Leader,
Then the Vision*

PRINCIPLES OF
BUY-IN LEADERSHIP

I n Chapter 10, we discussed the Law of Connection: "Leaders touch a heart before they ask for a hand." This heart connectivity was defined as a type of "liking" of the leader.

CONNECTION vs. BUY-IN

Now in Chapter 14, we are discussing the Law of Buy-In: "People buy into the leader, then the vision." What is the difference between these two laws?

First, they are sequential. The Law of Connection (the leader reaches those he desires to lead) tends to occur *before* the Law of Buy-In (the followers embrace a leader and his vision) is activated.

Second, the connection law pertains to the actions of the leader. The leader is the one doing something (touching people's hearts). In the buy-in law, it is the follower who is doing something (buying in).

And last, the Law of Connection is about likeability, even affability, a type of graciousness. But the Law of Buy-In is about credibility, trustworthiness, reliability, sincerity, a type of standing. The Law of Connection is about someone with whom you want to be. The Law of Buy-In represents someone with a cause for which you are willing to sacrifice.

𝓜

GREGORY THE GREAT:
A GREAT LEADER WITH GREAT VISION

At the inaugural point of the Middles Ages is one of the most successful leaders. In fact, the Middle Ages actually *begin* in A.D. 590 *due to the*
leadership of one named Gregory (A.D. 540–604).

Pope Gregory I is not called "great" by accident. His accomplishments are still impressive, fourteen hundred years later:

- exceptionally gifted leader (established bishop of Rome as head
  of the church)

- skillful administrator (numerous social programs; oversight of
  eighteen hundred square miles)

- competent financier (massive organization, estimated annual
  income $1.5 million)

- assionate communicator (preached to many)

- caring pastor of an enormous congregation (Rome)

- compassionate giver to the poor (instituted welfare programs)

- missions strategizer (sent Augustine of Canterbury to England)

He was also personally generous, fair, and zealous. (You may be
wondering if he had any weaknesses. He did. For one thing, he made
some serious theological mistakes. But with all those strengths, the guy
deserves to have *some* weaknesses, right?)

PRINCIPLE OF BUY-IN LEADERSHIP # 1:
The Credibility of the Leader Enhances the Credibility of the Vision

---

Gregory's generosity, sense of fairness, and zeal established credibility.
And people follow a credible leader. Without a doubt, Gregory I never

heard the phrase "the Law of Buy-In." But he certainly understood it. More importantly, he lived it. And that is why he is called "great," not simply because of what he *did*, but because of who he *was*.

⚜

BILL CLINTON:
THE HIGH COST OF VIOLATING A LAW

Let's observe this same law at work in more contemporary times—specifically in the presidency of Bill Clinton, elected to the White House in 1992. But this time, we will see the law working negatively.

The Law of Buy-In is (like the other laws) not just a guideline or a principle. It is a law. And when laws are broken, they break the people who broke them. Bill Clinton did not grasp the Law of Buy-In. James Carville, Lanny Davis, and Paul Begala, all Clinton advisors, tried to persuade Americans that character didn't matter. And shockingly, it appeared that they were right. After all, polls consistently and amazingly showed that while Americans did not trust Bill Clinton, they still thought he was doing a good job as president. The president's spin doctors skillfully, tirelessly, and constantly recited the mantra: "a person's personal life has no relationship to his ability to govern."

> **PRINCIPLE OF BUY-IN LEADERSHIP # 2:**
> *Loss of Credibility of the Leader*
> *Threatens the Credibility of the Vision*

But the American "gullibility tank" finally registered empty. Although it is true that the majority seemed to favor leaving Clinton in office after the impeachment, the Law of Buy-In took its toll on Al Gore, a sitting vice-president, who lost the election of 2000 during a time of unprecedented prosperity and peace. Although Gore has to own his election loss, most pundits attach a significant portion of Gore's loss to Clinton's behavior. And that is precisely what the Law of Buy-In is all about.

People accept the person first, then the vision. Unfortunately for Al Gore, he was the vicarious sacrifice on the altar of Clinton's trysts. A sufficient number of voters subconsciously regarded Gore as Clinton incarnate. The Law of Buy-In cannot be violated.

⚜

JOAN OF ARC:
PERSUADING A PRINCE AND A PEOPLE TO BUY IN

Once again, we move the calendar backward—some six hundred years—to the 1400s. From America, we return to Europe, specifically to France. And our focus will not be a president or a pope. It will be a seventeen-year-old girl. But we begin this story with a fascinating account of one of America's most popular authors—Mark Twain.

A floating page from a book caught Mark Twain's attention while he was walking toward his home in Hartford, Connecticut. It was a paper leaf from a history of Joan of Arc. His interest piqued, Twain began to read about someone he'd never heard of! That interest became something of an obsession. In time he would write one of his best, if least-known books, a highly imaginary account titled *Personal Recollections of Joan of Arc by the Sieur Louis de Conte (Her Page and Secretary).*[1] Twain found what millions of others have found: in significant ways Joan of Arc stands unique, truly one of a kind.

Louis Kossuth summarized this incredible biography: "Consider this unique and imposing distinction. Since the writing of human history began, Joan of Arc is the only person, of either sex, who has ever held supreme command of the military forces of a nation *at the age of seventeen.*"[2]

A simple peasant girl born in 1412 in a small French village, Joan grew up in the midst of the Hundred Years War between France and England. Much of France was ruled by the duke of Burgundy, an ally of England. He claimed the French crown. But patriotic Frenchmen were loyal to the Dauphin (*dauphin* means "eldest son of a French king") Charles, heir to the throne.

When Joan was twelve, she experienced a great revelation. In her

185

father's garden, she saw a great light and heard a voice. A bright light, an angel, left her on her knees, confident that God had given her a mission. The Archangel Michael assured her that Charles, the eldest son of the king, was "attended by heavenly angels. He told me that . . . it was our Lord's command."[3]

PRINCIPLE OF BUY-IN LEADERSHIP # 3:
People Will Embrace the Leader's Vision
Only When They See the Leader's Commitment to It

The next few years Joan listened and waited. She heard voices—saints' voices. When she was sixteen, she knew the time had come to help the dauphin, besieged by the English in the French city of Orleans. She would lead him to the city of Reims, where he would be officially crowned king. The voices told her that she would be given "men to go with me."[4] So she obeyed the voices, going to the nearby village official, telling her divine mission. Twice she asked for his help. Twice she was refused. Then she appealed again, and he was overcome by her supreme confidence in her mission and by her godly demeanor.

She was given a horse and bodyguard. She dressed herself in men's clothes and cut her hair short. "Go forward boldly," her voices commanded. So she rode through English territory to the castle of Chinon, the dauphin's current residence. She requested an audience with him, which he granted. But he determined to test her by dressing like everyone else in the assembly. Joan, who had never seen the dauphin, entered the hall and went immediately to him, kneeling before him. Charles, still testing her, pointed to a nearby aide, saying, "That is the king." But she was not deterred. "In God's name, noble prince, it is you and none other," she said.[5]

Charles then talked with her. He was deeply moved by her words. Ever unsure of himself, however, he insisted that some priests interrogate her. Perhaps her "voices" were not of God! The priests found her simple, sincere, godly, and worthy of trust.

Still not sure what to do, however, the dauphin delayed, procrastinating, afraid to believe her. Joan then issued an ultimatum: "I shall last

PRINCIPLES OF BUY-IN LEADERSHIP

a year and but a little longer; we must think to do good work in that year." Then Charles relented. He marshaled his forces and provided Joan with a suit of armor.

Joan asked emissaries to go to a chapel she had never visited to get a sword buried behind the altar. They found the sword that would be her weapon thenceforth. For a battle flag, she designed a white banner featuring the Lord Jesus, an angel at each side, with the words *Jesus Maria* prominently displayed.

Finally equipped, she and her army marched toward Orleans, which had been besieged for six months by the English. They had built a dozen tall stone bastions to expedite their endeavors. Ready to attack, Joan sent a message to the English: "The King of Heaven sends you word and warning by me, Joan the Maid, to abandon your forts and depart into your own country, or I will raise such a war cry against you as shall be remembered forever."[6]

PRINCIPLE OF BUY-IN LEADERSHIP # 4:
If You Want Your Followers to Sacrifice,
Then You Must Sacrifice First: Leaders Go First

She was not taken seriously. The English disdained her warning, and the battle began. Joan led her men into a brutal hand-to-hand engagement. Though she was injured by an arrow, she pulled it out and led her soldiers to victory, the great turning point of the Hundred Years War.

PRINCIPLE OF BUY-IN LEADERSHIP # 5:
Demonstrated Courage Increases Buy-In

The way now seemed clear to escort Charles to Reims, where he could be rightly crowned king of France. Joan urged haste, but Charles dragged his feet! He apparently enjoyed councils and committees, endless discussions that required no actions, no risks. "Noble Dauphin," she begged, "hold no more so many and such long councils, but come as quickly as you can to Reims and take the crown." He knew, as did Joan, that to get to Reims would involve more fighting, for the British held the country through which they must march. But Joan had no reservations. "Go bravely," she said; "all will go well."

Finally, Charles took Joan's advice. They fought their way victoriously to Reims, where on July 17, 1429, the great coronation took place. Just five months earlier she had left her small village, following her call. Joan, the simple shepherdess, a peasant woman, stood beside the newly crowned king, Charles VII, in the cathedral.

PRINCIPLE OF BUY-IN LEADERSHIP # 6:
Buy-In Is Enhanced When the Leader Represents the Best of Values in the Worst of Times

---

Mark Twain records this astounding account of the contrast between Joan of Arc and the times in which she lived:

> When we reflect that her century was the brutalest, the wickedest, the rottenest in history since the darkest ages, we are lost in wonder at the miracle of such a product from such a soil. The contrast between her and her century is the contrast between day and night. She was truthful when lying was the common speech of men; she was honest when honest was become a lost virtue; she was a keeper of promises when the keeping of a promise was expected of no one; she gave her great mind to great thoughts and great purposes when other great minds wasted themselves upon pretty fancies or upon poor ambitions; she was modest and fine, and delicate when to be loud and coarse might be said to be universal; she was full of pity when a merciless cruelty was the rule; she was steadfast when stability was unknown, and honorable in an age which had forgotten what honor was. She was all these things in an age when crime was the common business of lords and princes, and when the highest personages in Christendom were able to astonish even that infamous era and make it stand aghast at the spectacle of their atrocious lives black with unimaginable treacheries, butcheries, and bestialities.[7]

> ## PRINCIPLE OF BUY-IN LEADERSHIP # 7:
> *People Buy In Without Reservation*
> *When the Leader Has No Hidden Agendas*

Joan's courage was matched by her humility. Twain noted,

> No . . . suggestion of self-seeking can be found in any word or deed of
> hers. When she had rescued her King . . . she was offered rewards and
> honors, but she refused them all, and would take nothing. All she
> would take for herself—if the King would grant it—was leave to go
> back to her village home, and tend her sheep again, and feel her
> mother's arms about her, and be her housemaid and helper.[8]

> ## PRINCIPLE OF BUY-IN LEADERSHIP # 8:
> *The World Will Follow the One Who Finds*
> *a Way to Overcome the Odds*

Continuing his accolades, Mark Twain contrasted Joan of Arc's accomplishments to those of Caesar and Napoleon. Caesar, according to
Twain,

> carried conquest far, but he did it with the trained and confident vet-
> erans of Rome, and was a trained soldier himself; and Napoleon swept
> away the disciplined armies of Europe, but he also was a trained sol-
> dier, and he began his work with patriot battalions . . . but Joan of Arc,
> a mere child in years, ignorant, unlettered, a poor village girl unknown
> and without influence, found a great nation lying in chains, helpless
> and hopeless under an alien domination, its treasury bankrupt, its sol-
> diers disheartened . . . all courage dead in the hearts of the people
> through long years of foreign and domestic outrage and oppression,
> their King cowed, resigned to its fate, and preparing to fly the coun-
> try; and she laid her hand upon this nation, this corpse, and it rose and

followed her. She led it from victory to victory, she turned back the tide of the Hundred Years' War, she fatally crippled the English power, and died with the earned title of DELIVERER OF FRANCE which she bears to this day.[9]

Subsequent events would prove less happy for Joan, of course. Ultimately, largely because Charles failed to support her, she was burned to death as a heretic on May 30, 1431, at age nineteen. In time, however, a careful examination of her case by Catholic officials would lead them to reverse their appraisal of her. She was honored by being canonized—declared a saint—in 1920, 489 years after her death! So we remember her as Saint Joan, a gifted woman who persuaded men to follow her, a true patriot who helped liberate her people from foreign occupation.

GREEK ORATORY VS. HEBREW REVELATION

One illustration that clarifies the Law of Buy-In hinges on the use of two words: *oratory* and *revelation*.

In ancient Greece around 200 B.C., the ability to speak publicly was highly valued. Oratory was king. Training schools were developed to teach persons to *imitate* the greatest orators of the day. Emulation or imitation was the strategy, and it was, and still is, a good strategy.

In ancient Israel (the land of the Old Testament, around 600 B.C.), public communication was not primarily about oratorical skill. *Much* greater value was put on revelation. The ancient prophets, five and six hundred years before Christ's birth, would pepper their speeches with the phrase, "thus says the Lord." They had spent their time *listening* to God, not *imitating* other speakers. Their credibility came from paying the price to know what truth was.

Now what does that have to do with you? People will buy into your dream, your vision, if they buy into you. But they will buy in much more quickly if you, in your own world, will move from oratory (that is, imitating others) to revelation (that is, paying the price to be able to speak wisely to life's situations out of your personal reservoirs of integrity and knowledge).

"BEING" VS. "DOING"

> ### PRINCIPLE OF BUY-IN LEADERSHIP # 9:
> *If You Want People to Embrace You As Leader,*
> *Make Certain Something Is Truly There for Them to Embrace—*
> *"Being" Is More Important Than "Doing"*

Many a hopeful leader has lost his following because when the followers got really close to the leader, they found out there wasn't much to follow; they discovered there was too much fluff! And it shows. These leaders are content free. They are "cotton-candy leaders." Take a bite and it disappears. The leaders are puzzled about why people will not follow them. The answer is simple. They are Teflon leaders. No one sticks. And for good reason.

> ### PRINCIPLE OF BUY-IN LEADERSHIP # 10:
> *If You Must Choose Between Image and Substance,*
> *Always Choose Substance*

Other leaders gather a larger and larger following because, when the followers are with the leader, they sense that he is rich in substance and high in protein. He speaks out of the overflow of his life, adding understanding to the hearts and minds of the followers. These persons are Velcro leaders. People stick. And for good reason.

CELTIC VS. ROMAN

Every March 17, we celebrate St. Patrick's Day. St. Patrick's Day is not, or at least should not be, about leprechauns and shamrocks. It should be about St. Patrick. George Hunter III, a brilliant scholar from Asbury Theological Seminary, has studied St. Patrick's method of influencing people and drawing them into a vibrant faith in Christ. He contends that the Celtic way of evangelizing was to form close relationships with unbelievers, forming bridges of trust, even *before* they would embrace the Christian faith. These bridges of trust—deep relationships—made it possible for the Celtic people in Ireland to become Christian, even though they had remained resistant to every other religious movement that had previously tried to convert them.

In contrast, there was the Roman way of evangelizing: persuading, convincing, proclaiming, trying to get people to accept the teaching, and *then* forming relationships.

At the risk of oversimplification, the Celtic way was relationally based—built on trust, which, in turn, caused the decision to follow. The Roman way demanded a decision first, which, if made affirmatively, was rewarded with a relationship.

PRINCIPLE OF BUY-IN LEADERSHIP # 11:
Relationships Precede Buy-In

What does this have to do with you as a leader? Some of you are trying to get people to buy into your vision. They won't. They want you to give them a chance to buy into *you* first! You are using the Roman way. You need to switch to the Celtic way. Accept them as they are—that is, not yet buying into your vision. But move alongside them, letting them see your integrity and authenticity, then, having bought into you, they will buy into your vision. That is the Law of Buy-In.

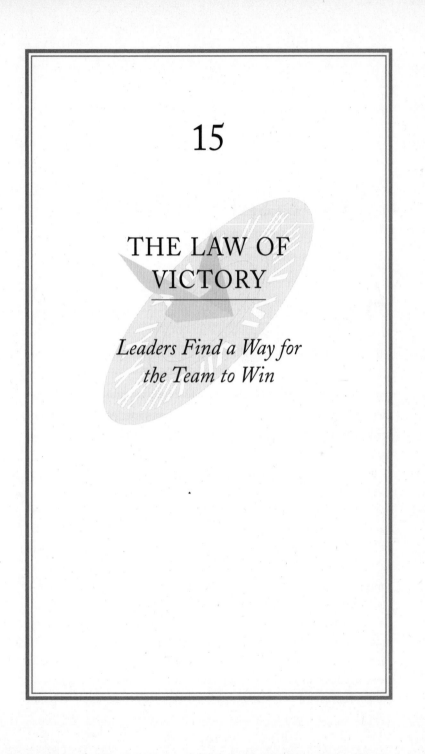

15

THE LAW OF VICTORY

*Leaders Find a Way for
the Team to Win*

PRINCIPLES OF
LEADERSHIP OF VICTORY

A ddressing the nation on January 29, 2002, President George W. Bush devoted much of his first official State of the Union address to national defense, particularly the war against terrorism. Warning the nation that there exists an "axis of evil," against which the United States must struggle for years to come, he insisted that there can be no compromise, no halfway settlements, no sponge-edged resolutions to this conflict. Only victory, decisive victory, will stop terrorism. "We will prevail in the war," said the president.[1] Few who heard him doubted his resolve.

GEORGE W. BUSH DEMANDS VICTORY

For twenty-five years growing numbers of terrorists had indeed doubted America's resolve. President Jimmy Carter did little but talk when radical Muslims took Americans hostage in Tehran in 1980. A few years later President Ronald Reagan, rather than risk war in the Middle East, simply withdrew American forces from Lebanon after several hundred marines were slaughtered in their barracks by an explosive-packed truck.

Under President Bill Clinton, the emboldened Islamics grew even bolder. Soon after Clinton assumed the nation's highest office, his one-time confidante and advisor, Dick Morris, said that the al-Qaeda launched a war on the U.S. that Clinton consistently chose to ignore.[2]

In February 1993, a month after Clinton's inauguration, a bomb intended to collapse the World Trade Center shook that great structure, killing a few and injuring scores of people. The president never visited the site, and he urged anyone concerned to beware of "overreacting." He did nothing to speed up the CIA investigation of the bombing, so it was three years before Osama bin Laden's involvement was even known.

Terrorists, meanwhile, cranked up their attacks. American embassies in Tanzania and Kenya were damaged by car bombs, killing numbers of innocent employees. A bomb killed American soldiers quartered in Riyadh, Saudi Arabia. An American warship, the *USS Cole*, was nearly sunk in Yemen, killing a dozen seamen and immobilizing one of the world's most sophisticated warships.

What was the response of the commander in chief? In every crisis, Morris says, President Clinton responded with strong words and weak will, other than lobbing missiles in the general direction of Afghanistan and a pharmaceutical factory in the Sudan.

We now know that detailed information was given to President Clinton, as early as 1995, about Osama bin Laden, pointing to him as a mastermind of the global terrorist network. Sudanese officials even offered to help the United States apprehend him.

The FBI director, Louis Freeh, wanted to do something about the terrorists. But Secretary of State Madeleine Albright deferred, lest a confrontation of some sort ensue, lest the administration lose points in the public opinion polls.

> **PRINCIPLE OF A LEADERSHIP OF VICTORY # 1:**
> *True Victory Is Not Halfway; It Is Not Merely Symbolic;*
> *To Really Be Victory, It Must Be Real and Complete*

Following the 1996 crash of TWA Flight 800, which took the lives of 230 people, President Clinton rushed a bill through Congress to "improve the security of air travel and carry forward our fight against terrorism."[3] A bill on the books, signed before the all-important TV cameras by a resolute president, was hailed by all. But sixteen months later the president had made no effort to implement it!

During his last year in office, President Clinton was urged, in a sixty-four-page report given to him by the National Commission on Terrorism, to follow through on some thirty-seven recommendations. One of the recommendations cited the need to impose sanctions on Afghanistan, to take action against the terrorist network based in that nation. Other reports urged the president to tighten up on the visas granted to immigrants to enter the U.S. and to monitor financial networks subsidizing terrorist groups. Preoccupied with other issues, Mr. Clinton ignored the report.

Decades of appeasement ended dramatically under President George W. Bush. September 11, 2001, transformed his presidency. But he was inwardly prepared for the crisis. Those who know him best acknowledge that there was a spiritual depth, a moral core, at the heart of the man. "Bush believes that the Lord prepares you for whatever He gives us," says an old Texas friend of the president.[4] As Bush noted in his message in the National Cathedral, days after the attacks, "We learn in tragedy that His [God's] purposes are not always our own."[5] But it is clear, he continued, that "freedom and fear, justice and cruelty, have always been at war, and we know that God is not neutral between them."[6]

What he, and we, have learned is the importance of one of the Christian virtues: courage! Courage dares to die rather than to tolerate injustice. Courage risks everything to uphold human dignity. Courage perseveres, through the darkest nights, to secure the triumph of righteousness.

Bush's campaign autobiography was titled *A Charge to Keep,* taken from the title of a familiar hymn that says: "To serve the present age, my calling to fulfill. Oh may it all my powers engage, to do my Master's will." President Bush likes to show White House guests a painting inspired by that hymn, and he often tells them, "I still have a charge to keep." To be true to that charge, to fulfill his duty as president, he knows that nothing less than total victory will ensure the safety of this nation and of a world so dependent upon it.

PRINCIPLE OF A LEADERSHIP OF VICTORY # 2:
*When You Are Calling for a Victory of Immense Proportions,
Divide the Challenge into Bite-Sized Increments*

In his 2002 State of the Union message, Bush reminded the nation that four months earlier ("in an hour of shock and suffering") he had called upon America to respond to a brutal attack. Remarkably, people had "begun to rebuild New York and the Pentagon; rallied a great coalition; captured, arrested, and rid the world of thousands of terrorists; destroyed Afghanistan's terrorist training camps; saved a people from starvation; and freed a country from brutal oppression." Still more: "The American flag flies again over our embassy in Kabul," denoting a hopeful alliance between the United States and Afghanistan.

> **PRINCIPLE OF A LEADERSHIP OF VICTORY # 3:**
> *Commitment to Pay the Price for Victory*
> *Is Proportional to the Perceived Legitimacy of the Cause*

America's armed forces had followed through on the commander in chief's orders. They "have delivered a message now clear to every enemy of the United States. Even 7,000 miles away, across oceans and continents, on mountaintops and in caves—you will not escape the justice of this nation. Our cause is just," said Mr. Bush, "and it continues. Our discoveries in Afghanistan confirmed our worst fears, and show us the true scope of the task ahead. We have seen the depth of our enemies' hatred in videos, where they laugh about the loss of innocent life. And the depth of their hatred is equaled by the madness of the destruction they design."

> **PRINCIPLE OF A LEADERSHIP OF VICTORY # 4:**
> *The Task of the Leader Is to Sustain the Vision*
> *Until Victory Is Realized*

Consequently, Bush continued, "our war against terror is only beginning." Literally tens of thousands of terrorists exist in our world, some of them "sleepers" sharing the ordinary experiences of ordinary Americans. Trained to kill, willing to die while killing, they will not be appeased.

They "view the entire world as a battlefield, and we must pursue them wherever they are."

And with President Bush leading, "our nation will continue to be steadfast, and patient, and persistent until the terrorist camps are destroyed and the nations that support them are brought to heel." Admittedly, he warned, "Our war on terror is well begun, but it has only begun. This campaign may not be finished on our watch, yet it must be and it will be waged on our watch. So," he stated emphatically, "we cannot stop short." Nothing short of victory is tolerable.

PRINCIPLE OF A LEADERSHIP OF VICTORY # 5:
The Task of the Leader Is to Maintain Momentum Toward Victory

---

Quoting from Todd Beamer, the brave young man who led the charge against the terrorists who had commandeered the plane that crashed in western Pennsylvania on September 11, President Bush ended his message to the nation with these words: "Let's roll." Clearly, he meant we must roll ahead, maintain our momentum, refuse to be slowed down, until victory is won.

⚅

DOUGLAS MACARTHUR:
"NO SUBSTITUTE FOR VICTORY"

The jump from the war on terrorism to the battles of WWI and WWII is not nearly as big as the other historical leaps we have made throughout this book. Our story line is still based in America, but takes us back fifty to seventy-five years. There is likely no biography that better meshes with victory than that of Douglas MacArthur.

"You couldn't shrug your shoulders at Douglas MacArthur," wrote David McCullough, a noted historian. "There was nothing bland about him, nothing passive about him, nothing dull about him. There's no question about his patriotism, there's no question about his courage, and there's no question, it seems to me, about his importance as one of the protagonists of the 20th century."[7]

MacArthur was a soldier from a line of soldiers. He was preeminently a soldier's soldier—and to soldiers like himself, there is a very simple rule to live by: "There is no substitute for victory." Those who understand the Law of Victory identify with MacArthur's sentiments.

His father, General Arthur MacArthur, was a bona fide Civil War hero, earning the congressional Medal of Honor for his valor at Missionary Ridge in Tennessee and serving ably during that conflict. Following the war, he was sent to various frontier army posts, and his son Douglas was born in Little Rock, Arkansas, in 1880. Subsequently, Arthur was stationed in New Mexico, which was still seething with Apache conflicts. Young Douglas found it full of adventure. "My first memory was the sound of bugles," he said in his autobiography, *Reminiscences*. "It was here I learned to ride and shoot even before I could read or write—indeed, almost before I could walk or talk."[8]

He also saw how his father functioned, ever exercising strong control over his commands. In 1893, the family was posted to San Antonio, Texas, where Douglas attended the West Texas Military Academy and, for the first time, demonstrated his academic potential. Subsequently, he received an appointment to West Point, arriving there in 1898. According to one account, he announced that he planned to graduate at the head of his class and ultimately become chief of staff of the United States Army!

PRINCIPLE OF A LEADERSHIP OF VICTORY # 6:
Victory Is Deliberate and Intentional; It Does Not Just Happen

---

He never lacked for ambition, and modesty rarely tempered his pronouncements. Vain he certainly seemed, but he was also extraordinarily talented. Like Muhammad Ali claiming he was "the greatest," MacArthur had a basis for his arrogance. He was not casual about his plans—he had an agenda for his life. His record at West Point was the finest compiled in the twenty-five years preceding him, and one of the finest ever in the academy's history. He graduated first in his class (with an average of

98.14 percent), and throughout his life, folks could hardly overlook his brilliance.

Following graduation from West Point, he was assigned, as a young lieutenant, to the Philippines, where his father had led American troops to victory over the Spanish (during the 1898 Spanish-American War) and subsequently served as military governor. Once accompanying a surveying party, he found himself "waylaid on a narrow jungle trail by two desperadoes, one on each side." Acting promptly, he said, "Like all frontiersmen, I was expert with a pistol. I dropped them both dead in their tracks, but not before one had blazed at me with an antiquated rifle."[9]

The same calm, collected courage would characterize his performance in World War I. When the war broke out, he became a brigadier general and led the Rainbow Division through some of the toughest fighting of the war. He led and inspired his men by his example.

PRINCIPLE OF A LEADERSHIP OF VICTORY # 7:
Victory Tends to Follow Persons Willing to Take Well-Calculated Risks

---

General George C. Kenney, who saw MacArthur in France in 1918, records the admiring comments of an infantry captain. "That's Douglas MacArthur," he said. "If he doesn't get himself knocked off by the Germans, that guy is going places. But he seems to think he's going to live forever. He goes on trench raids wearing that cap instead of a tin hat. He's already collected a couple of wound stripes, besides a flock of medals he earned the hard way."[10] Predictably, he returned home as the war's most decorated American soldier.

PRINCIPLE OF A LEADERSHIP OF VICTORY # 8:
Victory and Compromise Rarely Coexist

He also proved himself a constant advocate for complete victory—never a partial one. Marshal Foch, the French commander, weary of war, insisted that the Germans simply be pushed back to the Hindenburg

Line. The ranking American general, John J. Pershing, supported him. But when MacArthur's division made a dramatic breakthrough, he dashed to Pershing's headquarters, asking permission to push ahead into Germany. Pershing denied him permission, but his request reveals his fighting spirit—ever discontented with halfway compromises.

Between WWI and WWII, MacArthur served several significant assignments, including superintendent of West Point, and President Herbert Hoover appointed him chief of staff of the army in 1930. His adolescent ambition, announced when beginning his studies at West Point, was fulfilled! He was, at the age of fifty, the youngest officer ever appointed to that position.

MacArthur had no intention of simply enjoying the position. He continued his activism. During the 1930s, he struggled to get appropriations for the army, though it was a difficult task during the Great Depression. Congress was more interested in finding someone to blame for WWI than preparing for its sequel.

In 1935, he happily escaped Washington and returned to the Philippines, entrusted with helping build up the Philippine army, preparing that Asian nation for independence. While he was there, the Japanese attacked the Philippines shortly after they struck Pearl Harbor in December 1941. Though quickly overwhelmed, MacArthur's men fought bravely.

In General Kenney's opinion, "MacArthur's defense of the Philippines was one of the few creditable episodes of the first five months of the Pacific war; it stood out like a beacon of hope in comparison with the debacle at Singapore, the fall of the Netherlands East Indies, and the confusion in Washington."[11]

PRINCIPLE OF A LEADERSHIP OF VICTORY # 9:
Stubbornness for the Sake of Getting One's Way Is a Vice—Stubbornness for the Sake of Attaining Victory Is a Virtue

---

True to MacArthur's form, he fought hard. With few resources, he "delayed the Japanese schedule in the Philippines for weeks. Moreover, his stubborn resistance made the Filipinos feel that we were not going to abandon them, and when MacArthur said he would return they believed it. As a result, their widespread guerrilla activity pinned down many divisions of Japanese troops throughout the war."[12]

PRINCIPLE OF A LEADERSHIP OF VICTORY # 10:
Victory Often Allows the Leader to Keep His Word: Talk Is Cheap; Accomplishment Isn't

---

Ordered by President Franklin D. Roosevelt to leave Manila (thus leaving seventy thousand troops to surrender and suffer under the Japanese), MacArthur dramatically declared, "I shall return." During the next several years, serving as supreme Allied commander of the Southwest Pacific, he orchestrated troop movements through torrid New Guinea jungles, finally returning to the Philippines, ever remembering his promise. Wading ashore on a beach at Leyte in October 1944, he said, "I have returned." His ferocious commitment to "no substitute for victory" caused him to make good on his word.

MacArthur saw the occasion as an opportunity for a speech. While dismissed by his critics as "corny," it deeply moved the people to whom it was addressed: "Arise and strike! . . . For your homes and hearths, strike! In the name of your sacred dead, strike! Let no heart be faint. Let every arm be steeled. The guidance of Divine God points the way. Follow in His Name to . . . righteous victory."[13]

PRINCIPLE OF A LEADERSHIP OF VICTORY #11:
The True Heart of the Person Committed to Victory Is Often Misunderstood

---

There was always a certain arrogance, almost a messiah complex, evident in Douglas MacArthur. In public he seemed ever on parade, ever intent on making a lasting impression, perfectly poised for a photographer's portrait. Men serving under him learned that he demanded obedience and loyalty. But, Kenney says, "An old retired colonel who served with him for years summed up the feelings of practically every soldier who ever worked closely with him: 'Douglas MacArthur was a hard-boiled old softie.'"[14]

PRINCIPLE OF A LEADERSHIP OF VICTORY # 12:
Arrogance Tarnishes the Victor; Humility Exalts Him

As the Allies triumphed in the Pacific, MacArthur was sent to Japan to preside over that nation's final surrender. He then stayed on in Japan for five years, helping rebuild the land of his former foes. Few conquerors ever became so quickly loved.

In 1950, the North Korean Communists attacked South Korea. This war put MacArthur in command of an American-led United Nations force. After some initial losses, he outmaneuvered the Communists by landing at Inchon, behind enemy lines, and routed them. South Korea was quickly liberated, but then MacArthur aggressively pushed to the north, which prompted China to send troops to assist North Korea.

PRINCIPLE OF A LEADERSHIP OF VICTORY # 13:
Leaders Want Victory for Their Team More Than Anything

The general was willing to risk World War III, engaging Mao Tse-tung's newly forged Communist China. President Truman, however, was determined to avoid such a war. MacArthur unwisely made known his disagreement with his commander in chief, and Truman fired him—one of his most unpopular acts. Truman may very well have been right in his action. But it is clear that to the very end of his career, MacArthur *wanted victory in every conflict.*

Though unwisely released to the public, the general's letter to Joseph Martin, the House minority leader, expressed the core of his disagreement with his president. Communism, he believed, must be defeated! If it was not defeated then and there in Asia, Europe would ultimately fall. Then a worse war would ensue, should the United States choose to fight for freedom. "As you point out, we must win," MacArthur wrote. "There is no substitute for victory."[15]

Every team needs victories. They need wins. What are *you* doing to help them experience that? Leaders find a way for their teams to know the joy of victory.

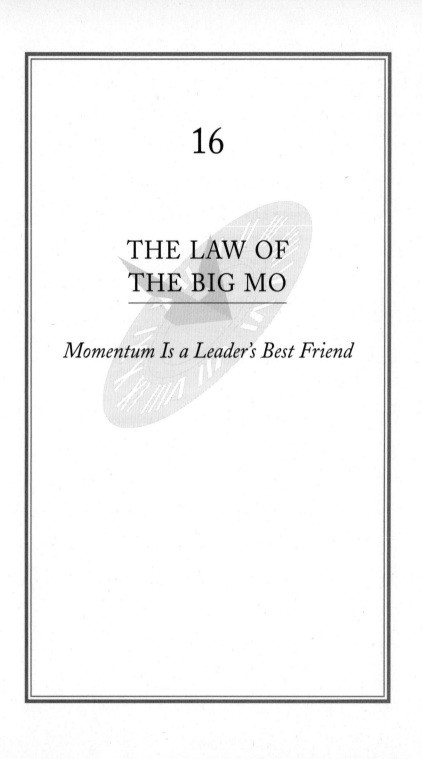

16

THE LAW OF
THE BIG MO

Momentum Is a Leader's Best Friend

Principles of
Leadership of Momentum

I t was a chilly Monday night, November 2, the night before the national election of 1992. President George Bush, the incumbent, was being challenged by the governor of Arkansas, Bill Clinton. Thrown into the mix was an independent candidate, Ross Perot, who later formed the Reform Party.

BILL CLINTON'S 1992 CAMPAIGN

Bill Clinton was barnstorming across America in a final-day, multicity, six-state, to-the-wire sweep. His last day of campaigning covered a full twenty-four hours, ending with a 6:00 A.M. rally in Little Rock, Arkansas. His next-to-the-last city was Fort Worth, Texas, with a stop at a small regional airfield—Meacham Field in the northern portion of the city. It was scheduled for 1:00 A.M. Yes, you read that right. One o'clock in the morning! I called my friends Dick Weinhold and Scott Fisher and said, "Let's go out and hear him speak." They love politics as much as I do, so they unhesitatingly agreed.

We wondered if we were crazy when we headed westbound on Highway 183/Airport Freeway, continuing farther west across extreme northern Fort Worth on I-820 in the midnight darkness. Exiting the freeway, we headed south down the unlit two-lane road toward the air-port—the site of the Clinton rally. Approximately a mile and a half from our destination, brake lights came on as the traffic slowed to a crawl and finally stopped. Looking at what our headlights would reveal, we saw cars on both sides of the road and people walking on the highway in the darkness. We realized that the little airport parking lot was overwhelmed, and we would have to park our car on the grassy shoulder of the road and walk the rest of the way—some ten or fifteen minutes.

It was almost eerie. With limited moonlight, we could barely see the stream of persons around us walking on the asphalt road toward the airport. Fortunately, a few forward-thinking persons had brought flashlights, which proved helpful to all of us. But in spite of the fact that we could not see people very well in the darkness, we could hear people—lots of people. And the closer we got to the airport, the larger and more compacted the crowd became. I soon realized that we were in a massive flow of people, all walking together in the darkness.

When we arrived at the airport, the sight was even more impressive. Generator-driven lights had been hastily positioned around the tarmac where the crowd was swelling in size. At approximately 12:30 A.M. on that cold November night (or, rather, morning), thousands of persons had gathered to hear Bill Clinton make his next-to-the-last campaign speech before the polls opened at 7:00 A.M., November 3, 1992.

Then we got a disappointing word. The Arkansas governor and his entourage were running late—a common problem throughout the Clinton campaign (and the later Clinton presidency). Instead of arriving at 1:00 A.M. as originally projected, he would be arriving at 1:30 or perhaps 2:00 A.M. What I observed next amazed me. No one cared! The crowd handled the news with aplomb. Not even a hint of irritation in anyone! The crowd seemed quite happy to be there, even with an extended wait. The time passed quickly as a string of down-the-ballot candidates were very happy to be introduced to such a large crowd only hours before voting was scheduled to begin.

PRINCIPLE OF LEADERSHIP OF MOMENTUM # 1:
Momentum Is Highly Contagious

And then finally, he arrived. Bill Clinton's plane taxied in. Doors opened. Then Governor Ann Richards, the "warm-up act," emerged first and delivered some scathing attacks on then President George Bush. When Bill Clinton stepped out of that plane, the crowd went wild.

I turned to my two Republican friends and said, "They taste victory. They smell it! They know that victory is in the air." Dick and Scott looked at me, said nothing, and nodded in agreement. Our assessment was right. Only hours later, Bill Clinton became the president-elect of the United States.

PRINCIPLE OF LEADERSHIP OF MOMENTUM #2:
The Passion of the Leader Increases Momentum

How did he win the election? Obviously, Ross Perot, the third party candidate, affected the outcome, possibly functioning as a bit of a political "spoiler." And the pundits analyzed all the possible reasons how a governor of Arkansas could unseat a popular sitting president.

PRINCIPLE OF LEADERSHIP OF MOMENTUM # 3:
Momentum Is Fueled by a Desire to Win

But I would like to bypass the more academic talk and cut to the chase: Bill Clinton and his assembled "War Room" campaign team *really wanted* the election, and they were willing to outwork their opponents. Many Americans responded to the vigor that Bill Clinton brought to the campaign. They were understandably enamored by it. And they voted for Clinton.

William Jefferson Clinton wanted to win. He *really* wanted to win. You could sense it. His passion to win was infectious. His campaign vibrancy was captivating. It was invigorating.

What I saw in the eyes of that crowd that chilly night was undeniable: they had momentum on their side, and they knew it. They really felt the Big Mo! And few things are more pervasive than momentum. Mo is your friend, as a leader. Embrace it. Cherish it when you have it.

JEREMIAH LAMPHIER AND AN 1857 NEW YORK PRAYER SERVICE

We leave the brilliantly fought 1992 political campaign to analyze a most unusual church service that is an amazing lesson on momentum. It really wasn't even a church service. It was just a small group of people who met to pray. But what occurred is so inexplicable that it is still discussed to this day.

Sometime in 1857, New York City resident Jeremiah Lamphier invited people to meet with him during the noon hour at the Dutch Reformed Church in Manhattan for the purpose of praying. He advertised it among New York City's one million population. Only six showed up. That could easily have been the end of the story. But it wasn't.

One week later, he invited persons to attend another noontime prayer service. Fourteen attended. Although it had doubled, it still was discernibly small and quite disappointing to Lamphier. The next week, the group grew to twenty-three. For some reason, Lamphier and his colleagues decided to meet daily rather than weekly. What happened next cannot be explained.

Soon the noon hour prayer meeting exploded in attendance. The Dutch Reformed Church was overflowing, so they moved to the Methodist Church on John Street. From there they moved to a public building. And then . . . the unthinkable happened. The meetings started multiplying, being held in many locations.

One inquisitive newspaper reporter wondered how many groups were actually meeting. He tried to make a quick visit to all of them in one noon hour. In the twelve prayer meetings that he was able to visit, he counted more than six thousand people in attendance.

But the noon prayer meetings didn't stop at six thousand. The "Layman's Revival," as it is called by historians, continued growing. Estimates were that ten thousand were being converted each week in the New York prayer meetings (not including all the already converted who were attending)!

Word about the prayer meetings spread, and they expanded for the next eighteen months, throughout 1857 and 1858. The movement flowed up to New England and across the Atlantic to Great Britain. From there it went to South Africa and on to South India. It is believed that the Layman's Revival resulted in more than one million persons embracing the Christian faith. Its impact was felt for the next four decades.

PRINCIPLE OF LEADERSHIP OF MOMENTUM # 4:
Sometimes Momentum Can Be Explained Only As Divine

How do you explain such a phenomenon? Candidly, you can't. It was as if God looked down and said, "I like that. I'm going to surprise them and make this grow." Not a very sophisticated answer? No, it isn't. But my explanation is as good as anyone else's.

PRINCIPLE OF LEADERSHIP OF MOMENTUM # 5:
Momentum Often Defies Any Explanation;
Enjoy It Rather Than Analyze It

Momentum has power. It is felt rather than explained. It is to be valued when you experience it. It feeds on itself, producing even more momentum. Momentum is a leader's dream.

❧

HARRIET BEECHER STOWE— ABOLITIONIST MOMENTUM

One of the most intriguing studies of momentum pertains to the power of the written word—in this case, an book published in 1852 that changed a nation!

Midway through the Civil War a tiny middle-aged woman entered the White House to meet President Abraham Lincoln. Greeting her, Lincoln allegedly said: "So this is the little lady who made this big war!"[1] Though the war, of course, had multiple layers of causation, slavery was clearly the emotional impetus of the conflict.

For nearly a century Americans had been troubled by the slave issue. During the War for Independence, when colonists talked much about freedom and the "natural rights of man," some folks acknowledged the irony of fighting for freedom from England while keeping African slaves in bondage. During the Revolution, some northern states outlawed slavery—though admittedly they had few slaves within their borders. Slavery was much debated in 1787 at the Constitutional Convention, which decided to outlaw the foreign slave trade within twenty years, though the main issue was how to enumerate the slaves when calculating representation in the House of Representatives.

Eminent southern slave owners, such as Thomas Jefferson, often lamented slavery's existence, blending "the most unremitting despotism" with "degrading submissions." In his *Notes on Virginia*, published in 1785, Jefferson anguished: "Indeed I tremble for my country when I reflect that God is just: that his justice cannot sleep for ever; that . . . an exchange of situation is . . . possible . . . it may [come] . . . by supernatural interference! The Almighty has no attribute which can take side with us in such a contest."[2]

During the early decades of the nineteenth century the slave question could never be quite suppressed. Antislavery societies abounded, in both the North and the South, searching for ways to ultimately eliminate the institution.

Political compromises—the Missouri Compromise in 1820 and the Compromise of 1850—tried to defuse sectional tensions and maintain an uneasy peace. For all the discussion, however, only a few folks, prior to 1850, supported abolitionism—the immediate abolition of slavery. By and large Americans were willing to tolerate slavery in the South, hoping that someday, somehow, it would gradually fade away.

But the accord established by the Compromise of 1850 quickly dissolved within the next decade, and large numbers of Northerners began to support the abolition of slavery, regardless of what it would cost. Angrily responding, large numbers of Southerners rallied to support their "peculiar institution."

The hot button that ignited passions in both sections was a novel, *Uncle Tom's Cabin*, by Harriet Beecher Stowe. Few literary works have ever exerted such power, and the momentum that led to the Civil War mounted like an avalanche.

Harriet was the daughter of a prominent preacher, Lyman Beecher. Though born in Connecticut, she lived for eighteen years in Cincinnati, an important Underground Railroad shelter. She had helped runaway slaves and certainly knew of their sorrows, though (other than a few days on a Kentucky plantation, visiting a school friend) she never actually spent time in the South.

She married a college professor, Calvin Stowe, and in 1850 they moved to Brunswick, Maine, where he taught at Bowdoin College. By that time she had embraced the radical abolitionist position flamboyantly evident in the preaching of her famous brother, Henry Ward Beecher.

A letter from her sister-in-law prodded Harriet to do something about her convictions. Taking the letter as a summons, she resolved, while the letter was still in her hand, "I *will* write something." So she sat at her desk and began to write, but she later declared, on many occasions, "The Lord Himself wrote it."[3]

When she began writing, she envisioned a few "sketches" and sent them to the *National Era,* a Washington, D.C., newspaper. Once the sketches appeared, however, readers demanded more . . . and more! Every community, it seemed, had at least one abolitionist who subscribed to the *National Era,* and he passed along his copy to many others.

The stories grew in popularity. Readers immersed themselves in the sketches and, rather like soap opera fans today, anxiously awaited each weekly installment. So in time she wrote forty episodes, devoting a year to their composition, all the while keeping house and rearing her children.

Then a Boston publisher, Jewett, arranged to publish the stories as a book, and it was issued in 1852. The public was ready; 6,000 copies sold almost overnight. Soon Jewett had three power presses running, twenty-four hours a day, six days a week. Within the first year 300,000 copies of *Uncle Tom's Cabin* had sold, and Jewett said the public's palate was still insatiable.

> ## PRINCIPLE OF LEADERSHIP OF MOMENTUM # 6:
> *Momentum Grabs the Emotions*

The market for the book crossed an ocean. Soon foreign publishers began to issue copies of the novel, for despite its literary limitations it appealed to man's universal hungers and ideals—for freedom and love and mercy.

Dramatists transformed the story into plays, which attracted large audiences. Songwriters composed lyrics, emotionally charged renditions of characters such as Uncle Tom, and folks sang about him as they worked. One entrepreneur even issued a card game titled "Uncle Tom and Little Eva."

Stowe's novel became something more than a novel. It served as a catalyst for conflict. Northerners tended to take its portrayal of slavery as factual; Southerners insisted it was jaundiced and skewed, sheer abolitionist propaganda. Though originally read and discussed in the South, it was soon suppressed, considered a toxic tome endangering the region.

> ## PRINCIPLE OF LEADERSHIP OF MOMENTUM #7:
> *Momentum Is a Change Agent*

As the nineteenth century came to an end, a New York analyst, Kirk Monroe, said, "The abolition of slavery was not, and could not be, accomplished by any one person. It was the result of united efforts . . . But the greatest and most far-reaching of all these influences was *Uncle Tom's Cabin*."[4]

⚜

GEORGE PATTON'S POST–D-DAY DASH TO BERLIN

Viewers of the film *Saving Private Ryan* witnessed some of the commitment—and bloody cost—of the Allies' invasion of Normandy on June 6, 1944: D-Day. Though the United States had declared war in December

213

1941, the country entered the European phase of World War II in 1943, leading the Allies' retaking of North Africa and successfully occupying Sicily and invading Italy, but the Nazi forces in Western Europe had not been tackled.

Responding to Joseph Stalin's pressure, the Allies opened a second front, a "western front" in Europe. That was done to help relieve the Russians, who had absorbed the massive Nazi assault that drove to the very heart of their homeland, stalling it at Stalingrad, and were slowly regaining lost territory. The Allies invaded France.

The fighting was fierce on D-Day in Normandy—ever memorializing sites such as Omaha Beach and Utah Beach. The Germans were entrenched in their concrete bunkers, and many of them were seasoned veterans. But the Allies, led by General Dwight D. Eisenhower, launched an overwhelming assault. Thousands of planes dropped both bombs and paratroops. Amphibious units landed tanks and equipment. Brave soldiers swarmed over the beaches and gained the victory, establishing a solid beachhead. Within a few weeks a million Allied soldiers were in France. D-Day was a dramatic victory, a brilliantly executed breakthrough. More important, it tipped the *morale* of the war to the Allies.

Many "experts" expected a long, protracted conflict, much as had taken place on the eastern front, where Russian armies slowly moved westward, suffering ghastly casualties. The mighty German war machine, which had swept through virtually all of Europe, still had millions of well-equipped soldiers, ready to defend the Third Reich, anxious to preserve Hitler's regime. By that time in the war, the Allies were generally optimistic, for they had (thanks to the United States) a vast superiority of men and materials. Yet few expected a rapid conclusion to the conflict.

Once the troops were ashore in Normandy, however, the Allies advanced quickly, often with surprising ease. Especially notable was the movement of the American Third Army under General George S. Patton. Patton's troops had not taken part in the Normandy invasion. Knowing the Germans fully expected him to be involved when the Allies actually crossed the English Channel, Eisenhower used Patton as a decoy, keeping his whereabouts secret and his assignment unannounced. His troops were kept in reserve on D-Day.

> ## PRINCIPLE OF LEADERSHIP OF MOMENTUM # 8:
> *Once You Have Momentum,*
> *Do All You Can to Maintain It; Treat It Like a Valued Treasure*

After the beachhead was secured, Patton's corps came ashore and launched a spectacular advance. From Normandy, he led his men south into Brittany, and then dashed east toward Paris, covering six hundred miles in two weeks, triumphantly riding through the liberated French capital. Within three months of D-Day, Allied troops were on the German border.

> ## PRINCIPLE OF LEADERSHIP OF MOMENTUM # 9:
> *Winning Fosters Momentum, Which, in Turn,*
> *Produces More Winning*

On June 5, 1944, shortly before departing England for France, Patton had addressed his troops bluntly:

> You are here today for three reasons. First, because you are here to defend your homes and your loved ones. Second, you are here for your own self respect because you would not want to be anywhere else. Third, you are here because you are real men and all real men like to fight. When you, here, everyone of you, were kids, you all admired the champion marble player, the fastest runner, the toughest boxer, the big league ball players, and the All-American football players. Americans love a winner. Americans will not tolerate a loser. Americans despise cowards. Americans play to win all of the time. I wouldn't give a hoot in hell for a man who lost and laughed. That's why Americans have never lost nor will ever lose a war; for the very idea of losing is hateful to an American.[5]

Then Patton declared to his men that "Death must not be feared . . . Death, in time, comes to all men." Everyone facing battle felt fear. But fear must be stared down.

PRINCIPLE OF LEADERSHIP OF MOMENTUM # 10:
Leaders Inspire Responses That Help Create and Sustain Momentum

---

Suitably inspired, both by Patton's rhetoric and by his daring example, the young Americans followed him into battle. Once the enemy was retreating, he had insisted, they must notch up the pressure:

> "Sure, we want to go home," he said. "We want this war over with. The quickest way to get it over with is to go get the bastards who started it. The quicker they are whipped, the quicker we can go home. The shortest way home is through Berlin and Tokyo. And when we get to Berlin, I am personally going to shoot that paper hanging . . . Hitler. Just like I'd shoot a snake!"[6]

PRINCIPLE OF LEADERSHIP OF MOMENTUM # 11:
Leaders Learn to Seize the Moment

He also insisted that men on the move had no time to seek shelter. "My men don't dig foxholes," he bragged. "Foxholes only slow up an offensive. Keep moving. And don't give the enemy time to dig one either. We'll win this war, but we'll win it only by fighting and by showing the Germans that we've got more guts than they have; or ever will have."[7]

PRINCIPLE OF LEADERSHIP OF MOMENTUM # 12:
Contentment Is an Enemy of Momentum

Patton never wanted his subordinates to inform him they were "holding" their positions. "Let the Germans do that," he said. "We are advancing constantly and we are not interested in holding onto anything" other than what they could wrest from the enemy. "Our basic plan of operation," he said, "is to advance and to keep on advancing regardless of whether we have to go over, under, or through the enemy."[8]

> PRINCIPLE OF LEADERSHIP OF MOMENTUM # 13:
> *Momentum Causes Persons to Accomplish*
> *What They Ordinarily Could Not*

Patton knew his critics would complain that he pushed his troops too hard. But few men cared less about critics! He stated, "I believe in the old and sound rule that an ounce of sweat will save a gallon of blood . . . Pushing means fewer casualties. I want you all to remember that."[9] When it was all over, when the victory was won, he said, his men would be supremely proud to have fought alongside George Patton in the great Third Army. And so they were!

The momentum gained at D-Day, translated into relentless advance by inspiring leaders like Patton, explains the rapid collapse of Hitler's Third Reich. Once a battle's won, momentum must be sustained until the war is over.

⚜

THE NEW YORK YANKEES

Momentum is hard to define. But everyone can "feel" it when you have it. And there is one team, above all teams, that has known the feeling of momentum. That team is the New York Yankees.

In 1903, baseball officials decided to try something new—a postseason series, with the winner taking the best of nine. The Boston Red Sox squared off against the Pittsburgh Pirates. In the eighth game, Boston won their fifth victory. They were winners of the first World Series.

One hundred years later, the World Series is as American as it gets. And so is one particular team: the New York Yankees. The Yankees have, by far, won more World Series titles than any other team. In fact, you could cut their wins in half, and *they would still have the most titles*. In the past century, the Yankees have won twenty-six World Series. The Cardinals and Athletics are tied for second position with nine each. The Dodgers trail with six.

How is this possible? How can one team so dominate the sport? The reasons may be varied and complex. But at the risk of being simplistic, they have momentum on their side.

PRINCIPLE OF LEADERSHIP OF MOMENTUM # 14:
Momentum Is a "Culture" That Is Attitudinal

The ball club is characterized by a commitment to excellence. Admittedly, the team has had dry spells, seasons when the coveted title eluded it (1970–76; 1979–85; 1987–95). Yet the Yankee organization has a tradition. When you "put on the pinstripes," you're expected to win! Members of the New York club have championship on their minds. No Yankee team member can simply think, *I'm just glad I get to play in the big leagues.* When they walk into America's most famous baseball stadium, they think, *Win!* And that produces a phenomenon, quite difficult to explain, called momentum.

What about you and your organization? Most of you who are reading this are not playing for the Yankees and never will. But what are you doing to help create momentum in your organization? How can you create a "culture" of momentum? In what ways can you generate an innate sense of momentum when people "put on the pinstripes" of your organization? If you successfully answer that question, you have enhanced your leadership skills significantly.

⚜

THE NEW ENGLAND PATRIOTS

Super Bowl XXXVI was played on February 3, 2002, in New Orleans. It provided one of the most gripping examples of the Law of Momentum I have ever seen. The St. Louis Rams were favored by 14. But something "tipped the scales" in favor of the New England Patriots *before* the game even began! And it was a most unlikely game-changing event. It was the introduction of the teams.

Anyone watching that game will remember that moment. St. Louis's starting lineup was introduced first—in the normal player-by-player format, ending with two-time NFL MVP, Quarterback Kurt Warner.

Then it was the Patriots' turn, the underdog, the less talented team—or so most people thought. The announcer, forgoing the usual mention of each player, simply said "The New England Patriots are being introduced as a team." And onto the field the team came—as one! It was a spectacular moment. General Manager Mark Shapiro of the Cleveland Indians, a friend of Patriots Director of Player Personnel Scott Pioli, commented on that electric moment: "I had goose bumps."

> **PRINCIPLE OF LEADERSHIP OF MOMENTUM # 15**
> *Momentum Is Enhanced When The Cause Becomes Bigger Than The Egos Of The Persons Involved*

This team had given up the glory of being seen *individually* on global television by more than a billion people—*for the sake of oneness.* It was an overpowering statement. I sat there stunned. As one who was rooting for the Rams, I knew that moment that St. Louis was in trouble. It was no longer an "even playing field." The Patriots, in an act of individual self-sacrifice, had shifted the momentum in their favor. The "all team" introduction was more than a symbol. It was a statement of who they were and how they were going to play. And they did.

> **PRINCIPLE OF LEADERSHIP OF MOMENTUM # 16**
> *Unity and Focus Can Overcome Raw Talent*

One sports writer put it this way: The Patriots "came out together. And stayed together. And played together. And won together. Now, they're celebrating together."

And celebrating together is exactly what all teams do that have the big mo—momentum. All of us love momentum. We want it. We dream of it. And when it happens, we would love to bottle it up and keep it. That is not possible.

But what is possible is this: Follow the principles that most enhance the opportunities for momentum. You cannot always produce momentum, but you can lead in a way that actually stops it.

Here is what we do know:

(1) Violating healthy leadership laws and principles will keep you from experiencing momentum. So don't do those things.

(2) Do lead by healthy leadership laws and principles. Although that does not guarantee momentum, it vastly increases the probability for it. In the areas that you can control, lead right. Give great leadership in the ways you can. Then commit the rest to God.

(3) Stay faithful to healthy leadership laws and principles even when you are not experiencing momentum. Do not yield to the temptation to cut corners in an attempt to manufacture momentum. If you are doing the right things—and if you are doing things right, then reward will eventually come. Be willing to plant, water, fertilize and cultivate (in some cases, for a long time), before you experience the harvest of momentum.

17

THE LAW OF PRIORITIES

*Leaders Understand That Activity Is
Not Necessarily Accomplishment*

PRINCIPLES OF LEADERSHIP OF PRIORITIES

It was May of 1978. I was on the second floor of the library at Drew University in Madison, New Jersey, doing research for my doctoral dissertation. Suddenly, outdoors I heard music. I knew that Drew's graduation ceremony, rich in tradition, had begun.

THE POWER OF PRIORITIES

Drew University is referred to as "the College in the Forest" because it is nestled in a breathtaking cluster of massive oak trees. In the middle of this picturesque campus is a small pond. Alongside the pond and through the trees is a walking path—actually a strip of asphalt—which lowers (along the pond) and raises like a blue ribbon amidst the bright green grass and towering oaks.

On that path, Drew's graduates proudly march each spring until they arrive at the backside of an antebellum-style mansion with an enormous porch that serves as the platform for the school's outdoor commencement. Looking out the window that May day, I saw the rows of white chairs that had been placed in neat rows across the lawn filled with proud parents and well-wishers. In the distance I saw the graduates and faculty coming toward the outdoor auditorium.

Undergraduates came first, followed by students who were completing their master's degrees. Then I saw the doctoral candidates. And what

I saw jolted me. There, in the midst of the Ph.D. graduates, was Tim. Tim had arrived at the university a year after me, and yet he was graduating well ahead of me. He had completed two years of full-time course work and had passed his comprehensive exams (four tests, eight hours each). He had successfully defended his rationale for his selected dissertation topic and had written the dissertation. He had defended his dissertation before his examining committee and made any necessary post-defense dissertation corrections.

> **PRINCIPLE OF LEADERSHIP OF PRIORITIES # 1:**
> *Prioritized Living Means Seeing the Goal*
> *and Then Adjusting Everything Accordingly*

Of those six steps, I had completed the first three, but had not done any of the last three. Finishing my dissertation certainly was *a* priority; it now had to become *the* priority.

At the second-floor library window, I stood still—watching him walk all the way to his seat. And in that moment, I made a resolution. I said it in a low murmur. "God," I said, "with Your help, there will never be another graduation here at Drew University without me in it!" That was it. That was my prayer, or my statement of resolution.

But talk is cheap. In order to live out that declaration, I would have to make changes in my life. And overhaul my schedule. I promptly cleared out anything I was doing June 1 through September 1, *except* writing my dissertation.

> **PRINCIPLE OF LEADERSHIP OF PRIORITIES # 2:**
> *Your Priorities Are Revealed by Your Conversation,*
> *Your Calendar, and Your Checkbook*

I knew that I would have to function during my best hours. I am *not* a morning person. I am a night person. So I would have to write during my peak hours, even though they were not conducive to living in the "real world." My best "beginning time," for optimum performance, is 9:30 A.M. (I have many meetings that start before that time, but I am never at my best. I am only operating at 85 percent before that time. This is really troubling when I fly from my home on the West Coast to the East Coast and have to speak for 7:00 A.M. events while my "body clock" says it is 4:00 A.M. in San Diego. I do it often but only by great willpower!) I knew that I could stay fresh with maximum output till 2:30 A.M. So that is exactly what I did—every day, every *single* day (except Sunday) for the summer of 1978. But I didn't merely write for seventeen hours. I followed a set schedule. By the end of May, I knew exactly how many pages I needed to write every day. And I followed it like clockwork.

PRINCIPLE OF LEADERSHIP OF PRIORITIES # 3:
Priorities Are Revealed Not by Words But by Actions

There are many "ABD's" around the country. In case you are not familiar with the term, it stands for "All But Dissertation," and it describes the condition of hundreds—perhaps thousands—of doctoral students who will never receive their Ph.D. degrees because they have not written their dissertations. Why? The answer to that may be varied, but most of them—perhaps 90 percent of them—are *not willing to prioritize.* They will not set a schedule and then follow it. A doctoral program is, in part, an endurance test. And you cannot complete it *unless you are willing to prioritize.*

One year passed quickly. Drew University's May 1979 commencement came. I had dreamed of walking through the forest. I had imagined what the selected commencement speaker—Jesse Jackson—might say, assuming that he might use the phrase for which he had become famous at that time: "I am somebody!"

But I never got to take the graduation walk through the forest. Nor did I get to hear the rousing graduation speech that I knew Jackson would bring. Why? Was it because I did not finish my doctoral dissertation? No. I *did* finish it. But northern New Jersey was hit with a tremendous rainstorm that day. The graduation was forced into a seriously overcrowded and perfectly unattractive gymnasium. And our speaker, Jesse Jackson, became ill and had to cancel. So, Alan Alda, of *M*A*S*H* fame, a neighbor of Drew University, was the graduation fill-in. The graduation, lacking the majesty of the outdoor forest atmosphere, along with some belligerent undergraduates who chose to be rowdy in response to Alda's appearance, made for a rather unimpressive event. But I did not care. I was so happy! I had finished the task at hand. True to my prayer, Drew University did *not* have another graduation without me. I was included! And I received the coveted Ph.D. degree. Priorities do count!

📖

SOCRATES' FIRST THINGS

We now travel to four hundred years before Christ. Shift to the ancient Greek philosopher Socrates. If we were to interview Socrates regarding this law of leadership, he would choose to call the establishment of proper priorities by another name: "first things." So committed was Socrates to his first things that he died for them. Few philosophers in history have given their lives to demonstrate their beliefs, but Socrates—"the patron saint of philosophy"—did so dramatically.

> **PRINCIPLE OF LEADERSHIP OF PRIORITIES # 4:**
> *When Writing Your Priorities Down, God Is Not Simply Number One; God Is the Paper On Which You Are Writing*

Although obviously Socrates was not writing from a Christian perspective, we can see that his priorities reflected his deep belief in the value of improving the soul. In 399 B.C., at the advanced age of seventy, on trial before a jury that would condemn him to death, Socrates said,

> Men of Athens, I honor and love you; but I shall obey God rather than you, and while I have strength I shall never cease from the practice and teaching of philosophy, exhorting any one whom I meet and saying to

him after my manner: You, my friend . . . are you not ashamed of heap-
ing the greatest amount of money and honor and reputation, and caring so little about wisdom and truth and the greatest improvement of
the soul, which you never regard or heed at all?[1]

Socrates' calling was for the soul of mankind. In his final speech, he
continued,

> I do nothing but go about persuading you all, old and young alike, not
> to take thought for your persons or your properties, but first and chiefly
> to care about the greatest improvement of your soul. I tell you that virtue
> is not given by money, but that from virtue comes money and every other
> good of man, public as well as private. This is my teaching."[2]

During the time of Socrates, there was a group of thinkers known as the
Sophists. They were professional teachers who stressed rhetorical style
and emotional appeals. They manipulated others in order to win a case.
Speaking of them, Socrates said, "Never mind the manner . . . but think
only of the truth of my words, and give heed to that: let the speaker
speak truly and the judge decide justly."[3]

Socrates' tenacious pursuit of the truth, his radical commitment to
"first things," marked "a turning point in the history of civilization," Max
Eastman says. "He taught that all good conduct is conduct controlled by
the mind, that all the virtues consist . . . in the prevailing of mind over
emotion."[4]

PRINCIPLE OF LEADERSHIP OF PRIORITIES # 5:
Outer Beauty Is a Good Thing, But Inner Beauty Is a Necessity

---

Socrates would not have won any beauty contests. The man who stood
before the Athenian jury was, on the surface, unimpressive. The famed
comic dramatist Aristophanes took delight in pillaring him in his plays.
He was bald-headed, bearded, with a flat snub nose and thick, fleshy
lips. He himself remarked on "a stomach rather too large for conven-

ience,"[5] and he was so "extraordinarily ugly," he and his friends often joked about it.

He dressed simply, generally walking about barefoot and wearing an old, tattered coat. By trade he was a stonecutter, but he never cared much for such work and spent much of his time talking—and talking—with anyone in Athens willing to discuss ideas. "The unexamined life is not worth living," he said. He sought to help folks find how to live rightly. "Know thyself," he demanded: know what you think and why you think it. What are the first principles, the basic truths, that shape your life?

> **PRINCIPLE OF LEADERSHIP OF PRIORITIES # 6:**
> *Learn Where Others Have Shipwrecked Their Lives—*
> *Then Stay Away from Those Rocks*

His obvious physical limitations perhaps encouraged him to turn his attention inward, to finer qualities of the soul, as did the absence of many purely external assets. Socrates warned:

> Many are ruined by admirers whose heads are turned by the sight of a pretty face . . .
> Many are led by their strength to attempt tasks too heavy for them, and meet serious evils . . .
> Many by their wealth are corrupted, and fall victims to conspiracies . . .
> Many through glory and political power have suffered great evils.[6]

> **PRINCIPLE OF LEADERSHIP OF PRIORITIES # 7:**
> *Before You Try to Lead Others, Lead Yourself*

Socrates believed that people needed to rightly live in accord with first things. In order to do that, they needed self-control, the classical virtue of *temperance*. To him, self-control was foundational to all of life. One of his most loyal students, the general Xenophon, summed up his master's views: "Should not every man hold self-control to be the foundation of all virtue, and first lay this foundation firmly in his soul?"[7]

PRINCIPLE OF LEADERSHIP OF PRIORITIES # 8:
Self-Discipline Is One of the Leader's Best Friends

In a discussion recorded by Xenophon, Socrates rejected the views of a young man named Antiphon who imagined "that happiness consists in luxury and extravagance. But my belief is that to have no wants is divine; to have as few as possible comes next to the divine."[8] He insisted that self-control, not self-indulgence, led to happiness. Excess in eating, drinking, sleeping, working, leaves one miserable. But disciplined eating, drinking, sleeping, working, enable one to attain his true end as a rational creature.

As Socrates explained, certain things should be highly valued:

- enjoying the delights of learning something good and excellent
- regulating his body well
- managing his household successfully
- being useful to his friends
- being useful to his city

These traits, Socrates contended, yield "not only very great benefits but very great pleasures."[9] Only the self-controlled enjoy such pleasure, he argued. In contrast, undisciplined persons know no such joy because they are slaves to whatever temporary pleasure is nearby.

PRINCIPLE OF LEADERSHIP OF PRIORITIES # 9:
Cultivate the Soul, the Inner Self

Socrates hoped to help men think more rationally, and to do so he constantly tried to carefully define terms and construct logical arguments. He thought of himself as a physician of the soul. A recent writer, Giovanni Reale, says that "no one prior to Socrates had understood by *soul* what Socrates understood by it, and after Socrates the whole of the West . . . the soul for Socrates was identified with . . . *the conscious self, it is intellectual and moral personhood.*"[10]

Knowing "true beauty and goodness" was his passion, for only truth, goodness, and beauty are medicine for the soul. So when he prayed, he asked simply for "good gifts, for the gods know best what things are good."[11]

PRINCIPLE OF LEADERSHIP OF PRIORITIES # 10:
When Living Life, Discover the Main Thing—
Then Keep It the Main Thing

The life of Socrates reveals a sustained commitment to ultimate things, "first principles." Making the main thing the main thing made him one of the most influential men in history. Devoting his life to truth, goodness, and beauty left a bright legacy, ever reminding folks who followed him of what's truly meaningful and worth pursuing.

LIFE'S FUNNEL

April 20, 1974, is the only time I remember locking myself outside my house. I was hurrying to leave to speak for a Methodist youth group in Crosswicks, only about five minutes from our home in Yardville, both suburbs of Trenton, New Jersey. As I closed the front door behind me, I heard the phone ringing on the inside. It was then that I realized I didn't have the house keys. I stood outside the front door, the phone ringing some twenty times, while trying to figure out how I could regain entrance to my own home. With the last phone ring, I looked at my watch, realized that I had better get to my speaking engagement, and determined to figure out how to get into the house when I returned.

Four hours later, my wife and I returned to the house. We somehow managed to get inside, but were barely in when the phone rang again. Carol answered it in the kitchen. I answered it from the master bedroom of the tri-level home. It was my father calling. His voice was somber. What he said next forever altered our family. "Your brother Bob," he stated, "has been killed in a plane crash." What he said next I do not recall.

My wife, with much more presence of mind, stayed on the phone in an attempt to understand the details. Although usually priding myself on being able to keep it together, I lost it. I can recall only two things: realizing I was laying in the middle of the bedroom floor (no longer standing as I had been when I received the call), and hearing a sound come out of my inner being such as I had never heard before. My nineteen-year-old brother Bob was dead, along with Rick, our twenty-year-old cousin, and nineteen-year-old Dave, Bob's college roommate.

Roland and Sue Wills, not knowing of our family tragedy, arrived at our home while we were still on the phone. They became our comforters in the moment of crisis. They assisted us in packing for our trip back home to Kansas. Dave Erickson, a close pastor-friend from nearby Lambertville, New Jersey, arrived within one hour and sat with me through the long, dark night, not leaving until the rays of the 6:00 A.M. sun were clearly visible.

Early the next morning we flew from Philadelphia to Kansas City, where we met my parents and siblings, along with cousin Rick's parents and siblings. We drove to an open pasture near the small Kansas town of White City, where twenty-five dazed family members stood around a ten-by-twenty-foot burned-out area—the only evidence of what had been the point of impact of the small aircraft. That day blurred into the next and the next, which began the funeral services held at MidAmerica Nazarene University (college for the three boys) and in the high school auditorium of our hometown of Concordia, Kansas.

A flurry of events surrounded the flights, hundreds of conversations with friends and family members, funeral services that ended with the burial at the picturesque Walnut Grove Cemetery, surrounded by pastures, overlooking the river valley where one could easily see our farmstead approximately one-quarter mile to the north. In all those experiences, I can recall only the comments of two persons, one of which is the purpose for my telling you this story. And that one comment has become a riveting point of my life.

The late Dr. Curtis Smith, then president of MidAmerica Nazarene University, was the speaker at the funeral service for the three collegians. (The pilot, who also lost his life, was remembered in his home community in western Kansas.) I don't recall anything that he said, except one profound sentence toward the end of the funeral sermon: "The older one gets, the more one discovers that fewer and fewer things are really important." My mind locked in on that statement. *How interesting,* I thought. *And, I suspect, how true.*

PRINCIPLE OF LEADERSHIP OF PRIORITIES # 11:
*The Older One Gets, the More One Discovers That
Fewer and Fewer Things Are Really Important*

Consider the implications of the reality that "the older one gets, the more one discovers that fewer and fewer things are really important." If that statement is true (and it is), then what are the things that will be really important to me as I grow older? When one is 10 years of age, *everything* seems so important. That is still true at 20 years of age. It is less so at 30. And at 40, one is much more faced with the question, What is really important? But at 50, that is considerably more pronounced. According to those I've interviewed, that continues to intensify at ages 60, 65, 70, 75, and beyond.

PRINCIPLE OF LEADERSHIP OF PRIORITIES # 12:
*Order Your Life Around the One Single Thing That Is Going to Matter
Most When You Take Your Last Breath on Earth*

Here is the key issue: What *one single thing* is going to make a difference to me just before my last breath? Answer: Am I prepared for the afterlife, the next life? Am I ready to meet my Maker? And if that is the most important issue at that point, why not live like it *now* so that I can give my life away for the things that *really* count, thus avoiding giving my life away for the things that really *don't have* lasting value?

And what, may I ask, will be your concern just two breaths before your last breath? Are *your family members* ready to meet their Maker? And if that question is all that is important (and it is), why not construct and order your life so that issue is valued *now*?

18

THE LAW OF SACRIFICE

A Leader Must Give Up to Go Up

PRINCIPLES OF
LEADERSHIP OF SACRIFICE

In September of 2001, I received a phone call from Marcus Vegh of Progressive Vision, San Clemente, California, asking me to record a ninety-minute video in which I would cover two thousand years of church history. He explained that he needed the Video Compact Disk (VCD), which he would then translate into to the Mandarin language for the purpose of training many Chinese young adults for cross-cultural ministry and church planting. I asked the usual questions. His answers amazed me.

WILLING TO SACRIFICE EVERYTHING!

Some months before he had conversed with a representative of six bishops, the leaders of approximately 20 million Christians who are part of China's flourishing illegal, underground church. They had discovered that there were currently only 118,000 known, identifiable Western missionaries. They realized that 118,000 missionaries *cannot* do the task of spreading the Christian message. Many more are needed.

These six bishops, along with the people under their spiritual care, decided that they could do something about this missionary shortage. They set a goal to send out 100,000 missionaries in a five-year period, a staggering goal considering that that number nearly equals the total currently sent by the entire Western Christian world. The training strategy was set with the selection process of those between the ages of fifteen and twenty-five. Don't think of the immaturity of American youth when you hear this. These Chinese youth function much like very mature adults, unlike some Americans who seemingly endlessly prolong their adolescence into their thirties.

PRINCIPLE OF LEADERSHIP OF SACRIFICE # 1:
Count the Cost; Then Pay It

Chinese can travel with ease in many countries in the difficult "10/40 window" (the rectangular "window" that extends from West Africa to East Asia, from ten degrees north to forty degrees north of the equator) where Western Christians experience resistance. The 100,000 young-adult Chinese are preparing for an intensive month-long training (by VCDs) and then will buy *one-way tickets* to the cities of southern Asia, the Middle East, and North Africa for the purpose of sharing their faith in Christ. Ordinarily, it is very expensive to locate a new missionary in a foreign land, easily costing $100,000 per family. How much financial support do these Chinese young adults expect? None. Absolutely none. They feel that they can live on $1 per day, which they will earn working as common laborers. They ask for *nothing* except some help in training. And *they are willing to risk their lives* for this cause.

PRINCIPLE OF LEADERSHIP OF SACRIFICE # 2:
When People Sacrifice for a Cause,
It Convicts Others to Get Involved in That Cause

When Marcus finished explaining this to me in the September 2001 phone call, I hung up the phone, sitting there a bit dazed. I had read many accounts of sacrifice in the course of church history. But I had never heard of such stunning sacrifice by such a large group in this age group in present times. I consented to record the training videotape. But I felt so unworthy to teach *them*. I felt that *I* was the one who had much to learn!

FRANCIS ASBURY:
SACRIFICING BY EXAMPLE

John Wesley possibly rode more on horseback than any known figure in history. His circuit riding—preaching from town to town—is well recorded, documented daily by his exhaustive diaries.

In 1771, he sent twenty-six-year-old Francis Asbury of England to the colonies of America for the purpose of evangelizing. But some of those men under Asbury's direction in the New World were not so enthused to ride on horseback every single day, with no home, in all kinds of weather, to preach every place they could gather a small crowd.

> **PRINCIPLE OF LEADERSHIP OF SACRIFICE # 3:**
> *Leaders Sacrifice First*

One day, exasperated by the hesitancy of some, he said, "I'll show you how." Francis mounted his horse and virtually rode the rest of his life, covering the seaboard repeatedly. So ever-present was he that letters got to him that were sent from England simply addressed "To Francis Asbury, in America."

> **PRINCIPLE OF LEADERSHIP OF SACRIFICE # 4:**
> *When the Leader Sacrifices, So Do the Followers*

His modeling was so contagious that some have suggested that five thousand young circuit riders followed his example. Most did not live long lives. Their constant exposure to the elements destroyed their health. In usually severe conditions, it was often said that "the only ones out in such weather were the crows and the Methodist circuit riders!" As a result of this sacrifice, Methodism exploded across America at a remarkable pace.

JIM ELLIOT: THE ULTIMATE SACRIFICE

Jim Elliot was a handsome and bright student at Wheaton College in the early 1950s. Even as a collegian, he was a gifted writer, speaker, teacher, and—athletically—a wrestler. But most of all, Jim was determined to make his life count. As he prayed, he felt God directed him to go to South America and present the gospel to people who had never heard of Christ.

In the winter of 1952, he boarded a freighter for South America. In October of 1953, he married Elisabeth, a young woman who felt equally called to the South American jungles. In the fall of 1955, a young missionary pilot, Nate Saint, who shared Jim's vision, located an Auca village and started making friendly overtures to the isolated group by dropping gifts from the plane. They repeated this day after day, until they felt they had won the hearts of the dangerous tribesmen.

> **PRINCIPLE OF LEADERSHIP OF SACRIFICE # 5:**
> *Sacrifice Can Be Risky*

In January of 1956, Saint, Elliot, and three other young missionaries landed their small plane on a beach of the Curaray River in eastern Ecuador. At first, it appeared that their attempts to befriend the tribe had succeeded. But on January 8, 1956, the Aucas did to the five young missionaries the same thing they had done to some Shell Oil Company employees. They speared them and hacked their bodies to pieces.

America was shocked. The news riveted a nation. Five outstanding men killed—leaving wives and children behind. Jim Elliot was only twenty-eight years of age! His dream had been cut short. But his real dream was about to be fulfilled.

> **PRINCIPLE OF LEADERSHIP OF SACRIFICE # 6:**
> *The Present Generation Always Stands On the Sacrifices of Those Who Have Gone Before It*

The surviving family members continued to try to reach out to the Aucas—this time successfully. One by one, they came to know the Christ for whom the five men were willing to die. Even more amazing, the South American Indian who killed Jim Elliot later traveled all over America speaking, relating his acceptance of the gospel, alongside Elisabeth Elliot, the wife of the man he had murdered! The speaking duo, a seemingly "odd couple," shared the story of peace, reconciliation, forgiveness, and healing.

At the time of the writing of this book, an Auca named Mincaye, one of the killers of the Jim Elliot–Nate Saint entourage, has been touring America sharing about his Christian conversion, accompanied by Steve Saint, Nate Saint's now-grown son, who was a child at the time of his father's death.

PRINCIPLE OF LEADERSHIP OF SACRIFICE # 7:
Don't Clutch; Live Life with an Open Hand

How is one to understand such things? The most succinct explanation comes from the writing of Jim Elliot himself, taken from his personal journal (which has been preserved, on the original papers, in his own handwriting), entered November 28, 1949, while he was a college student. Here are Jim's probing, convicting words: "He is no fool who gives up what he cannot keep to gain what he cannot lose." *No one has ever summarized the Law of Sacrifice better!*

WILLIAM TYNDALE:
LOSING A LIFE, BUT WINNING THE CAUSE

William Tyndale could have enjoyed the life of a scholar. Instead he died a martyr. Many know his name. They know he's important. But they know little of his life of profound sacrifice.

Born in 1494, Tyndale was a brilliant linguist with a passion to translate the Greek New Testament into the English language, something the English-speaking world lacked. His bishops warned him not to do it, however, because they believed that the "common person" should *not* have the Bible in a language they could understand. In hiding in Europe, William saw his dream come true in February 1526 when six thousand copies of the English New Testament were completed.

> ### PRINCIPLE OF LEADERSHIP OF SACRIFICE # 8:
> *Presumed Defeats Are Often Victories Waiting to Happen*

Bishop Cuthbert Tunstall didn't approve of the Scriptures being translated into English and hired August Packington to pay whatever was needed in order to buy up all the Bibles and destroy them. Tyndale cooperated willingly in the plan. Why? Paid an exorbitant amount, he knew he would be able to afford to do a higher quality translation and be able to produce far more Bibles. And that is exactly what he did.

In a very short time, Tyndale was peppering England with Bibles, hidden in sacks of flour and bales of cotton. And he kept on the move so that King Henry VIII of England could not find him, that is, until a man named Henry Phillips turned him in. His pursuers found him on May 21, 1535.

> ### PRINCIPLE OF LEADERSHIP OF SACRIFICE # 9:
> *Dream Beyond Your Life*

William Tyndale was strangled, and they burned his body at the stake in 1536. As he gasped his last breath, he cried out, "Lord! Open the king of England's eyes." And that prayer was answered! Two years later, in 1538, the king reversed himself and issued a royal injunction that required a copy of the Bible to be available in every parish church in England. Tyndale won the cause, but lost his life in the process. Leading can cost—dearly.

ANDREW JACKSON'S SACRIFICES

Certainly not every story of sacrifice ends in death. And Christian missionaries are not the only examples of sacrifice. Few realize the level of sacrifice required to serve in public life. And few sacrificed more than President Andrew Jackson.

The presidency cost Andrew Jackson his wife, his fortune, and his health. Most presidents retire from the White House better off than when they were elected. Almost alone of America's chief executives, Andrew Jackson left the White House poorer than he had entered it eight years earlier. But he left the presidency stronger than he found it. He presided over the rise of the common man and the transformation of American politics. He stood strong for his convictions, and even his staunchest critics admit he made a difference in this nation.

Though born on March 15, 1767, in the Carolinas, where he fought with Revolutionary soldiers at the age of fourteen, Jackson made his mark in Tennessee. He learned enough to pass the bar and became a successful frontier lawyer and judge. Various investments brought him considerable wealth, and he acquired a fine plantation near Nashville—the Hermitage.

When the state of Tennessee was formed, Jackson served as the first congressman from his state and later returned to Washington as a senator. When troops were needed, Jackson often recruited and led volunteers, as he did in the War of 1812, defeating the Creek at the Battle of Horseshoe Bend in 1814 and the British at New Orleans in 1815. His valor and leadership earned him two nicknames in that war—Old Hickory (for his physical toughness) and the Old Hero (for his triumph over the British).

By 1820, he wearied of public service and sought refuge at the Hermitage. But friends insisted he run for president in 1824, and he did, garnering more votes than any of the other candidates. He did not win a majority in the electoral college, however, and political maneuvering led to the election of John Quincy Adams. Angered by the election's outcome, Jackson then ran energetically for president the next four years and was elected in 1828.

The campaign was marred by vicious slanders. In particular, some of Jackson's foes dragged up the fact that when he wed his beloved wife, Rachel, in 1791, she was "married" to another man—Lewis Robards. She thought he had already divorced her, for so he had publicly declared, but he had quietly dropped the procedures while encouraging others to think the divorce had been finalized.

However innocent she was, Rachel was technically still married when she married Jackson, so she was a bigamist. Two years later, Robards initiated divorce procedures again, that time charging Rachel with adultery, since she was living with Jackson. Once the situation was clarified, the legal details were resolved, and the Jacksons were legally married in 1794. But his enemies loved to tell the story and spread slanderous innuendos.

PRINCIPLE OF LEADERSHIP OF SACRIFICE # 10:
Accept the Fact That Life Isn't Fair

Sadly enough, Rachel died in December 1828 before her husband was inaugurated. Jackson blamed her critics for her death. Men who maligned him he could handle—indeed he'd fought a few duels with his detractors! But men who would slander a lady, he thought, were beneath contempt. His anger boiled. But his heart was broken, and he entered the White House a widower. The love of his life was gone, and he never fully recovered from that loss. He experienced deep sadness, with brooding black moods, derived in part from the death of Rachel. He'd lost his wife to gain the presidency, he felt.

Aged sixty-two, gaunt and white-haired, the president who was inaugurated in 1829 ached incessantly. Old Hickory was as tough as nails. But he hauled many ailments with him to the White House.

To make matters worse, Jackson carried, next to his heart, a heavy lead bullet, left there as a result of a duel with Charles Dickinson, who'd insulted Rachel Jackson. Dickinson died in the encounter, but he'd launched a bullet that lodged so close to Jackson's heart that doctors could not remove it. Consequently, Jackson often suffered from chills, fever, and a pulmonary abscess that recurrently drained pus. In addition, he experienced chest pains, bleeding from his lungs, and uncontrollable coughing.

In 1813, as a result of another altercation, he'd been shot by Jesse Benton, the brother of Thomas Hart Benton, whom Jackson was trying to horsewhip in a Nashville tavern brawl. That bullet shattered Jackson's left arm and left him with a chronic infection that did not heal until 1832, when at last a surgeon removed the lead ball.

The president also suffered from dysentery, aggravated by his carelessness in eating and drinking. Savage headaches plagued him so severely that at times his vision blurred. And all of the problems were certainly not relieved by the home remedies he employed—medicines often worse than his ailments.

Obviously, Jackson's ill health didn't stem from being president, for many of his ailments came from his own ill-tempered ways. That he even survived two terms as president is remarkable, and he ultimately lived until 1845. But it is also clear that the demands and pressures of the presidency aggravated his physical problems. A president can hardly indulge in much rest and relaxation. He assumed the office, knowing that it would prove costly to him physically. And it did.

PRINCIPLE OF LEADERSHIP OF SACRIFICE # 11:
Always *Avoid Dishonest or Compromised Gain*

But there's more. Jackson lost money serving as president. In part the cause was his own honesty. Old Hickory believed government service should not enrich officeholders. In his first annual message to Congress, Jackson lamented that some wanted to enrich themselves by holding offices, to care for their own fortunes rather than the Republic's. Some were corrupt, others simply so self-seeking they failed to consider the public interest.

PRINCIPLE OF LEADERSHIP OF SACRIFICE # 12:
*If You Will Control Your Own Desire for Power,
Others Won't Have To*

To deal with this, Jackson instituted his own form of term limits. He proposed to rotate people through the government on a regular basis. If one served only a few years and went home, perhaps he'd understand that he was to serve the people rather than fleece them. And Jackson, at least, followed his own advice.

While president, Old Hickory often entertained lavishly in the White House at his own expense! He neglected his own business affairs in Tennessee, which deteriorated while he was absent. Then he gave generously to charitable causes—unlike many rich politicians who relish expending others' monies, taken through taxation.

> ## PRINCIPLE OF LEADERSHIP OF SACRIFICE # 13:
> *A Good Name Should Be Chosen Above Riches*

Andrew Jackson left Washington in 1837, having sacrificed much of his wealth to serve his country. Being a public servant rarely means sacrificing much of anything. But to Jackson, serving meant sacrificing one's comfort and advantage in order to rightly guide the ship of state.

SAM HOUSTON'S SACRIFICE

Often we find ourselves jumping many centuries as we examine some of the lives of great persons who illustrate the various laws of leadership. This time, however, we will continue the time line as we learn from the sacrifice of one who was strongly affected by Andrew Jackson: Sam Houston, born twenty-six years after Jackson, on March 2, 1793.

> ## PRINCIPLE OF LEADERSHIP OF SACRIFICE # 14:
> *If You Lose Friends by Telling and Living the Truth,*
> *They Were Not Friends You Should Keep Anyway*

The story of Sam Houston, the father of the Texas Republic, tells us much about the courage and character of America's frontiersmen. In significant ways his preface to his autobiography sums up his life: "This book will lose me some friends. But if it lost me all and gained me none, in God's name, as I am a free man, I would publish it."[1] Dealing with Houston, you realize you're dealing with an oddity in human history: a principled politician.

Reared in Tennessee, he ever exuded an adventurous, romantic spirit. As a boy, he ran away from home and lived for a while with the nearby Cherokee, who adopted him into the tribe and gave him a native name, *Co-lon-neh,* which means "the Raven." During the War of 1812, he responded to Andrew Jackson's call and served as an officer in the infantry. At the Battle of Horseshoe Bend in 1814, he caught a bullet in the arm while leading a charge against the embattled "Redstick" Creeks.

Houston was now a bona fide war hero, enjoying Jackson's support. He rose rapidly in Tennessee politics, serving as congressman and governor. Jackson apparently hoped his young protégé would in time move to the White House as president of the United States.

PRINCIPLE OF LEADERSHIP OF SACRIFICE # 15:
Most of Life's Real Values Are Learned in the Crucible of Pain

---

Such dreams dissipated when Houston abruptly resigned from his position as governor of Tennessee. Apparently, he was overwhelmed with sorrow when he discovered that the woman he had recently married had accepted his proposal *only* because her politically ambitious father insisted. Knowing that she actually loved another man broke Houston's heart.

In anguish, Houston left for Indian Territory, where he lived for a year with some of his old Cherokee friends and drowned his sorrows in alcohol. Then he moved south to Texas, joining hundreds of other Americans settling there, where tensions were slowly building with the newly established Republic of Mexico.

When the Texans revolted against Mexico, Houston naturally assumed a leading role. He managed to put together an ill-equipped "army" of 700 men to oppose General Santa Anna, who had invaded Texas with 4,000 trained troops.

> ## PRINCIPLE OF LEADERSHIP OF SACRIFICE # 16:
> *Leaders Give Up the Right to "Blame-Shift"*

Houston's strength is revealed in a letter he wrote while preparing his men for action: "On my arrival on the Brazos, had I consulted the wishes of all, I should have been like the ass between two stacks of hay. Many wished me to go below, others above. I consulted none—I held no councils of war. If I err, the blame is mine."[2] Vintage Sam Houston—taking control and accepting responsibility—he brought to the crisis precisely what Texas needed.

The situation certainly looked grave. Mexican soldiers had killed 371 Texans at Goliad, a mission one hundred miles southeast of San Antonio, and another 187 at the Alamo, in San Antonio. Frontiersmen like Davy Crockett fought bravely but were simply outnumbered and overwhelmed. Triumphantly, Santa Anna now pursued Houston, confident he would annihilate him as well.

But Houston surprised them totally at the Battle of San Jacinto, on April 21, 1836, near the city that now bears his name. Shouting, "Remember the Alamo!" "Remember Goliad!" the Texans charged the enemy's camp and within minutes killed 630 Mexicans, wounding 200 others and taking 330 prisoners (Santa Anna included). The Mexicans were routed. The war ended. Texas gained her independence!

Following the great victory, of course, Houston loomed large in Texas. When the new republic was formed and elections held, he was elected president of the Texas Republic. Prevented by the constitution from succeeding himself, another man was the second president, but Houston was elected to a second term three years later. Without question he was the most eminent man in Texas.

When Texas joined the United States, a move fully approved by Houston, voters sent him to Washington as his state's first senator, proving himself "one of the most independent, unique, popular, forceful and dramatic individuals ever to enter the Senate chamber."[3] You certainly could never ignore him! Dressed in a military cloak and panther-skin waistcoat, occasionally wearing a Mexican blanket and wide-brimmed sombrero, he looked to some like a "magnificent barbarian." A national celebrity as the father of Texas, he stepped forth as a national leader, touted by some as a presidential candidate (reviving old Andy Jackson's dream).

Houston was a Southern Democrat, like Jackson, and equally committed to the Union, which he considered "his guiding star." As a congressman from Tennessee in 1820, he had supported the Missouri Compromise as a way to maintain peace between the sections. As a senator from Texas, he'd also supported the Compromise of 1850 for the same reason. Opposing South Carolina's John C. Calhoun, Houston declared: "I know neither North nor South; I know only the Union."[4]

> **PRINCIPLE OF LEADERSHIP OF SACRIFICE # 17:**
> *Cherish Truth, But Know That It Will Cost*

Then came the deeply divisive Kansas-Nebraska Bill of 1854, which opened up two new territories north of the Mason-Dixon line to slavery. It allowed settlers there to decide whether or not to adopt slavery. Houston opposed the bill, the only Southern Democrat to do so. His position elicited the wrath of the Richmond *Enquirer,* which, referring to Houston, declared that nothing can save "the traitor from the deep damnation which such treason may merit."

No editor could intimidate Houston, however. He loved the South, but his love would not lead him to betray his conscience. "It was," he said, "the most unpopular vote I ever gave [but] the wisest and most patriotic."[5]

At that point many Texans believed Houston had sided with the abolitionists. He had "betrayed his state in the Senate." The Texas legislature voted to condemn Houston's opposition to the Kansas-Nebraska Act. His own party disowned him. The Dallas *Herald* called for his resignation: "Let him heed for once the voice of an outraged, misrepresented, and betrayed constituency, so that Texas may for once have a united voice and present an undivided front in the Senate."[6]

> **PRINCIPLE OF LEADERSHIP OF SACRIFICE # 18:**
> *When Defeated While Standing for Genuine Truth,*
> *Know That It Is More of a Delay Than a Defeat—*
> *Because Truth Always, Eventually Emerges*

True to form, Houston refused to resign and returned to Texas to defend himself. He denounced both "the mad fanaticism of the North" and "the mad ambition of the South." Then he decided to run as an independent for governor in 1857, without resigning his Senate seat. His fellow Texans rejected him, giving him his first defeat in politics!

Again editors urged him to resign from the U.S. Senate. He refused. So the Texas legislature, a few months later, replaced him with a more belligerent proslavery Southerner.

> **PRINCIPLE OF LEADERSHIP OF SACRIFICE # 19:**
> *Give Your Life Away to a Cause Bigger Than Yourself*

Houston's career was apparently over, but as he left the Senate, he did so "with clean hands and a clean conscience." Defiantly, he said, "I wish no prouder epitaph to mark the board or slab that may lie on my tomb than this: 'He loved his country, he was a patriot; he was devoted to the Union.'"[7]

But he wasn't quite dead, not yet! He returned home and in 1859 ran again for governor, again as an independent. Powerful interests opposed him. No newspapers supported him. Against all odds he won!

> **PRINCIPLE OF LEADERSHIP OF SACRIFICE # 20:**
> *Die to Self; Check Your Ego at the Door*

While secessionists across the South sought to divide the Union, Houston battled to preserve it. He called a special session of the legislature to consider the issue. Houston sat on the platform, almost alone in opposing it. One historian, Wharton, writes: "To those who tell of his wonderful charge up the hill at San Jacinto, I say it took a thousand times more courage when he stalked into the Secession Convention at Austin and alone defied and awed them."[8]

Texas seceded, but the state did so defying Houston's will. Following the convention, the governor stalked the state, trying to rally the people to the Union. Angry crowds tossed stones and shouted him down. In the midst of one speech a man charged him, threatening to kill him, but Houston, placing his hands on his two pistols, stared him down.

PRINCIPLE OF LEADERSHIP OF SACRIFICE # 21:
"Opinion Poll Leaders" Have Temporary Popularity;
Principled Leaders Have Permanent Legacies

At seventy years old, he still had backbone and bravado. He lost the political battle, but he preserved his integrity. As Texas seceded from the Union, Houston resigned as the governor. He paid a price for his convictions. Writing out his resignation, he explained that he was "stricken down because I will not yield those principles which I have fought for."[9]

JOHN HUSS

Honestly, it is *not* my intention to be morbid in this chapter. But let's face it, sacrifice can hurt. It costs.

John Huss's friend Jerome returned home to Prague (in the present-day Czech Republic) from England's Oxford University with books containing the radical teaching of the late Dr. John Wycliffe. Wycliffe was viewed by church authorities as "radical" and untrustworthy. But Huss was excited by what he saw. By 1402, he began preaching some of Wycliffe's views twice a day to receptive audiences.

Church and political authorities were not certain how to stop Huss's popularity and his preaching. Under the guise of a supposed theological debate, Huss was tricked into coming to the town of Constance, Germany, in November 1414. There, he thought, he would finally have an opportunity to explain his views, which included his confidence in Christ for salvation and his belief in the full authority of the Bible. Although promised "safe conduct," Huss was thrown in prison soon after he arrived.

PRINCIPLE OF LEADERSHIP OF SACRIFICE # 22:
Avoid Shortcuts If They Cost You Your Integrity

The events surrounding his death were meticulously recorded by Poggius Bracciolini, who had originally served Huss the summons that had required him to appear before the Constance council. Bracciolini was overwhelmed by Huss's dignity and grace. He watched as they dragged Huss through the streets of Constance on July 6, 1415, facing the jeering of an inebriated crowd, which had been supplied free, cheap liquor for Huss's execution.

Arriving at the place where his body was to be burned, Huss was given one last opportunity to renounce his firm belief in Christ as the provider of salvation and his confidence in the truth of the Bible. He would not.

PRINCIPLE OF LEADERSHIP OF SACRIFICE # 23:
Sacrifice Reveals Quality in Character

The fire was lit, and Huss began singing, "Jesus Christ, Thou Son of the living God, have mercy upon me." He sang it a second time. He started the phrase a third time. He never finished the phrase. Poggius Bracciolini recorded the events, ending with these gripping words: John Huss "was just too good for this world."

And he *was* "too good for this world." You see, sacrifice is one of the "tickets" that lets you in the door of leadership. This ticket costs. It isn't cheap. But if you want in, you must have one.

Here is my question: Assuming you want to be a leader or to improve your leadership skills (and you apparently do, or you would not be reading this book), have you purchased your ticket? Are you willing to sacrifice in order to lead? Oh, I admit, there have been those who have led who have not sacrificed. But they don't lead long. Or they leave a bad taste in everyone's mouth when they are gone. Do you want to be a true leader? Then be prepared to sacrifice.

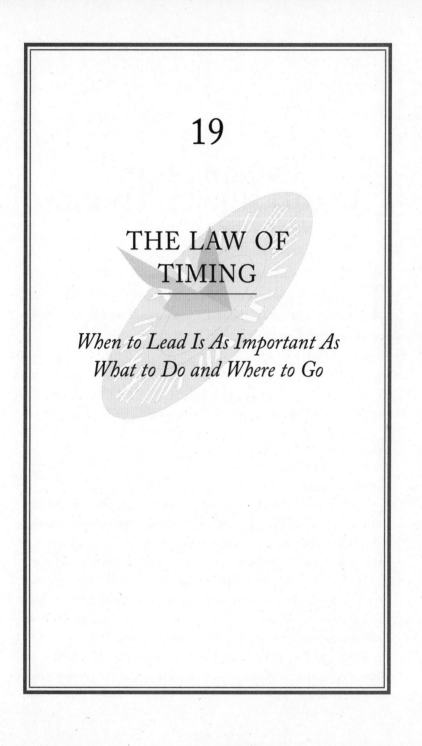

19

THE LAW OF
TIMING

*When to Lead Is As Important As
What to Do and Where to Go*

PRINCIPLES OF
LEADERSHIP BY TIMING

T iming really is everything. We are all aware that the only difference between a foul ball and a home run is timing. And what's
true of swinging a bat is also true of living life.

🎜

MARTIN LUTHER:
THE POWER OF CONVERGENCE

When a modern-day college professor posts an article on a Web site for
the purpose of provoking a chat room discussion, he doesn't expect to
change the world.

But that is exactly what happened to one college professor (Martin
Luther) on October 31, 1517, when he posted an article (the Ninety-five
Theses) on a place used for presenting articles for academic debates (the
castle church door) for the students and faculty of Wittenberg University.
Unknown to him, someone took the document down and took it to a
printing press (the Gutenberg press had been invented prior to this).
Within three weeks copies were disseminated throughout much of
Germany. A theological and political firestorm followed.

What had Luther said that was so controversial? For starters, he
questioned the authority of the pope, contending that the Word of God,
the Bible, was the "last word" on issues. He also contended that "works"

252

(that is, doing something) could not earn one salvation and entrance to heaven. Luther stressed that God had provided His Son, Jesus, to die for our sins. Thus, grace—that is, what Jesus did on the cross—caused us to be forgiven of our sins. When we have faith in Christ, His death counts for us. We are forgiven of our sins. The pope was furious with Luther, and as a result, he ordered Luther to appear before one council after another.

But what is significant for our purposes is not *what* Luther said, but that *he was able to say it!* Others had tried desperately to say the same things. But they paid a dear price for it.

PRINCIPLE OF LEADERSHIP BY TIMING # 1:
Although You Will Pay a Price for Being Too Early with an Idea,
You Are Likely Paving the Way for Others Who Will
Come After You with the Same Idea

Peter Waldo, in Lyons, France, was harassed and persecuted constantly for teaching what Luther would later teach in the 1500s. John Wycliffe taught some of the same concepts at Oxford in the late 1300s. They banished him. And to add insult to injury, forty-four years after his death, they exhumed his body, burned what remained, and dumped the ashes in a river to intentionally dishonor him! John Huss, to whom Martin Luther was sometimes compared, was burned at the stake in Constance, on the German-Swiss border, in 1415 for saying what Luther later said.

How did Martin Luther survive teaching what he taught? And not only survive but thrive? Luther's teachings went everywhere. They spread all across Europe. They touched off a type of revolution, although it is labeled a reformation—the Protestant Reformation.

PRINCIPLE OF LEADERSHIP BY TIMING # 2:
Convergence Is the Coming Together of Things in Such a Way
That You Can't Take the Credit for It

The answer to that question is found in timing. I firmly believe in providence, that is, God's involvement in things on this earth. But I also believe that He uses numerous things to bring about His will at a given time, and that applies to the spread of the Reformation as well. Several things came together that caused Luther's teaching to take hold of the Continent:

- First, the "taxation" from Rome to build St. Peter's Basilica was causing resentment.

- Second, closely related to the first reason, the political hold of the pope was straining the German population.

- Third, German nationalism was growing.

- Fourth, Frederick the Elector in Saxony, Germany, needed an excuse to ignore Rome.

- Fifth, Frederick the Elector was impressed with Luther and provided him political protection, making it impossible for the pope to harm him.

- Sixth, Frederick the Elector saw the controversy as a way of further establishing his young school—Wittenberg University, which was founded in 1502.

- Seventh, the newly invented printing press made it possible to disseminate Luther's views.

It is not an accident that Luther's teachings spread like a wildfire. Those who had previously tried to articulate a similar message were stamped out. But Luther's could not be stopped. The difference is found in one word—*timing*. And due to that timing, the entire known world was changed by the Protestant Reformation—the single most pivotal event in the 2000–year history of Christianity.

THE POWER OF TIMING—MUSICALLY SPEAKING

You have been patient and read many "heavy" historical accounts in the previous pages. Let's lighten the topic considerably. We shift our focus from theological disputes in the 1500s to the music that many of you grew up on in the last fifty years.

Music is like a river. It can be directed certain ways, but it cannot be stopped. Few things are more powerful, more gripping, more emotive than music. And nothing is more pervasive than a music style whose time has come.

You might not think of Elvis Presley, the Beach Boys, the Beatles, the Rolling Stones, Madonna, or U2 as leaders, but they are. Remember, as I stated in Chapter 2, leaders have *influence,* and be assured, these musicians had or have enormous influence. Some of them admittedly had negative influences on America's youth, but nevertheless, they have been influential.

ELVIS PRESLEY

Born in a two-room house on January 8, 1935, in Tupelo, Mississippi, Elvis Presley went on to become one of the most—if not *the* most—important pop icons of the twentieth century. Several musical "streams" converged in Elvis's music:

- gospel music he heard in church
- the gospel quartets in the all-night "sings" common in the South
- black R&B he heard on Beale Street in Memphis
- the tearful quality of the South's country music

Presley had the charm, charisma, and boyish good looks that helped him land the starring role in thirty-three successful films. But it was his music that captured hearts from 1956 to the present. The statistics are mind-boggling:

- Elvis charted more songs on *Billboard's* Hot 100 than any other artist (149).
- He spent more weeks at the top of the charts than any other artist (80).

- He had the greatest number of consecutive #1 hits (10).

- Elvis is second only to the Beatles in total of #1 hits (18).

- He has the second most multiplatinum records (19), exceeded only by the Beatles.

- He has more gold records than any other artist (81), exceeded only by Barbara Streisand.

- He has more platinum records than any other artist (43), exceeded only by the Beatles.

No wonder they call him the King.

Music and social historians have attempted to analyze the almost instant popularity of Presley's music: For some, it signaled a type of pre-1960 rebellion that seemed to grip American youth, a rejection of Mom and Dad's values. According to this theory, Elvis's music allowed youth to be as brash, cocky, and independent as he was.

For others, "Elvis the Pelvis" (no below-the-waist camera shots while on *The Ed Sullivan Show*) was a precursor of the sexual revolution.

Still others claimed the music revolution that Elvis brought had racial themes. According to them, it gave whites a chance to sing "black" music.

PRINCIPLE OF LEADERSHIP BY TIMING # 3:
Simple, Replicable Things Are Better Received by Far More People Than Complex Things

---

Obviously, the question still stands: *Why* did we like it so? Because it was simple, and it offered an addictive beat. The masses like it very simple. Complex songs, with complex chord patterns and complex intervals (from one note to the next), don't sell. They're just too hard to remember, replicate, or perform.

Furthermore, Presley's rise to fame coincided with the rapid rise in the interest in and availability of the guitar, one of the few instruments, other than the piano, that is multitonal (many tones or notes, such as a chord) but still leaves your vocal cords free to sing (as opposed to a saxophone or trombone, for example).

The big band sound that was popular in the 1940s was not replicable by an early 1960s ninth-grade boy sitting in his room. It took an orchestra. But give that ninth grader a guitar and he could turn his room, with a little imagination, into a concert hall, singing "You Ain't Nothin' But a Hound Dog" or "Heartbreak Hotel"—especially if he had a mirror to look at!

PRINCIPLE OF LEADERSHIP BY TIMING # 4:
When You Succeed, Remember That There Were Many Other Persons and Forces at Work That Got You Where You Are

---

Several other factors converged that helped Elvis become the King:

- the exceptional promotional skills of Colonel Tom Parker (Presley's agent)

- the establishment of radio in every home

- the new popularity of television in the mid-1950s

- the uncontested status of *The Ed Sullivan Show*, with up to 53 million viewers each Sunday night

---

PRINCIPLE OF LEADERSHIP BY TIMING # 5:
Watch Leaders Who Consistently Anticipate What Is Coming Next, and Learn from Them

---

Now back to our key point. Timing is everything. Elvis *felt* what so many *felt*. But the key is, *he felt it first.* Most leaders have the gift of "pre-feeling" (I know there is no such word) things. Leaders sense things very early. They lead the pack. If Presley had performed his songs in 1945, he would have been too early. If he had done it in 1965, it would have been too late. He walked into a musical vacuum, presumably without initially knowing it.

Timing is everything. He was first. And the rest of us followed. His music, both in lyrics and in musical style, was an idea whose time had come.

THE BEACH BOYS

Only five years after Elvis burst on the national scene, five young California men—Brian Wilson, Carl Wilson, Dennis Wilson, Al Jardine, and Mike Love—musically ignited the nation. In the words of one fan Web site, "When the aforementioned three brothers, one cousin and a school friend formed a casual singing group in Hawthorne (California) in 1961, they unconsciously created one of the longest-running, compulsively fascinating and bitterly tragic sagas in popular music."[1]

To anyone growing up in the 1960s, there is no sound quite like "Surfer Girl," "Good Vibrations," "California Girls," "409," "Surfin' Safari," and "I Get Around." All these songs—and many more just like them—spoke of fun, freedom, sun, beaches, beautiful girls, and hot cars. In their heyday, the Beach Boys ruled.

PRINCIPLE OF LEADERSHIP BY TIMING # 6:
Most Often, Major Social Changes Can Be Neither Anticipated Beforehand Nor Explained Afterwards

---

Once again, the nagging question: *Why?* Why was their music so popular?

- Whereas youth of the 1940s and early 1950s worked most of the time, suburban youth of the late 1950s and the 1960s had many more luxuries, not the least of which was lots of extra time on their hands, including time to hang out and listen to music.

- The youth of the 1960s had much more spending money, usually in the form of allowances.

- Young people had their *own* cars in the late fifties—a new

258

phenomenon—complete with radios that allowed them to listen to their own music.

- Technological advances included transistor radios that were affordable and easily carried.

- Record companies realized the money that youth now had.

- Television focused a spotlight on southern California (especially its beaches) as paradise, which made the Beach Boy's songs even more contagious.

- The popularity of the never-aging Dick Clark and his "American Bandstand" TV show, which aired nationally for three decades, from 1957 to 1987, skyrocketed.

- Radio stations emerged with enormous wattage blanketing a major section of the U.S. (such as Oklahoma City's KOMA which could be heard nightly from Texas to the Canadian border), aiming for the youth audience.

PRINCIPLE OF LEADERSHIP BY TIMING # 7:
Being Too Early Is As Bad As Being Too Late

Had the Beach Boys written their songs in 1950, no one would have heard them. Had they written their primary works *after* the Beatles, no one would have cared. (In fact, that was one of the major struggles the Beach Boys later faced). But they wrote them from 1962 until 1964 (the year of the Beatles' "invasion" of America), producing 8 albums with 84 songs (63 of which were written by Brian Wilson). Timing is everything. And because of the phenomenal timing, the Beach Boys are still listened to.

THE BEATLES

As everyone knows, the Beatles took America by storm in 1964 and went on to become the biggest-selling group ever. Read the list of songs.

See if you can get all the way through without a tune going through your head: "I Want to Hold Your Hand," "A Hard Day's Night," "Yesterday," "Hey Jude," "Michelle," "I Saw Her Standing There," "And I Love Her," "Eight Days a Week," and "Let It Be."

If you made it through all of these without humming a tune, you were born before 1945, or you were born on another planet. The Beatles' music is seemingly all-pervasive. They have sold a staggering 1 billion records and tapes. They hold the record for #1 hits on the single charts in both Britain (17) and the U.S. (20). They had nearly three dozen platinum (1,000,000 in sales) albums and more than a dozen multi-platinum (more than 2,000,000 in sales) albums.[2] In addition, they have racked up a staggering 5 diamond (10,000,000 in sales) awards. Why? Timing. For starters, the Beatles represented a complete break with the past. Unlike the seemingly wholesome image of some southern California surfer types like the Beach Boys, out to have fun, the Beatles were brash, antiestablishment types. Their music had some light fun, but it also had some social sub-themes: politics, rebellion, and drugs.

The Beatles offered a break from the past in almost every way. No longer was the hair combed back like Elvis's. It was allowed to just hang forward. No longer were we confined to the same three basic chords of each key. The music was considerably less predictable. The Beatles' popularity arose at the same time as the Vietnam War protests. And their music played to a generation stunned by the assassination of President Kennedy.

What if Beatles-type music had been attempted in the 1940s? Someone probably *did* try. But we never heard of him. Watch the reruns of the Beatles appearing on *The Ed Sullivan Show* in 1964. Exciting? Well, somewhat. But a little passé now, wouldn't you agree? Why? Timing. Because timing is everything.

MADONNA

Elvis came and went. His intense popularity had subsided and risen again long before his premature death in August of 1977. The Beach Boys' popularity peaked and plummeted in a short time span, followed by a series of drug problems and emotional struggles. The Beatles morphed through numerous phases, broke up, did solo careers, and have had a reduced (but significant) impact through the years. But the musical "cat with nine lives" is most certainly Madonna (Madonna Louise Veronica Ciccone).

Many singers, leaders, athletes, politicians, and businesspersons have had staying power. But no one has had as many stages as the ever-emerging "stages" of Madonna, complete with cone bras, Marilyn-esque appearance, a "material girl" look (whatever that is), a ghetto cowgirl makeover, an Evita look-alike, complete with motherhood and a touch of yoga.

Her "song history," from 1983 to the present, contains many phases:

- "Like a Virgin"—rough and raunchy

- "Material Girl"—Marilyn Monroe-ish

- "Like a Prayer"—religious (or irreligious?) and overtly racial

- "Vogue"—cones, underwear as outerwear, antiestablishment

- "Human Nature," "Justify My Love"—explicit sex (both songs were banned from MTV)

- "Ray of Light," "Power of Goodbye"—embracing the Hindu religion; the Evita Peron look; pregnant

- "Music"—enjoying motherhood, somewhat calming down; pregnant again; ghetto cowgirl

---

PRINCIPLE OF LEADERSHIP BY TIMING # 8:
In a Rapidly Changing Culture, Every Leader, Institution, and Organization Must Reinvent Itself (Approximately Every Four Years)

What does Madonna have that we should want? Nothing! Except one thing. She understands timing. Her ability to adapt is stunning. Generally speaking, the older one gets, the harder it is to change. But not for Madonna. Remember, she is not a young woman anymore. At the time of this writing, she is turning forty-four! Yet the reinvention keeps occurring. Her sense of timing has kept her on top of the charts for years. By now, she should have been a has-been on the nostalgic circuit. But she isn't. She has continued to produce a constant conveyor belt of new followers.

As much as I don't like to admit it, she is an influencer. That makes her a leader. And she has maintained her leadership edge by her exceptional sense of timing—knowing what will come next and when it is time to change.

Every organization, business, school, and church can learn something from her: change when you need to. Most church leaders (including me) admittedly don't admire Madonna. But they could learn from her. Every church *must* change its methodology in order to stay true to its mission. And what is true in a church is as true in every other organization as well.

※

NAPOLEON BONAPARTE:
THE MISCALCULATION

It might seem strange to contrast Madonna, the contemporary singer, to one of the world's best-known leaders, Napoleon Bonaparte, from the nineteenth century. But bad decisions made in the final years of his life provide one of history's most glaring examples of a violation of the Law of Timing.

PRINCIPLE OF LEADERSHIP BY TIMING # 9:
When You Succeed, Don't Believe Your Own Press Releases—
It Will Destroy You

Consolidating power after the chaos of the French Revolution, Napoleon Bonaparte proclaimed himself emperor of France in 1800. Once secure at home, he set out to conquer Europe. And when Czar Alexander I displeased him, he determined to conquer Russia with a vast army that outnumbered Russia's defenders.

In the spring of 1812 Napoleon launched his invasion. For a full month, the French were hot on the trail of the Russians. Yet they occasionally met only token resistance.

Realizing that he needed to secure the territory already occupied,

Napoleon decided to pause. For fifteen days he fretted and stewed that he was unable to overcome the Russians.

PRINCIPLE OF LEADERSHIP BY TIMING # 10:
Seek Counsel—Even with Regard to Timing

His veteran generals urged patience, hunkering down for winter where they were. Rather than consider their wisdom, however, Napoleon attacked the Russians. Historian Philippe-Paul de Segur lamented that Napoleon confused "his impatience for the inspiration of genius!"[3] And that confusion would cost him dearly. The French marched to Smolensk, where the Russian General Barclay appeared ready to engage them. But Barclay was bluffing! After drawing up his battle lines, he retreated, leaving Smolensk ablaze. Entering the city, de Segur says, Napoleon "realized that here . . . the mirage of victory which lured him on, which he seemed so often on the point of grasping, had once more eluded him. He determined, however, to continue pursuing it."[4]

Finally, on September 5, the Russian army under General Kutuzov stood firmly at Borodino. The two armies, both then numbering around 120,000 men, prepared for action. The battle began early on September 7, and it was a mighty contest. The battle was something of a draw, but Napoleon lost heavily—40,000 men and 43 generals were killed or wounded. "The victory, so long and ardently sought, so dearly purchased, was incomplete."[5]

PRINCIPLE OF LEADERSHIP BY TIMING # 11:
There Is No Such Thing As Good Timing for a Bad Strategy

Distressed but not deflated, Napoleon marched to the outskirts of Moscow, again facing Kutuzov. But Kutuzov and his men and the Russian people left the city, and what's more, they set fire to it so that the conflagration drove the French outside Moscow's gates.

September slipped into October. Provisions grew scarce. Hostile

THE LAW OF TIMING

Russian units, especially the Cossacks, harassed the French army. Napoleon kept hoping Alexander would surrender, but he would agree only to an armistice.

The days grew colder. Many French soldiers had earlier discarded their heavy winter coats when the days were so insufferably hot. Their boots were worn out, their clothes threadbare. Then the Russians attacked, and Napoleon ordered a counterattack at Kaluga.

PRINCIPLE OF LEADERSHIP BY TIMING # 12:
The Leader Who Fails to Understand Timing
Will Always Be at the Mercy of the Leader
Who Does Understand Timing

The Russians lost heavily, but so did the French. The Russians easily replenished their ranks. The French could not. Napoleon had been outwitted, and he had to face the truth. He said, "The time has come now for us to turn all our thoughts to saving the remains of the army."[6] The withdrawal from Russia began.

Snow and piercing wind assaulted the French. The survivors struggled on, only to be caught by the Russians at Krasnoye, where a fierce (if minor) battle ensued. Back through Smolensk, to the banks of the Dnieper River. It was freezingly cold but not yet solid enough to support the retreating troops. Casualties and chaos!

The Russian Kutuzov and his 80,000 men paused at the river. Only remnants of Napoleon's army managed to get across. So much for the vaunted Grand Army! On December 13, 1812, what little was left reached the Russian frontier. Rarely has such a large, well-equipped fighting force been so utterly annihilated.

PRINCIPLE OF LEADERSHIP BY TIMING # 13:
Bad Timing Costs the Leader Credibility

Not long after his Russian disaster Napoleon would be sent into exile from his country. He finally returned in triumph again, only to be defeated at Waterloo in 1815. The Russian campaign of 1812 was his undoing. And he failed mainly because of his lack of a sense of proper timing. He had seriously underestimated and miscalculated.

🍋

LEADERSHIP:
THE DIFFERENCE BETWEEN CHRONOS AND KAIROS

There is nothing so powerful as an idea whose time has come. One of the most powerful demonstrations of that concept occurs in a place most leaders might not think to look: the account of the birth of Jesus Christ.

Galatians, the ninth book located in the New Testament portion of the Bible, records an interesting phrase: "When the fullness of the time came, God sent forth His Son" (4:4 NASB). In another part of the New Testament is a phrase referring to the life of Christ: "The time is fulfilled" (Mark 1:15 NASB). Both places use the Greek word *kairos*. Although a bit difficult to translate, it essentially means "time." But not just any "time." It means "when everything has come together," "when everything fits," or "when the time is just right."

There is another word for "time" in the Greek language. It is *chronos*. But *kairos* is not the same as *chronos*. Whereas *kairos* refers to the "fulfillment" of things, *chronos* refers to tick-tock time, as in "What time is it?" as you look at your wristwatch.

PRINCIPLE OF LEADERSHIP BY TIMING # 14:
Leaders Understand More Than the Puzzle;
They Know How and When the Pieces Fit Together

Many historians have pondered why it is that one person—Jesus—could have had so much impact so quickly. Although Christianity was persecuted through much of the Roman Empire initially, it became the *officially* established religion of the entire Roman Empire by A.D. 380. How was that possible? The answer (in addition to God's providence) is timing!

Several things came together perfectly—shall we say *kairotically*—at

265

the time of Christ's birth, which helped the message of Christianity spread rapidly:

- The Roman government created a sense of "oneness."

- The peace of Rome, and its phenomenal road system, allowed freedom of movement.

- Many Roman soldiers embraced Christianity and spread it throughout the entire empire.

- Greek was a universal language spoken by almost everyone, thus enhancing communication.

- Greek philosophy had effectively destroyed the pagan religions.

- Greek philosophy proved to be empty to the population, thus creating a void for Christianity to fill.

- The Jewish faith, the "cradle" in which Christianity was born, assumed the existence of God, which, in turn, helped the Christian message to spread faster.

- The Jewish faith taught that a Messiah would come someday, thus creating an expectancy for Christ.

- The high standards of the Jewish Ten Commandments paved the way for the moral teachings of Christ.

All of these things worked together to cause the message of Christianity to explode across the known world. These conditions had not converged until the time of Christ.

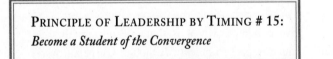

PRINCIPLE OF LEADERSHIP BY TIMING # 15:
Become a Student of the Convergence

Understand not just *chronos*, but *kairos*. Understand that when there is "a fullness of time," when things are right, when every piece of the puzzle fits, that is *kairotic* leadership. And it is winning leadership because the leader understands the *when* as much as he understands the *what* or *where*.

20

THE LAW OF
EXPLOSIVE GROWTH

To Add Growth, Lead Followers—
To Multiply, Lead Leaders

PRINCIPLES OF LEADERSHIP OF EXPLOSIVE GROWTH

Robert Coleman could have been simply another seminary professor with four academic degrees. Little did he know that his Ph.D. studies at the University of Iowa would develop into one of the premier leadership development books that would be translated into nearly one hundred languages and sell almost five million copies. Nor could he have imagined that it would become the "manifesto" for training Christian workers around the globe.

⚖

ROBERT COLEMAN:
THE INFLUENTIAL LEADERSHIP DEVELOPMENT BOOK

Written in 1963, *The Master Plan of Evangelism* has been hailed as one of the most significant books in recent times. Billy Graham, in the foreword, stated that "few books have had as great an impact on the cause of world evangelization in our generation as Robert Coleman's *The Master Plan of Evangelism.*"

What is the genius of that book? Why is it read as much today as it was in the mid-1960s when it was first released? Because it teaches us how to train leaders. Every pastor, every school official, every business-

268

man or woman, every political leader—every person in leadership—can learn much from this groundbreaking work.

PRINCIPLE OF LEADERSHIP OF EXPLOSIVE GROWTH # 1:
Leaders Understand the Steps for Producing Another Leader

Robert Coleman, one of my professors in the 1970s at Asbury Theological Seminary and later a professor at Trinity International University's graduate school, became globally known because of his analysis of the method by which Jesus trained the twelve disciples. According to Coleman, Jesus changed the world by establishing a principle of discipling people in such a way that they would disciple others, who would, in turn, disciple others. He surmised that Jesus followed an eight-pronged strategy:

1. selection
2. association
3. consecration
4. impartation
5. demonstration
6. delegation
7. supervision
8. reproduction

PRINCIPLE OF LEADERSHIP OF EXPLOSIVE GROWTH # 2:
*Leadership Development Is Less a Commitment to a Program
As It Is a Commitment to a Person or Persons*

Each of these had a specific purpose that would ultimately produce a disciple or, in our case here, a leader:

1. In *selection*, the leader finds persons who are really willing to grow and concentrates most of his time on them, without totally neglecting others who are not selected for potential leadership.

2. During the *association* phase, the leader spends a great amount of time forming deep relationships with those he has selected and selects some (even among this group) who will form the core into whom he will invest the most.

3. The *consecration* stage is a time when the expectations are more clearly shared; the standard is racheted up; some fall away; and those left are willing to pay the price.

4. *Impartation* is the stage in which the leader demonstrates a life of sacrifice, love, and passion; the leader releases power to the followers to do what they are charged to do.

5. The *demonstration* period is a time in which the leader leads by "doing," providing the followers with on-the-job training; the followers have the joy of seeing the leader model what they are about to become; the relationship foundation allows for the teaching to be done naturally and informally, yet constantly, as opposed to a sterile classroom experience. This is the "watch me do it" stage.

6. *Delegation* means the followers now do what they were shown *without* the leader present to assist them; they work in teams of two or more, attempting to emulate the leader. There will be many bumps and bruises at first, but that is an important part of the learning experience. This is the "I'll watch you do it" stage.

7. *Supervision* is the season in which the leader watches them, instructs them, and brings gentle but needed correction; this is an exciting phase when the follower is in the full stage of development. This is the "go do it and come back and report" stage.

8. In the *reproduction* phase, we will no longer refer to them as "followers"; for our purposes, they are now "leaders" in their own right; the original leader has now multiplied himself

several times over and enjoys great satisfaction. This is the "go and train others, just as I trained you, using these eight steps, beginning by selection" stage.

PRINCIPLE OF LEADERSHIP OF EXPLOSIVE GROWTH # 3:
The Real Test of a Leader's Capacity to Reproduce Himself Occurs After the Leader Is Gone

---

According to Coleman, this was the strategy by which Jesus trained His original twelve followers into becoming the world-changers that they became. Ten of them were so devoted to Jesus that they, according to tradition, were willing to die for Him, and they were martyred.

Peter, it is said, was crucified because of his commitment to Christ. When they proceeded to kill him, he insisted that they hang him upside down (even more excruciating) as he said he was not worthy to die the same way Jesus had! John was one who did not die a martyr's death—miraculously surviving being boiled alive in a huge container of oil! Only Judas proved to be a disappointment. That defection should be an encouragement to some of you when someone you have invested yourself in does not continue in what you taught him.

The essence of Coleman's thesis is the same as that in John Maxwell's twentieth chapter in *The 21 Irrefutable Laws of Leadership:* if you only lead followers, you will add; if you raise up leaders, you multiply.

PRINCIPLE OF LEADERSHIP OF EXPLOSIVE GROWTH # 4:
You Will Have More Impact If You Develop Disciples Than If You Entertain Crowds

---

Virtually every time someone discusses Coleman's thesis, he or she relates an oft-used illustration that demonstrates the power of multiplication:

- If I were to lead one person to Christ this year and disciple him for a year, there would be two of us;

- then the next year the two of us would disciple one person each, making a total of four;

- then the third year the four of us would disciple one person each, making a total of eight.

As you can see, by working with only one person each year, the total number would double each year.

At this point in the illustration, a key question is asked: "How long would it take to disciple the earth's entire population of six billion?" One might think that such a slow method would take many years, perhaps one hundred or one thousand. Not so! It would take approximately thirty-three years! That is the power of multiplication, even if you raise up only one leader per year. Lead followers and you will add; lead leaders and you will multiply.

⚜

GENGHIS KHAN'S EXPLOSIVE EMPIRE

The Law of Explosive Growth works, whether you are Jesus Christ taking the world by love or whether you are a leader determined to take the world by force. There are many who have taken the world by force, by the sword: Alexander, Muhammad, Genghis Khan, Napoleon, and Hitler, to name a few. But the Law of Explosive Growth—that is, focusing on training up leaders—is a constant. Let's look at one of these figures, Genghis Khan (ca. 1161–1227).

General Douglas MacArthur of World War II fame felt that if the only military reading a soldier had was that of Genghis Khan, he would still have "a mine of untold wealth from which to extract nuggets of knowledge useful in molding an army."[1] Why would MacArthur, a twentieth-century American, so highly praise a thirteenth-century Mongolian warrior? Part of the answer is found in Khan's ability to focus on leading strong leaders.

Genghis Khan's father, a tribal chieftain, was killed when Genghis was thirteen. Pursued by his enemies, young Temujin (another name for

Genghis Khan) evaded capture, won to himself his father's followers, and by the age of twenty was a chieftain. His prowess on a horse and in battle had been fully proved.

During the next thirty years, he brought together an alliance of Mongolia's thirty-one nomadic tribes, a total of two million people, mixing brutality against his enemies and inordinate generosity to his supporters. He had also put together a mighty military machine. Though he never had more than 200,000 soldiers, during the next sixteen years his Mongolians exploded under his guidance and conquered one of the largest empires recorded in history.

At an important gathering in 1206, at a great assembly of his people, he was proclaimed "Ssutu-Bogdo" (the God-sent). Here Temujin was renamed Genghis Khan, which roughly translated means "limitless strength." He shrewdly appealed to their pride and declared, "This race . . . is the most sublime people in the world . . . And it is my will that henceforward it shall bear the name of Koko-Mongols—the Heavenly-Blue Mongols."[2]

Khan explained that "heaven has appointed me to rule all the nations," the reason being that before he ruled, there was complete chaos. He described the lack of order:

> Children do not hearken to the words of their fathers, younger brother disobeyed elder brothers, the husband had no confidence in his wife, and the wife did not heed her husband's commands. Inferiors did not obey superiors, and superiors did not fulfill their duties to inferiors; the rich did not support the rulers, and there was no content anywhere. The race was without order and without understanding; that was why, on all hands, there were malcontents, liars, thieves, rebels, and robbers.[3]

But when Khan came to rule, "all came under his command and he will rule them by fixed laws that rest and happiness shall prevail in the world."[4] Now there was a man with a plan!

Genghis Khan planned to establish a realm, under the rule of law, that would endure for a thousand years if his successors followed his precepts. In order to accomplish that he designated those who would help him lead. He then appointed strategic officials, such as judges, to serve him, showing an almost unerring appraisal of character and ability.

His leadership skills proved very adequate in selecting and placing key persons in roles of authority. He succeeded in much he proposed. In fact, Michael Prawdin makes the stunning claim that under Khan's rule, "murder, robbery with violence, theft, and adultery disappeared from among the Mongols, and their conception of honour rose so high that no one justly accused ever denied the deed, while many came voluntarily to the judge acknowledging their offenses and demanding punishment."[5]

PRINCIPLE OF LEADERSHIP OF EXPLOSIVE GROWTH # 5:
When Developing Leaders, Take No Shortcuts

Genghis Khan then organized the kingdom, putting together an efficient communications network and administration. And, above all, he marshaled an army. And what an army! Once again his ability to select quality leaders proved highly successful. He appointed a general staff and began a war college to raise up leaders for his officers' corps.

PRINCIPLE OF LEADERSHIP OF EXPLOSIVE GROWTH # 6:
Successful Leadership Development Begins with Careful Selection of Those Being Developed

---

Khan knew precisely what he looked for in leaders and how to organize them. He chose 10,000 for his personal guard. "These men," he said, "my body-guard, who will be in close contact with me, must be tall, strong, and adroit."[6] Under them were the soldiers, the mounted warriors (organized in units of 10, 100, 1,000, and 10,000) with whom Genghis Khan would ride to rule his world.

> **PRINCIPLE OF LEADERSHIP OF EXPLOSIVE GROWTH # 7:**
> *Leadership Development Replicates the Leader's Strengths*
> *(and Weaknesses)*

Khan produced warriors as tough as he was! A Mongol on a horse was a marvelous fighter. The horses, toughened on the windswept steppes, seemed tireless. The horsemen, virtually reared riding and fighting, could sleep in their saddles and proved powerful in battle.

No one could withstand them. Edwin Muller stated that "the Mongol attack won by superiority in weapons, speed in bringing those weapons into contact with the enemy, and then by rapidity and accuracy of fire. The armies of China, the dashing warriors of Islam, the knights and men-at-arms of Christendom, all broke before the Mongol hail of arrows."[7]

> **PRINCIPLE OF LEADERSHIP OF EXPLOSIVE GROWTH # 8:**
> *Well-Trained Leaders Know Precisely What the Agenda*
> *Is and How to Accomplish It*

Now that Genghis Khan had completed the training, he laid out the strategy they would follow. First he marched east and attacked China. The Mongols pierced the Great Wall, hardly pausing, and battled their way, overcoming reverses and difficulties, across northern China to capture Yenking (now Beijing) in 1215.

The Chinese emperor fled for his life, and Genghis Khan replaced him, but he drew into his service a number of talented Chinese who kept his kingdom together there. He also recruited thousands of Chinese army engineers and technicians who proved invaluable in coming days.

Returning home to Mongolia, Genghis then looked to the west, where Muslim kingdoms awaited. The Khorezmian Empire, uniting central Asia and Persia, tragically erred by executing some of Genghis Khan's ambassadors in 1218. A Mongol chronicler noted: "With this command, the Shah signed his own death warrant. Each drop of the blood he then shed was paid for by floods of his subjects' life-blood. Each hair of the victims' heads was paid for by a thousand heads."[8]

The Mongols attacked and conquered in two years. He and his men occupied and plundered the beautiful capital of Samarkand, sending the shah packing south, where he died on an island in the Caspian Sea, a tragic end for one of the mightiest men of his day.

There was terror, too, in the Mongol conquest of the Khorezmian Empire. In the end the empire simply disappeared. Never before had Genghis Khan ordered such sheer destruction of an enemy. Resistance resulted in annihilation. In a city that dared oppose him, he butchered 500,000 civilians.

PRINCIPLE OF LEADERSHIP OF EXPLOSIVE GROWTH # 9:
Leaders Who Equip Leaders Have Considerably More Influence Than Those Who Simply Gather Followers

---

Genghis Khan died at the age of sixty-six, in 1227. In less than two decades, he had imposed his will upon a vast land. "From the Sea of Japan to the Caspian," says Prawdin, "from Korea to the Caucasus, Jenghiz Khan's word was law."[9]

PRINCIPLE OF LEADERSHIP OF EXPLOSIVE GROWTH # 10:
*Leaders Who Train Other Potential Leaders
Produce a Culture of Accomplishment*

His descendants kept expanding the empire, occupying most of Russia and pushing into Eastern Europe. Under Kublai Khan, the grandson of Genghis, the Mongols reached the apex of their expansion. But it was all the result of following Genghis Khan's prescriptions.

Explosive expansion under Genghis Khan occurred for several reasons. First, he had incredible energy, even into old age. He never relaxed, never retired or indulged himself. Second, he clearly knew what he wanted to do, and he did precisely that. Third, he understood the absolute importance of organization, and he not only established it, but he appointed the finest people to run it. Fourth, he insisted on precise training for his leaders and absolute discipline.

Genghis Khan experienced the Law of Explosive Growth the same way that every other person has: *selecting leaders of leaders, who, in turn, lead others.* Consequently, he multiplied his impact many times over.

ᘔ᙭

DERRIC JOHNSON

Derric Johnson was one of the most impactful pastors I have ever known. I was a college freshman when his influence on me began. In time, he became the music consultant for Disney World in Orlando, where he worked for 25 years. In addition, he was in demand as a speaker / music arranger all over America.

Derric was a regular "pied piper." Everyone wanted to follow him. He could easily have focused on gathering a crowd. But he didn't. He focused on making leaders. His goal? To inspire 1,000 college students to want to go into fulltime Christian ministry—pastors, associate pastors, missionaries, youth workers, musicians, etc. I suspect he, now in his seventies, is close to his goal.

How do I know this story? Because I am one of "Derric's thousand." Thank you, Derric. Thank you for not merely adding followers, which you could easily have done. Thank you for multiplying yourself by raising up young leaders. All one thousand (or however many there are now) of us say "thank you."

But that's Derric. What about you? Add—by gathering a crowd? Or multiply—by raising up leaders? It's your call.

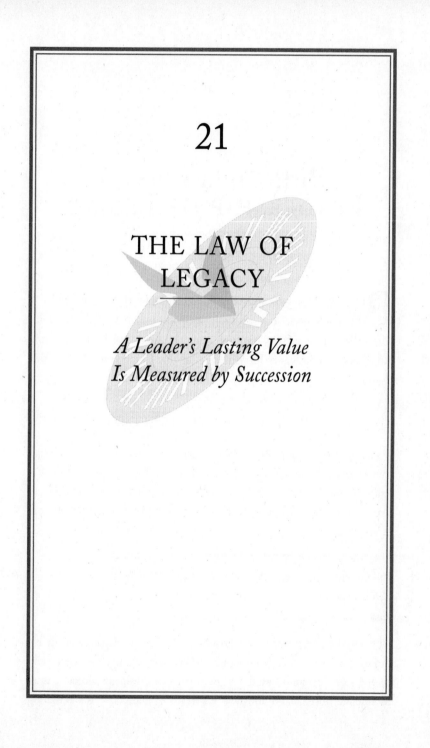

21

THE LAW OF
LEGACY

*A Leader's Lasting Value
Is Measured by Succession*

PRINCIPLES FOR A
LEADERSHIP OF LEGACY

Previously I have reminded you that I am uniquely qualified to write this book because I am the only person to have followed John Maxwell in a leadership position since the time that he has become America's leading leadership expert. And that is especially true of this chapter.

THE SUCCESS OF THE SUCCESSOR

If you have read John's *21 Irrefutable Laws of Leadership,* you may recall that he ends the final chapter—the one on the Law of Legacy—with a story about the transfer of leadership from John to me at Skyline Wesleyan Church. You read it from his perspective. Let me tell you my perspective.

PRINCIPLE FOR A LEADERSHIP OF LEGACY # 1:
Affirm Your Successor—Publicly and Privately

The outgoing pastor of a church can have enormous impact—positively or negatively—on the incoming pastor. Just one negative comment, said to the right person(s) at the right time, can create an almost insurmountable obstacle for the new leader to overcome. If the outgoing leader stays visible or in any way tries to subtly "direct" things, the new leader has his hands effectively tied behind his back.

> ## PRINCIPLE FOR A LEADERSHIP OF LEGACY # 2:
> *You Can Undercut Your Successor by What You Say*
> *Or by a Telling Silence*

But John Maxwell, who was at Skyline Church fourteen years, believes that you don't succeed unless you have a successor. And he lived that out in 1995 when he left Skyline Church and I came aboard. Allow me to give you just one example. With the arrival of any new leader there are always those who understandably prefer the previous leader. John was still living here in San Diego at the time (he later moved INJOY to Atlanta) and was still attending the church on Sundays when he wasn't traveling. When someone would come to John with some complaint regarding me, he would say, "Now, before you tell me what you want to talk to me about, you need to know one thing: Jim is *my* pastor, and whatever he says, I support." Then he would pause intentionally, letting that soak in. He would continue, "*Now*, what do you want to talk about?" The person would change the subject. John had made it clear: I will help my successor succeed by supporting him. And he did!

> ## PRINCIPLE FOR A LEADERSHIP OF LEGACY # 3:
> *The Real Mark of Leadership Security Is Wanting Your Successor*
> *to Achieve Beyond Your Accomplishments*

In addition to John, Orval Butcher, the founding pastor who had led Skyline Wesleyan Church for twenty-seven years (1954-1981), was (and still is) attending the church. (In Skyline's forty-eight-year history, it has had only three senior pastors.) If either one of them had uttered one negative comment about me, it could have made my job so much more difficult. But they did not. Instead, they spoke positively about me and still do! Every single time I am with Orval Butcher (now eighty-four years of age) or John Maxwell, they repeatedly affirm me. I could not have made it without their support. They have helped me succeed. They seem to enjoy my successes as much as if those successes are their own. And in a very real way, my successes are their successes. They set me up to succeed.

PRINCIPLE FOR A LEADERSHIP OF LEGACY # 4:
If Your Successor Fails, It Might Be Because of You;
And If That Is the Case, That Failure Is Your Failure

Leaders, I hope you hear what I am saying. There is nothing more important in this whole chapter than the preceding paragraph. You have in your hand the ability to help your successor succeed or fail. I have seen it in businesses, schools, and churches—both positively and negatively. It is a terrible sight to watch the outgoing leader undermine the incoming leader. If you, as a leader, have a tendency to do that, it comes out of your own insecurities and is something you need to conquer immediately. Just think how gratifying it would be for you to experience the joy of seeing *your* successor someday write about you the way I have just written about Orval Butcher and John Maxwell. Learn from them. Emulate them. You will be glad you did. And your successor, to quote a section of Proverbs from the Old Testament, will "arise and call [you] blessed" (31:28).

⚜

YOUR LEGACY LIVES WHEN YOU ARE NO LONGER ALIVE

One northeastern family lineage offers a most fascinating example of the Law of Legacy:

- Solomon Stoddard was a brilliant, highly successful pastor at Northampton, Massachusetts, in one church from 1672 until his death in 1729; he was the author of the Halfway Covenant and the leader of five spiritual "harvests," as he called them.

- His grandson, Jonathan Edwards, succeeded him as pastor. Edwards is likely the greatest philosopher-theologian this nation has ever produced. In 1758, he became the president of Princeton University.

- Edwards's grandson, Timothy Dwight, served as Yale University's eighth president, from 1795 to 1817. He learned the entire alphabet in one lesson and was reading the Bible by the time he was four. He entered Yale at age thirteen and graduated at age seventeen.

- Dwight's grandson, also named Timothy Dwight (sometimes called Timothy Dwight, "the Younger"), became the president of Yale in 1886 and was respectfully called the "father of the university."

These four generations of grandfather-to-grandson lineage cover well over two hundred years of spectacular service. But there is more.

PRINCIPLE FOR A LEADERSHIP OF LEGACY # 5:
How You Live, Talk, Think, and Act Has an Impact on Future Generations Long After You Are Gone

---

Princeton Theological Seminary, which I attended in the 1970's, has a rich theological heritage. One of the most famous professors in its history was Benjamin B. Warfield, who taught there from 1887 to 1921. According to a widely circulated report, he did an analysis of 1,394 descendants of Jonathan Edwards and discovered that there were

- 13 college presidents

- 65 college professors

- 30 judges

- 100 lawyers

- 60 physicians

- 75 army and navy officers

- 100 pastors

- 60 authors of prominence

- 3 United States senators

- 80 public servants in various capacities

Warfield also traced 1,200 descendants of Max Jukes, an atheist living at the same time as Jonathan Edwards. He discovered that 310 died as paupers; 150 were criminals (including 7 murderers); more than 100 were alcoholics; and half of the female descendants ended up as prostitutes. At the time this study was done, 540 of Jukes's descendants had cost the state $1.25 million.[1]

Jonathan Edwards's spectacular influence branches out in many other directions as well. He profoundly influenced the young evangelist George Whitefield in the mid-1700s; Whitefield went on to become the moving force in the First Great Awakening in America and the Evangelical Awakening in England in the years following 1737.

PRINCIPLE FOR A LEADERSHIP OF LEGACY # 6:
Your Legacy Will Always Be the Replication of Who You Are

As I mentioned, Timothy Dwight, grandson of Jonathan Edwards, was a president of Yale. One of his students was Lyman Beecher, considered to be the "father of more brains than anyone in America." Here is another amazing family lineage:

- Lyman became president of Lane Seminary in Ohio.

- His daughter Harriet Beecher Stowe wrote the landmark book *Uncle Tom's Cabin* (referred to in an earlier chapter).

- His daughter Catharine founded the Western Female Institute, an antecedent institution to Miami University in Oxford, Ohio.

- His son Henry Ward Beecher became one of the most influential thinkers/speakers in the country, serving as the preacher at Brooklyn's Plymouth Church.

- His son Edward became the first president of Illinois College in 1830.

- His daughter Isabella Beecher Hooker was heavily involved in the right-to-vote cause for women, organizing the first conventions of their kind in Connecticut and Washington, D.C.[2]

Leaders, such as Edwards, Dwight, and Beecher, live the Law of Legacy: a leader's lasting value is measured by succession. Without succession, there is no success.

⚜

CHARLEMAGNE'S SUCCESSORS

Charlemagne was the greatest king of the early Middle Ages. Few figures in human history accomplished as much in their lifetimes. And few persons provide a more glaring example of the failure to understand the Law of Legacy as Charlemagne.

Following the collapse of the Roman Empire, the kingdom of the Franks (German-speaking tribes in present-day France and Germany) emerged under King Clovis as one of the strongest new "nations." When Clovis's successors weakened, some "mayors of the palace" assumed control. One of them was Charles Martel, grandfather of Charlemagne. Martel successfully repelled the Muslim advance at the Battle of Tours in A.D. 732, which saved Europe from Islamic control. In 752, Pepin III, father of Charlemagne, was crowned king.

When Pepin died in 768, his two sons divided the kingdom, but after the death of Carloman in 771, Charles became the sole king of France. Charles (or Charlemagne) was twenty-nine years old, and he set out to consolidate and enlarge his kingdom. Ultimately, he brought all of

Europe, from the north of Spain to Hungary, including the northern half of Italy, under his control. He christianized Bavaria and Saxony, and protected Italy and northern Spain from Muslim attacks.

Though impressive as a warrior, he seemed more interested in effective administration. Charlemagne held assemblies, issued edicts, and made decisions. He dealt with agriculture, education, and religion. Through it all he upheld justice and cared for the people's needs. And he hungered for knowledge and orchestrated an intellectual awakening, known as the Carolingian Renaissance.

On Christmas Day in the year 800, something very significant happened. Charlemagne had come to Rome to rescue the pope from his foes. He knelt in prayer before St. Peter's altar, and Pope Leo III placed a jeweled crown upon his head. Charlemagne had become emperor of Rome (actually the Holy Roman Empire), something unknown in that city since 476, the date of the fall of Rome!

PRINCIPLE FOR A LEADERSHIP OF LEGACY # 7:
Accomplishment Without Succession Is Futile

Charlemagne spent his last decade supervising his realm, assisting the church in its endeavors, making sure his political and educational reforms were secure. At his death in 814, he had achieved what only a handful of men can rival. But there was one fatal flaw in the foundation of this great movement: failure to grasp the principles by which a legacy is passed on.

His sole surviving son, Louis, aged thirty-six, succeeded him. Those who knew Louis praised his personal goodness, his liberality, his refinement. He also was, Will Durant says, "modest, gentle, and gracious."[3] He insisted on high moral standards in the palace and the church. Durant continues, "Wherever he found injustice or exploitation he tried to stop it, and to right what wrong had been done."[4] But no sooner did Louis become king than he began to divest himself of his power! In 817 he publicly announced (and indirectly anointed) as his successors his three sons, Lothair, Pepin (who preceded his father in death), and Louis (also called Ludwig).

In 818 he (recently widowed) married Judith, "apparently chosen by the emperor in the ninth-century equivalent of the modern beauty contest," Stewart C. Easton says.[5] She gave him another son, Charles the Bald, who grew up and began to push (with his doting father's support) for *his* claims to the throne! Over the next twenty years an unending series of crises, civil wars, and power struggles beset King Louis.

PRINCIPLE FOR A LEADERSHIP OF LEGACY # 8:
He Who Cannot Control His Home Cannot Control the World

Charles' three oldest sons defeated him in battle in 833 and insisted he abdicate the throne and do public penance. Eventually, the people came to Louis's side, and he regained his throne. True to his nature, he forgave his offspring. Yet after going to battle once again (fighting son Louis this time) to preserve his realm, King Louis became sick and died in 840. Louis had inherited one of the largest and inwardly peaceful empires ever delivered into a man's hands. But Louis left it in chaos.

As one might expect, Louis's sons were not interested in their father's wishes. They fought each other to a stalemate before dividing Charlemagne's empire into three parts in A.D. 843. The disharmony and fragmentation proved predictably fatal, and by 888 the empire had vanished.

During the ninth century Viking expeditions vented their fury, sacking French cities such as Rouen, Nantes, and even Paris. At the very time a strong leader like Charlemagne was needed, his son and grandsons failed at their most important assignment: protecting the homeland!

Listen to the tragic description that came from one church council in 909: "The cities are depopulated, the monasteries ruined and burned, the country reduced to solitude . . . Men devour one another like the fishes in the sea."[6] Such results when men occupying positions of power fail to ensure a legacy of strong, good leadership.

CONSTANTINE AND HIS MOTHER, HELENA

Constantine is the most significant emperor of the first few centuries after Christ, and his legacy lasted for more than a millennium. He (b. ca. A.D. 272) is rightly called "the Great," for he altered the course of history. By tolerating and endorsing Christianity, he charted the course of European Christianity. He claimed control of the western half of the Roman Empire in A.D. 306. Constantine followed his deceased father, Constantius I, who succeeded the dreaded Emperor Diocletian, one of the most savage persecutors of Christians.

Young Constantine proved himself an able soldier, serving alongside his father, who died in Britain. Loyal soldiers promptly declared young Constantine "Augustus," and he began consolidating his power in Britain and France.

But Constantine had a rival, his tyrannical brother-in-law Maxentius. Constantine wisely garnered the support of the Senate in Rome, leading to a struggle for the imperial throne. Marshaling his troops, he marched on Rome, defeating Maxentius at the Battle of Milvian Bridge in 312.

What occurred the evening before the skirmish altered history! That night Constantine had a dream (a burning cross emblazoned with the Greek words *en toutoi nika*—"in this sign conquer"). The next morning he heard a voice telling him to brand his soldiers' shields with the letter *X*, with a vertical line through it curled at the top like a shepherd's staff, symbolizing Christ. Though he apparently knew little about Christ, this motto now defined him: *Hoc Vinces*—"in this sign you will be victor."

Successful in battle, Constantine thenceforth sought to honor the "God of the Christians" who had granted him the victory. Eusebius, who knew him well, wrote a *Life of Constantine* twenty years after the event and said that the emperor and his soldiers saw a cross in the sky in broad daylight—and this was confirmed by the emperor himself, on oath.

Whatever happened in 312, it totally transformed Constantine's life. Entering Rome, he granted mercy to Maxentius's followers. When the city erected a statue of him, he insisted it have a cross in his hands. The great triumphal arch, still standing near the Colosseum in Rome, credits his victory to a "divinity." He refused to participate in pagan rites, customary for preceding emperors. He also ordered, with the Edict of Milan in 313, that Christians (as well as devotees of other faiths) be allowed to freely worship. Persecution of Christians ceased throughout the empire. No longer would Rome execute believers.

It was an amazing moment for all Christian believers—many had been maimed and tortured over the years, and others had lost their lives. What a happy day! Christians were now safe. Even the emperor had embraced their beliefs. What an amazing turnaround!

Triumphant in the West, Constantine soon moved eastward. In 324 he united the entirety of the empire. To rule the vast region more effectively, he moved his capital from Rome to a new city, Constantinople (now Istanbul, Turkey), in 330.

> PRINCIPLE FOR A LEADERSHIP OF LEGACY # 9:
> *Everyone Leaves Some Legacy, Either a Good One or a Bad One.*
> *Either Way You Will Have a Legacy*

The emperor proved to be a true friend to the spread of Christianity. Soon Constantine began to subsidize Christian churches, providing for the copying of Bibles and construction of sanctuaries, appropriating funds to care for the poor, extending legal protection to women, slaves, and children. He decreed Sunday to be an official holiday, prohibiting public or commercial business. He was the first emperor to forbid the stealing of young girls, many of whom were confined to brothels.

In the words of Warren H. Carroll, "During the years 315–321 he issued laws prohibiting the torture and killing of slaves by their masters; safeguarding tenants from unjust treatment by their landlords; safeguarding children from major physical abuse by their parents; and protecting convict prisoners from cruel treatment, including abolition of the practice of branding them on the face."[7]

This is not to say he became an exemplary Christian, for in both his public and his private life he all too frequently acted brutally. He was, first and last, the emperor! And he shrewdly recognized how he could profit from enlisting the growing numbers of Christians in his cause.

PRINCIPLE FOR A LEADERSHIP OF LEGACY # 10:
If Your Private Life Doesn't Measure Up to Your Public Image,
Don't Lower Your Public Image Down to the Level of
Your Private Life; Raise Your Private Life Up to the Level
of Your Public Image

Yet Constantine prayed daily, shutting himself up in a secluded place. He provided his sons with a Christian education. He delighted in discussing religion with Christian bishops, and he called the first ecumenical council of the church, which met at Nicaea in 325. That council crafted the enormously important creed that stands at the heart of "orthodox" faith. While many readers may not be familiar with the Council of Nicaea— now Iznik, Turkey—Christians are indebted to it for the understanding of the nature of Christ and an understanding of the Trinity.

PRINCIPLE FOR A LEADERSHIP OF LEGACY # 11:
If You Want Something to Last,
Build It on a Good Foundation

The system Constantine established and headquartered in Constantinople developed into what was called the Byzantine civilization. The Byzantine Empire refers to the eastern half of the Roman Empire, which lasted another one thousand years after Rome fell in the 400s. Instead of the Roman Catholic Church, this portion of Christianity consisted of Eastern Orthodox Christianity, which had divided from Rome in 1054. This empire continued until overrun by Muslims in 1453. Basically, Constantine established a very firm foundation, which lasted an extremely long time!

> **PRINCIPLE FOR A LEADERSHIP OF LEGACY # 12:**
> *To Have an Enduring Legacy, Partner with God,*
> *and Get with His Agenda*

One writer stated that Constantine

> was a masterly general, a remarkable administrator, a superlative states-
> man . . . His Christianity, beginning as policy, appears to have gradu-
> ated into sincere conviction. He became the most persistent preacher
> in his realm, persecuted heretics faithfully, and took God into partner-
> ship at every step . . . By his aid Christianity became a state as well as
> a church, and the mold, for fourteen centuries, of European life and
> thought. Perhaps . . . the grateful Church was right in naming him the
> greatest of the emperors.[8]

Constantine's mother, Helena, also left a lasting legacy. She was born a
commoner, a barmaid (or an innkeeper), who may have been no more than
Constantius's legal concubine. She apparently became a Christian after
Constantine's triumph in 312. However humble her origins, Constantine
deeply revered her and gave her the affirming title of Augusta.

> **PRINCIPLE FOR A LEADERSHIP OF LEGACY # 13:**
> *Give*

Her devout Christianity stood revealed in her commitment to supporting the church. She distributed large offerings to poor and destitute
people. She gave generously to church building projects.

> **PRINCIPLE FOR A LEADERSHIP OF LEGACY # 14:**
> *Look for Ways to Bless Those Who Will Come After You*

If you tour Israel, you will hear her name often. Many of today's most important Christian sites were first identified by her. Anyone touring the Holy Land today immediately senses the spectacular legacy she left behind. Following her son's success in unifying the empire, she traveled to Palestine and sought to glorify God by discovering and restoring sacred sites. Without training, Helena became something of an archaeologist, unearthing in 326 (according to tradition) the true cross upon which Jesus was crucified. She built a church in Bethlehem, covering the Grotto (cave) of the Nativity. The Church of the Nativity, the site of countless pilgrimages, is one of the oldest churches in the world—but tragically has recently become the epicenter of Muslim extremism.

Helena built another church on Mount Calvary, outside the walls of Old Jerusalem—the Church of the Holy Sepulchre. In Egypt she oversaw the construction of a church in Fostat, where the holy family spent time when Jesus was a child.

PRINCIPLE FOR A LEADERSHIP OF LEGACY # 15:
If You Want to Leave a Good Legacy, Live in Humility and Purity, and Pray for Strength and Wisdom

---

More important, she was a woman of deep faith, modest, never condescending, as she could have been, for she was the mother of the emperor. She mingled with worshipers at the church that she faithfully attended. She spoke openly of her love for God. And her conduct matched her words.

The son was an emperor who fused church and state, establishing Christianity in the Roman Empire, which ultimately divided into Byzantium and Europe. The mother was a godly woman, whose influence lingers in Holy Land shrines as well as the catalog of saints.

THE GLOBAL LEGACY

It still amazes me. There was a man who lived and died many years ago—yet one-third of the earth's population still talks about Him. Why? Why would two billion of the earth's inhabitants identify with Jesus, a person who lived more than two millennia ago in the tiny country of Israel, where most of us have never been and will never go? I find that fascinating. I certainly know the correct theological or religious response: He's the Son of God; in fact, He *is* God. And I believe that.

But here is what amazes me. There is no single person on all the earth who has captured the attention (in this way) of 2 billion persons. Islam, with its founder, Muhammad, attracts more than 1 billion followers—perhaps as many as 1.4 billion. But Islam has used the sword, coercion. It has had extensive armies for much of its fourteen-hundred-year history. Jesus did no such thing. Jesus never led an army. He never had a sword. Unlike Muhammad and his sixty-six different battles, Jesus never fought. Yet a couple of billion people choose to voluntarily follow Him, or at least identify themselves with Him in some way!

On Easter, churches are filled to capacity. Think about it—filled to capacity over the entire globe! Why? Because they believe (and I do, too) that there is actually a connection between a death on a cross—so far away, so long ago—and them. Amazing!

They believe that He rose from the dead (and I do, too) and that there is some connection between His resurrection—so far away, so long ago—and their daily lives. Even the ones who are forced to go to Easter services by an insistent mother or grandma somehow feel and know that it is right that they are there at church singing about Someone who died, and rose, *two thousand years ago.*

What makes it so amazing is that Jesus really did not do a lot of things like the things done by the people mentioned in the pages of this book. Compared to the world's "greats," He really didn't accomplish all that much.

He was never president. He was never governor. He wasn't even a mayor.

He was never a college president. He was never a professor. No one ever called Him a great philosopher. He never pastored a large church. He never even graduated from high school.

Jesus never owned a business. He never owned His own house. He never even owned His own form of transportation.

He never wrote a book. That becomes more shocking when you consider that one particular book *about* Him, the Bible, has remained a best-seller continually and globally! And every single day, teams of persons are translating the Bible into yet more languages and more of the world's dialects. There have been more books written about Him than about any person in all of history. Yet He Himself never wrote one.

He never saw a movie. He never saw a television. Yet the *Jesus* film—the story of His life—has been seen by more persons than any other movie or video ever released, approaching four billion, two-thirds of the earth's population.

He was not highly educated. He did not attend the high-brow Jerusalem institutions that were the "Harvards" of the day.

Occupationally, He was a carpenter. He likely built tables and benches in a tiny "Joseph & Son" operation. And He didn't stay in that job past age thirty.

After age thirty, He was an itinerant—always on the move. He hung out with an odd collection of fishermen, tax collectors, and small business owners. His entourage included a few wealthy widows, who had to periodically financially underwrite His traveling band.

He did not rub shoulders with the politically powerful. Kings rarely heard His name mentioned. No emperor ever met Him. He never made it to Rome. The only time He really had contact with political authorities was when they were irritated with Him and the mob that His reactions had created.

His birthplace was strikingly unimpressive. He was born in a tiny town, in a type of cave, filled with the smell of manure. His parents had to hide Him for the first few years of His life for fear He would be killed.

They then returned to their hometown of Nazareth, which probably never had a population of more than three hundred at the time. Most towns had walls around them. But Nazareth was so poor that raiding armies knew not to even bother stopping there. There were no fortifications at all because there was nothing to defend! Even the locals admitted, "What good can come out of Nazareth?"

And if the town was not impressive, neither was the area surrounding it. Galilee was looked down on by those from Judea, down south. Jerusalem was the center for intellect. The area around it—Judea—was for the elite. Even the distinct northern Galilean accent was a clue that these were not the educated types.

And His boyhood home? It was probably a small cave. Sort of half cave, half lean-to, a bit of a dugout in the side of a hill. Nothing impressive about that either.

His travels were even less impressive. Other than the trip to Egypt when He was an infant, He never even made it out of the country. The extent of His travels? Essentially the distance from the Sea of Galilee up north to Jerusalem down south, with a few other points thrown in. And how far is that? Well, it would take you an hour in a car. The bottom line: He never traveled. He never knew New York or Los Angeles or Tokyo or London or Paris or Madrid. He never saw any of the sights you have seen. Never.

He was a grand religious leader, right? Hardly. He never oversaw a prominent synagogue. He certainly did not officiate at the temple. He never made it onto the Sanhedrin, the religious "supreme court" of the day.

And what about the crowds? Well, this is a bit more encouraging. At one point He attracted five thousand men alone. If you count probable wives and children, it might reach twenty thousand. Now that's impressive! Great news, right? Wrong! Most of them dissipated. The crowd was nowhere to be found when the leaders came after Him.

Although they loved Him on Palm Sunday, the crowds turned against Him by Friday of the same week. How upset were they with Him? Enough to kill him!

And you would think that at least the Resurrection would draw several thousand followers. It didn't. Even though He made many appearances *after* the Resurrection, He still didn't draw much of a crowd. Only 120 people in a second-story rented room. That's it! One hundred and twenty after three-and-a-half years of hard work! Quite unimpressive.

What's worse, some of His own family members regarded Him as a lightweight. His own brother James—or half brother, actually—didn't even take Him seriously until *after* He had ascended to heaven.

He was the Messiah, God's Promised One. But He didn't capitalize on the public relations potential. He could have made a splash in the

Jerusalem Times if He had arranged a press conference in the heart of Judea. But no, He didn't.

He "squandered" the announcement of His messiahship on a Samaritan (they were considered half-breeds, racially inferior), on a woman (no one took women seriously in that day), on a woman with a lousy reputation (she was at the well getting water at the "disrespectful" hour), a woman with five divorces—count them, five!—a woman who was in a live-in arrangement! What lack of PR savvy! He missed His big chance! He blew it on her!

And the healings! Now they could have drawn the crowds. But time after time, He told people He healed *not* to tell anyone. Come on!

And His closest friends? When He came to the toughest moment of His life, what did they do? They fell asleep! Couldn't even stay awake one hour!

And after He had taught them all about love, what did they do? They fought! They fought about who was the greatest! Their moms wanted "my boy" to be first! His teachings didn't even soak in with His closest buds.

What about Judas? Traveled with Jesus for more than thirty-six months, then *sold* Him! What kind of a friend is that? Couldn't Jesus have picked a better bunch to run with?

And then in that final hour, in the most painful moment imaginable, when He was on the cross, there were only Mom and John and maybe a couple of others. Even one of the *criminals* on the next cross rejected Him! And His heavenly Father? Well, Jesus asked Him, "Why have You left Me?" How much more abandoned could One be?

And yet, this One—this One who had never written or traveled or studied or owned anything or been elected to anything—*this One has moved all of human history.*

Calendars are set according to Him: B.C. "before Christ," and A.D., referring to after His birth.

Remember, I am *not* talking to you as a pastor, who is supposed to say religious things; I am talking as an amateur historian who is mystified by the reality of this one life. Historically speaking, I stand in awe of Him.

What amazes me is that every single day nearly 200,000 persons embrace Him. They start following Him! It has been two thousand years since He was even on the earth, and 1 million more persons start following Him every six days!

Go to any country on the earth. People there are talking about Him.

It is illegal to worship Him in many parts of the earth. But they keep doing it. It is illegal to mention Him in many of our public schools. But people keep saying His name.

Most of His original buddies were killed for following Him. They couldn't be talked out of it. Multitudes have been killed through the centuries since then just for serving Him. And they won't stop!

More persons have been killed for following Him in the last 100 years than in all the preceding 1,900 years. More than 160,000 persons will be killed for following Him just this year! That's one every three minutes.

In the length of time it has taken you to read this section about Him, somewhere on planet earth, three or four persons have been killed just for following Him.

In the length of time it has taken you to read this chapter, about ten persons have been killed just for believing Him.

In the length of time it has taken you to read this book, hundreds have been killed just for worshiping Him.

When in all of history have you ever heard anything like this? Where in all of the earth have you ever heard any comparable story?

How does one explain this historically? Sociologically? Politically? Why do people follow Him—two billion of them, with more joining every second?

PRINCIPLE FOR A LEADERSHIP OF LEGACY # 16:
Give Yourself Away

Because He left a legacy. And that legacy compels us—billions of us. That legacy is Himself. He gave Himself for us! And as a result, we, too, are His legacy.

One person said Christians are "plainclothesmen" (and "plainclothes*women,* too) infiltrating the entire world. Christians are plainclothesmen in the Jesus Revolution—the only revolution that will ultimately conquer the hearts and minds of mankind.

Someday every person will kneel before Him. Someday every person will say the name "Jesus" with awe and reverence, realizing who He really is.

Followers of this One Jesus are to be (and have been for 2,000 years) contagious carriers of Him. His disciples infectiously carry the good news—the spectacular news—that He brought: By embracing and believing in Him and what He did, every person can be set free of the bondage and garbage of his or her life. Along with Himself, that freedom is His legacy. And that is why two billion of us—with more coming on board every day—follow Him.

This story that I have just told you is the most amazing example of the "law of legacy" ever known to humankind.

NOTES

CHAPTER 1

1. Samuel Eliot Morison, *The Oxford History of the American People* (New York: Oxford University Press, 1965), 417.
2. Quoted in Paul Johnson, *A History of the American People* (New York: HarperCollins, 1997), 481.
3. *The Great Democracies,* vol. 4 of *A History of the English Speaking Peoples* (New York: Dodd, Mead, 1958), 262.
4. Quoted in T. Harry Williams, *The Union Restored* (New York: Time Inc., 1963), 152.
5. Ibid.
6. Ibid.

CHAPTER 2

1. Quoted by Lisa Beamer, *A Reason for Hope* (Wheaton: Crossway, 2001), 10.
2. Ibid.
3. William Barker, *Who's Who in Church History* (Grand Rapids, MI: Baker, 1977), 114.
4. Scout.org/wso
5. Ibid.

CHAPTER 3

1. Albert Outler, *Evangelism in the Wesleyan Spirit* (Nashville, TN: Tidings, 1971), 18.
2. Warren Candler, *Wesley and His Work* (Nashville, TN: Publishing House of the M. E. Church, South, 1912), 55.
3. Norman W. Mumford, "The Organization of the Methodist Church in the Time of John Wesley," part 1, *London Quarterly & Holborn Review* 171 (January 1946): 35–40.
4. Henry Bett, *The Early Methodist Preachers* (London: Epworth Press, 1935), 9.
5. Winston Churchill, *The Age of Revolution* (New York: Dodd, Mead, 1957), 260.

6. *Oxford History of the American People*, 318.

7. Churchill, *Age of Revolution*, 260.

CHAPTER 4

1. Cited in John Eidsmoe, *Columbus & Cortez: Conquerors for Christ* (Green Forest, AR: New Leaf Press, 1992), 90.

2. Quoted in Lewis Hanke, *Aristotle and the American Indian* (Bloomington: Indiana University Press, 1959), 124.

3. Vol. 39 of *Great Books of the Western World* (Chicago: Encyclopaedia Britannica, 1952), 271.

4. Quoted in Stephen B. Elmer, "Columbus: Discovering the Discoverer."

5. "Custer, George Armstrong," in *Dictionary of American Biography*, 7.

6. Quoted in Robert Paul Jordan, "Ghosts on the Little Bighorn," *National Geographic*, December 1986, 789.

CHAPTER 5

1. Samuel Eliot Morison, *Oxford History of the American People* (New York: Oxford University Press, 1963), 377

2. Ibid.

3. Ibid.

4. Johnson, *A History of the American People*, 183–84.

5. Ibid.

CHAPTER 6

1. J. William Jones, *The Life & Letters of Robert E. Lee* (Harrisburg, VA: Sprinkle Publications, 1978; reprint of 1906 ed.), 25.

2. Quoted in J. Steven Wilkins, *The Call of Duty* (Elkton, MD: Highland Books, 1997), 45.

3. Ibid., 39.

4. Quoted in J. W. Jones, *Personal Reminiscences* (Richmond, VA: United States Historical Society Press, 1989), 223–24.

5. Quoted in Wilkins, *Call of Duty*, 297.

6. Quoted in H. W. Crocker III, *Robert E. Lee on Leadership* (Rocklin, CA: Prima Publishers, 1999), 4.

7. Dylan Loeb McClain, "Media Talk: Scandals Don't Much Harm An Already Bad Reputation," *New York Times*.

8. Naftali Bendavid, "Clinton Could Have Been Charged, Counsel Says," *San Diego Union-Tribune*, 7 March 2002.

9. Oren Harari, "Behind Open Doors," *Modern Maturity*, January/February 2002, 50.

CHAPTER 7

1. Mark Galli and Ted Olsen, *131 Christians Everyone Should Know* (Nashville, TN: Broadman and Holman, 2000), 31.

2. J. D. Douglas, *Who's Who in Christian History* (Tyndale, 1992), 31.
3. "He's Our Man; Evangelicals Can Embrace a Rich Inheritance from Aquinas: A Conversation with Norman Geisler," *Christian History* 23, no. 1.
4. Speech, House of Commons, 13 May 1940, in Winston Churchill's *Their Finest Hour* (Boston: Houghton Mifflin, 1949), 25.
5. Plutarch, "Alexander and Julius Caesar," in *The Lives of Noble Grecians and Romans*, vol. 14 of *Great Books of the Western World* (Chicago: Encyclopaedia Britannica, 1952), 543.
6. Ibid.
7. Ibid., 551.
8. Ibid., 560.
9. Ibid.
10. Will Durant, *The Life of Greece* (New York: Simon and Schuster, 1939), 544.
11. Ibid., 542.
12. Ibid.
13. Ibid.
14. Plutarch, *Lives*, 563.

CHAPTER 8
1. Quoted in Alvin M. Josephy Jr., *The Patriot Chiefs* (New York: Viking Press), 314.
2. Ibid., 322.
3. Ibid., 339–40.

CHAPTER 9
1. *Christianity Today*, 15 June 1998, 72.
2. Quoted in Sam Wellman, *C. S. Lewis*, 130.
3. Ibid., 132.
4. Tasunke Witko (Crazy Horse), as remembered by Ohiyesa <http://maier1.best.vwh.net/native/ohiyesa.htm>.
5. Mari Sandoz, *Crazy Horse: The Strange Man of the Oglalas: A Biography* (Lincoln, NE: Bison Books, 1961).
6. Ohiyesa <http://maier1.best.vwh.net/native/ohiyesa.htm>.
7. Galli and Olsen, *131 Christians Everyone Should Know*, 204.
8. Stephanie A. Crockett, "MLK Streets Not a Fitting Tribute to Slain Civil Rights Leader," BET.com, posted 18 January 2002.

CHAPTER 10
1. Jerald Brauer, *Westminster Dictionary of Church History* (Westminster Press: Philadelphia), 452.
2. Barker, *Who's Who in Church History*, 154.
3. Brauer, *Westminster Dictionary of Church History*, 453.
4. Quoted in Richard M. Ketchum, *Will Rogers: His Life and Times* (New York: American Heritage Publishing Company, 1973), 177.
5. Ibid., 178.

CHAPTER 11

1. Published by Zondervan, this book is still available more than thirty years after the author's death.
2. Quoted in William E. Leuchtenberg, *Franklin D. Roosevelt and the New Deal* (New York: Harper & Row, 1963), 64.
3. Ibid.
4. Ibid., 34.
5. Ibid.
6. Ibid., 35.
7. Quoted in Glyndon G. Van Deusen, *The Jacksonian Era* (New York: Harper Torchbooks, 1959), 31.

CHAPTER 12

1. Quoted in Stephen Ambrose's essay, "Character Above All," PBS web site.
2. James G. Randall, *Civil War & Reconstruction* (Boston: D. C. Heath, 1953), 292.
3. Ibid., 176–77.
4. Ibid., 459.
5. Quoted in William Jones, *Personal Reminiscences,* 156.
6. Ibid.
7. James L. Garlow, "John Wesley's Understanding of the Laity as Demonstrated by His Use of the Lay Preachers" (Ph.D. diss., Drew University, 1979), 89.

CHAPTER 14

1. Mark Twain, *Personal Recollections of Joan of Arc by the Sieur Louis de Conte (Her Page and Secretary)* (San Francisco: Ignatius Press, 1989; reprint of 1896).
2. Ibid., 5.
3. Louise Redfield Peattie, "Maid of Orleans," in *Great Lives, Great Deeds,* 400.
4. Ibid.
5. Ibid.
6. Ibid., 402.
7. Twain, *Personal Recollections of Joan of Arc,* 19.
8. Ibid.
9. Ibid., 20.

CHAPTER 15

1. "State of the Union Speech," *Washington Times National Weekly Edition,* 4–10 February 2002, 1.
2. Morris's *Wall Street Journal* column referenced by David Horowitz, FrontPageMagazine.com, 11 February 2002.
3. Http://www.townhall.com/columnists/ollienorth/printon20011008.shtml.
4. "Bush's Defining Moment," *Christianity Today,* 11 November 2001, 40.
5. Ibid., 42.
6. Ibid.

7. Cited in "MacArthur," *The American Experience*, PBS Online.
8. Ibid.
9. Ibid.
10. George C. Kenney, "The MacArthur I Knew," in *Great Lives, Great Deeds* (Pleasantville, NY: Reader's Digest Association, 1962), 449.
11. Ibid., 453.
12. Ibid.
13. Ibid., 456.
14. Ibid., 454.
15. Quoted in Merle Miller, *Plain Speaking: An Oral Biography of Harry S. Truman* (New York: Berkley Books, 1974), 327.

CHAPTER 16

1. Quoted in Forrest Wilson, "Her Book Brewed a War," in *Great Lives, Great Deeds*, 307.
2. Quoted in Jefferson, *Writings*, 289.
3. Wilson, "Her Book Brewed a War," 310.
4. Ibid., 315.
5. "General Patton's Address to the Troops," 5 June 1944, <*http://www.manly-web.com/realmen/pattonspeech.html*>
6. Ibid.
7. Ibid.
8. Ibid.
9. Ibid.

CHAPTER 17

1. Plato, *Apology*, trans. Jowett, in *Great Books of the Western World*, vol. 7 (Chicago: Encyclopaedia Britannica, 1952), 206.
2. Ibid.
3. Ibid.
4. Max Eastman, "The Wisest One," in *Great Lives, Great Deeds*, 62.
5. Xenophon, *Symposium*, trans. E. C. Marchant (London: Loeb Classical Library, 1959), 2.1.18.
6. Quoted in Douglas J. Soccio, *Archetypes of Wisdom*, 2d ed. (Belmont, CA: Wadsworth Publishing Company, 1995), 115.
7. Ibid., 116.
8. Ibid., *Memorabilia* 1.6.
9. Ibid., 116–17, *Memorabilia* 4.5.
10. *History of Ancient Philosophy*, vol. 1, trans. John Catan (Albany: SUNY, 1987), 216.
11. Ibid., 202.

CHAPTER 18

1 Quoted in John F. Kennedy, *Profiles in Courage* (New York: Harper & Row, 1964), 6.

2. Letter to Secretary of War, 29 March 1836, in *America's Frontier Story*, by John Rollin Ridge and Ray A. Billington (New York: Holt, Rinehart and Winston, 1969), 433–34.
3. Kennedy, *Profiles in Courage*, 122.
4. Ibid.
5. Ibid., 124.
6. Ibid.
7. Ibid., 131.
8. Ibid., 136.
9. Ibid., 138.

CHAPTER 19
1. www.beachboys.com/history.html.
2. www.silkhouse.co.uk/tytv/html/didyouknow/archive/music/musicsept.shtm.
3. Philippe-Paul de Segur, *Napoleon's Russian Campaign* (New York: Time Inc., 1958), 20.
4. Ibid., 33.
5. Ibid., 78.
6. Ibid., 145.

CHAPTER 20
1. Edwin Muller, "Terror of the World," in *Great Lives, Great Deeds*, 86.
2. Quoted in Michael Prawdin, *The Mongol Empire* (New York: Free Press, 1981), 87.
3. Ibid., 89–90.
4. Ibid., 90.
5. Ibid., 91.
6. Ibid., 96.
7. Muller, "Terror of the World," 92.
8. Prawdin, *Mongol Empire*, 155.
9. Ibid., 198.

CHAPTER 21
1. www.familyfirst.net/fathersd2000.asp.
2. http://newman.baruch.cuny.edu/digital/2001/beecher/lyman.htm.
3. Will Durant, *The Age of Faith* (New York: Simon and Schuster, 1950), 472.
4. Ibid.
5. *The Heritage of the Past* (New York: Holt, Rinehart and Winston, 1964), 515.
6. Quoted in ibid., 475.
7. *The Founding of Christendom*, vol. 1 of *A History of Christendom* (Front Royal, VA: Christendom College Press, 1985), 540.
8. Will Durant, *Caesar and Christ* (New York: Simon and Schuster, 1944), 664.

ABOUT THE AUTHOR

D R. JIM GARLOW is Senior Pastor of Skyline Wesleyan Church in San Diego, California. He travels and speaks at pastoral and leadership events as well as major conferences throughout America. Garlow is a graduate of Oklahoma Wesleyan University and Southern Nazarene University (B.A.and M.A.) and holds an M.Div. from Asbury Theological Seminary, a Th.M. from Princeton Theological Seminary, and a Ph.D. from Drew University.

OTHER BOOKS BY DR. JIM GARLOW

A Christian's Response to Islam (River Oak/Honor Books, 2002)
How God Saved Civilization (Regal Books, 2000)
The Covenant (Beacon Hill Press, 1999)
Partners in Ministry (Beacon Hill Press, re-released 1998)

VIDEOTAPE:

The Church Alive & Well—a "walk" through 2000 years of Christian History (1993)

For more information, go to *www.jimgarlow.com*

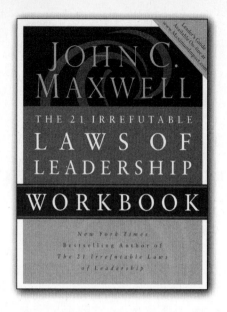

There's a reason why John Maxwell's *The 21 Irrefutable Laws of Leadership* has sold over 700,000 copies—the Laws hold true. Now this companion workbook is available for those who desire to grow as a leader and mentor others to do the same. Unlike other daily format guides, this revolutionary workbook teaches each of the 21 Laws using six steps:

1) Read: Brief case studies in leadership, taken from the original book, will illustrate each Law.

2) Observe: Using personal observation, readers find examples from their own career area.

3) Learn: This is the "meat" of the book—the detailed explanation of each Law.

4) Evaluate: Questions prompt readers to evaluate their leadership ability relative to each Law.

5) Discuss: The questions included here can be used in a mentoring group.

6) Act: This section contains an assignment or project for the reader to complete.

For anyone ready to take their leadership growth to the next level, *The 21 Irrefutable Laws of Leadership Workbook* is a much-needed resource.

ISBN 0-7852-6405-1

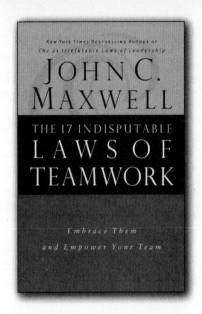

New York Times BESTSELLING AUTHOR OF
The 21 Irrefutable Laws of Leadership

JOHN C. MAXWELL

THE 17 INDISPUTABLE
LAWS OF
TEAMWORK

*Embrace Them
and Empower Your Team*

Everyone who works with people is realizing that the old autocratic method of leadership simply doesn't work. The way to win is to build a great team.

John C. Maxwell has been teaching the benefits of leadership and team building for years. Now he tackles the importance of teamwork head on, writing about teamwork being necessary for every kind of leader, and showing how team building can improve every area of your life.

Written in the style of the bestseller *The 21 Irrefutable Laws of Leadership*, this new book not only contains laws that you can count on when it comes to getting people to work together, but it tells them in such a way that you can start applying them to your own life today. And it's illustrated with great stories of team leaders—and team breakers—from history, business, the church, and sports.

ISBN 0-7852-7434-0

Leading from the Lockers
Based on John Maxwell's best-selling title
*Developing the Leader Within You, Leading
from the Lockers* offers tweens the tools they
need to develop as leaders before reaching
high school or college. Leadership takes
many forms, and today kids are assuming
roles as leaders in school, on their sports
teams, in church youth groups, and as peer
mentors. *Leading from the Lockers* covers the
topics of influence, priorities, integrity, problem solving, self-discipline,
and peer relationships. Color pages with vignette line drawings
enchance the text and give books an up-to-the-minute look.
ISBN 0-8499-7722-3

AVAILABLE MARCH 2003

A Leaders Promise for Every Day
Applauded as one of the world's most popular
leadership experts, John C. Maxwell distills
many of his winning concepts and scriptural
meditations into a daily devotional, following
the phenomenally popular format of *Grace for
the Moment* and *Hope for Each Day*. Delivered
with his trademark style of confidence and
clarity, Maxwell addresses a host of relevant
topics including success, stewardship,
teamwork, and mentoring.
ISBN: 0-8499-9594-9